The Happy Days Of The Empress Marie Louise

By

Imbert De Saint-Amand

The Happy Days Of The Empress Marie Louise
by Imbert De Saint-Amand

Copyright © 2024

All Rights reserved.

No part of this publication may be reproduced, stored in a retrieval system, or transmitted in any form or by any means, electronic, mechanical, photocopying or Otherwise, without the written permission of the publisher.
The author/editor asserts the moral right to be identified as the author/editor of this work.

ISBN: 978-93-62201-92-8

Published by

DOUBLE 9 BOOKS

2/13-B, Ansari Road
Daryaganj, New Delhi – 110002
info@double9books.com
www.double9books.com
Tel. 011-40042856

This book is under public domain

ABOUT THE AUTHOR

Imbert de Saint-Amand, a prolific French author and historian, is renowned for his insightful biographies and historical narratives. Among his most celebrated works is "The Happy Days of the Empress Marie Louise," a captivating portrayal of one of the most intriguing figures of the Napoleonic era. Through meticulous research and vivid storytelling, Saint-Amand brings to life the joys and challenges faced by Empress Marie Louise, providing readers with a fascinating glimpse into the inner workings of the French imperial court. With his signature attention to detail and engaging prose, Saint-Amand invites readers on a journey through history, immersing them in the opulence, intrigue, and romance of the Napoleonic era. "The Happy Days of the Empress Marie Louise" stands as a testament to Saint-Amand's talent as a historian and his ability to breathe life into the past, offering readers an unforgettable portrait of one of history's most enigmatic figures.

CONTENTS

INTRODUCTION 7

I	EARLY YEARS 26
II	1809 31
III	THE PRELIMINARIES OF THE WEDDING 38
IV	THE BETROTHAL 50
V	THE RELIGIOUS DIFFICULTY 59
VI	THE AMBASSADOR EXTRAORDINARY 65
VII	THE WEDDING AT VIENNA 71
VIII	THE DEPARTURE 77
IX	THE TRANSFER 81
X	THE JOURNEY 87
XI	COMPIÈGNE 94
XII	THE CIVIL WEDDING 99
XIII	THE ENTRANCE INTO PARIS 104
XIV	THE RELIGIOUS CEREMONY 108
XV	THE HONEYMOON 115
XVI	THE TRIP IN THE NORTH 121
XVII	THE MONTH OF JUNE, 1810 125
XVIII	THE BALL AT THE AUSTRIAN EMBASSY 129
XIX	THE BIRTH OF THE KING OF ROME 135
XX	THE RECOVERY 143
XXI	THE BAPTISM 149
XXII	SAINT CLOUD AND TRIANON 154
XXIII	THE TRIP TO HOLLAND 158

XXIV	NAPOLEON AT THE HEIGHT OF HIS POWER	163
XXV	MARIE LOUISE IN 1812	172
XXVI	THE EMPRESS'S HOUSEHOLD	180
XXVII	DRESDEN	190
XXVIII	PRAGUE	202

INTRODUCTION

In 1814, while Napoleon was banished in the island of Elba, the Empress Marie Louise and her grandmother, Marie Caroline, Queen of Naples, happened to meet at Vienna. The one, who had been deprived of the French crown, was seeking to be put in possession of her new realm, the Duchy of Parma; the other, who had fled from Sicily to escape the yoke of her pretended protectors, the English, had come to demand the restitution of her kingdom of Naples, where Murat continued to rule with the connivance of Austria. This Queen, Marie Caroline, the daughter of the great Empress, Maria Theresa, and the sister of the unfortunate Marie Antoinette, had passed her life in detestation of the French Revolution and of Napoleon, of whom she had been one of the most eminent victims. Well, at the very moment when the Austrian court was doing its best to make Marie Louise forget that she was Napoleon's wife and to separate her from him forever, Marie Caroline was pained to see her granddaughter lend too ready an ear to their suggestions. She said to the Baron de Méneval, who had accompanied Marie Louise to Vienna: "I have had, in my time, very good cause for complaining of your Emperor; he has persecuted me and wounded my pride,—I was then at least fifteen years old,—but now I remember only one thing,—that he is unfortunate." Then she went on to say that if they tried to keep husband and wife apart, Marie Louise would have to tie her bedclothes to her window and run away in disguise. "That," she exclaimed, "that's what I should do in her place; for when people are married, they are married for their whole life!"

If a woman like Queen Marie Caroline, a sister of Marie Antoinette, a queen driven from her throne by Napoleon, could feel in this way, it is easy to understand the severity with which those of the French who were devoted to the Emperor, regarded the conduct of his ungrateful wife. In the same way, Josephine, in spite of her occasionally frivolous conduct, has retained her popularity, because she was tender, kind, and devoted, even after she was divorced; while Marie Louise has been criticised, because after loving, or saying that she loved, the mighty Emperor, she deserted him when he was a prisoner. The contrast between her conduct and that of the wife of King Jerome, the noble and courageous Catherine of Wurtemberg, who endured every danger, and all sorts of persecutions, to share her husband's exile and poverty, has set in an even clearer light the faults of Marie Louise.

She has been blamed for not having joined Napoleon at Elba, for not having even tried to temper his sufferings at Saint Helena, for not consoling him in any way, for not even writing to him. The former Empress of the French has been also more severely condemned for her two morganatic marriages,—one with Count Neipperg, an Austrian general and a bitter enemy of Napoleon, the other with Count de Bombelles, a Frenchman who left France to enter the Austrian service. Certainly Marie Louise was neither a model wife nor a model widow, and there is nothing surprising in the severity with which her contemporaries judged her, a severity which doubtless history will not modify. But if this princess was guilty, more than one attenuating circumstance may be urged in her defence, and we should, in justice, remember that it was not without a struggle, without tears, distress, and many conscientious scruples, that she decided to obey her father's rigid orders and become again what she had been before her marriage,—simply an Austrian princess.

It must not be forgotten that the Empress Marie Louise, who was in two ways the grandniece of Queen Marie Antoinette, through her mother Maria Theresa of Naples, daughter of Queen Marie Caroline, and through her father the Emperor Francis, son of the Emperor Leopold II., the brother of the martyred queen, had been brought up to abhor the French Revolution and the Empire which succeeded it. She had been taught from the moment she left the cradle, that France was the hereditary enemy, the savage and implacable foe, of her country. When she was a child, Napoleon appeared to her against a background of blood, like a fatal being, an evil genius, a satanic Corsican, a sort of Antichrist. The few Frenchmen whom she saw at the Austrian court were émigrés, who saw in Napoleon nothing but the selfish revolutionist, the friend of the young Robespierre, the creature of Barras, the defender of the members of the Convention, the man of the 13th of Vendémiaire, the murderer of the Duke of Enghien, the enemy of all the thrones of Europe, the author of the treachery of Bayonne, the persecutor of the Pope, the excommunicated sovereign. Twice he had driven Austria to the brink of ruin, and it had even been said that he wished to destroy it altogether, like a second Poland. The young archduchess had never heard the hero of Austerlitz and Wagram spoken of, except in terms inspired by resentment, fear, and hatred. Could she, then, in a single day learn to love the man who always had been held up before her as a second Attila, as the scourge of God? Hence, when she came to contemplate the possibility of her marriage with him, she was overwhelmed with surprise, terror, and repulsion, and her first idea was to regard herself as a victim to be sacrificed to a vague Minotaur. We find this word "sacrifice" on the lips of the Austrian statesmen who most warmly favored the French alliance, even of those who had counselled and arranged the match. The Austrian ambassador in Paris, the Prince of Swartzenberg, wrote to Metternich, February 8, 1810, "I pity the princess; but let her remember that it is a fine thing to bring peace to such good people!" And Metternich wrote back, February 15, to the Prince of Swartzenberg, "The Archduchess Marie Louise sees in the suggestion made to her by her August father, that Napoleon may include her in his plans, only a means of proving to her beloved father the most absolute devotion. She feels the full force of the sacrifice, but her filial love will outweigh all other considerations." Having been brought up in the habit of severe discipline and passive obedience, she belonged to a family in which the Austrian princesses are regarded as the docile instruments of the greatness of the Hapsburgs. Consequently, she resigned herself to following her father's wishes without a murmur, but not without sadness. What Marie Louise thought at the time of her marriage she still thought in the last years of her life. General de Trobriand, the Frenchman who won distinction on the northern side in the American civil war, told me recently how painfully surprised he was when once at Venice he had heard Napoleon's widow, then the wife of Count de Bombelles, say, in speaking of her marriage to the great Emperor, "I was sacrificed."

Austria was covered with ruins, its hospitals were crowded with wounded French and Austrians, and in the ears of Viennese still echoed the cannon of Wagram, when salvos of artillery announced not war, but this marriage. The memories of an obstinate struggle, which both sides had regarded as one for life or death, was still too recent, too terrible to permit a complete reconciliation between the two nations. In fact, the peace was only a truce. To facilitate the formal entry of Napoleon's ambassador into Vienna, it had been necessary hastily to build a bridge over the ruins of the walls which the French had blown up a few months earlier, as a farewell to the inhabitants. Marie Louise, who started with tears in her eyes, trembled as she drew near the French territory, which Marie Antoinette had found so fatal.

Soon this first impression wore off, and the young Empress was distinctly flattered by the amazing splendor of her throne, the most powerful in the world. And yet amid this Babylonian pomp, and all the splendor, the glory, the flattery, which could gratify a woman's heart, she did not cease to think of her own country. One day when she was standing at a window of the palace of Saint Cloud, gazing thoughtfully at the view before her, M. de Méneval ventured to ask the cause of the deep revery in which she appeared to be sunk. She answered that as she was looking at the beautiful view, she was surprised to find herself regretting the neighborhood of Vienna, and wishing that some magic wand might let her see even a corner of it. At that time Marie Louise was afraid that she would never see her country again, and she sighed. What glory or greatness can wipe out the touching memories of infancy?

Doubtless Napoleon treated his wife with the utmost regard and consideration; but in the affection with which he inspired her there was, we fancy, more admiration than tenderness. He was too great for her. She was fascinated, but troubled by so great power and so great genius. She had the eyes of a dove, and she needed the eyes of an eagle, to be able to look at the Imperial Sun, of which the hot rays dazzled her. She would have preferred less glory, less majesty, fewer triumphs, with her simple and modest tastes, which were rather those of a respectable citizen's wife than of a queen. Her husband, amid his courtiers, who flocked about him as priests flock about an idol, seemed to her a demi-god rather than a man, and she would far rather have been won by affection than overwhelmed by his superiority.

It is not to be supposed, however, that Marie Louise was unhappy before the catastrophes that accompanied the fall of the Empire. It was in perfect sincerity that she wrote to her father in praise of her husband, and her joy was great when she gave birth to a child, who seemed a pledge of peace and of general happiness. Let us add that the Emperor never had an occasion to find fault with her. Her gentleness, reserve, and obedience formed the combination of qualities which her husband desired. He had never imagined an Empress more exactly to his taste. When she deserted him, he was more ready to excuse and pity her than to cast blame upon her. He looked upon her as the slave and victim of the Viennese court. Moreover, he was in perfect ignorance of her love for the Count of Neipperg, and no shadow of jealousy tormented him at Saint Helena. "You may be sure," he said a few days before his death, "that if the Empress makes no effort to ease my woes, it is because she is kept surrounded by spies, who never let my sufferings come to her ears; for Marie Louise is virtue itself." A pleasant delusion, which consoled the final moments of the great man, whose last thoughts were for his wife and son.

We fancy that the Emperor of Austria was sincere in the protestations of affection and friendship which he made to Napoleon shortly after the wedding. He then entertained no thoughts of dethroning or fighting him. He had hopes of securing great advantage from the French alliance, and he would have been much surprised if any one had foretold to him how soon he would become one of the most active agents in the overthrow of this son-in-law to whom he expressed such affectionate feelings. In 1811 he was sincerely desirous that the King of Rome should one day succeed Napoleon on the throne of the vast empire. At that time hatred of France had almost died out in Austria; it was only renewed by the disastrous Russian campaign.

The Austrians, who could not wholly forget the past, did not love Napoleon well enough to remain faithful to him in disaster. Had he been fortunate, the hero of Wagram would have preserved his father-in-law's sympathy and the Austrian alliance; but being unfortunate, he lost both at once. Unlike the rulers of the old dynasties, he was condemned either to perpetual victory or to ruin. He needed triumphs instead of ancestors, and the slightest loss of glory was for him the token of irremediable decay; incessant victory was the only condition on which he could keep his throne, his wife, his son, himself. One day he asked Marie Louise what instructions she had received from her parents in regard to her conduct towards him. "To be wholly yours," she answered, "and to obey you in everything." Might she not have added, "So long as you are not unfortunate"?

But who at the beginning of that fatal year, 1812, could have foretold the catastrophes which were so near? When Marie Louise was with Napoleon at Dresden, did he not appear to her like the arbiter of the world, an invincible hero, an Agamemnon, the king of kings? Never before, possibly, had a man risen so high. Sovereigns seemed lost amid the crowd of courtiers. Among the aides-de-camp was the Crown Prince of Prussia, who was obliged to make special recommendations to those near him to pay a little attention to his father-in-law, the Emperor of Austria. What power, what pride, what faith in his star, when, drawing all Europe after him, he bade farewell to his wife May 29, 1812, to begin that gigantic war which he thought was destined to consolidate all his greatness and to crown all his glories! But he had not counted on the burning of Moscow: there is in the air a zone which the highest balloons cannot pierce; once there, ascent means death. This zone, which exists also in power, good fortune, glory, as well as in the atmosphere, Napoleon had reached. At the height of his prosperity he had forgotten that God was about to say to him: Thou shalt go no further.

At the first defeat Marie Louise perceived that the brazen statue had feet of clay. Malet's conspiracy filled her with gloomy thoughts. It became evident that the Empire was not a fixed institution, but a single man; in case this man died or lived defeated, everything was gone. December 12, 1812, the Empress went to her bed in the Tuileries, sad and ill. It was half-past eleven in the evening. The lady-in-waiting, who was to pass the night in a neighboring room, was about to lock all the doors when suddenly she heard voices in the drawing-room close by. Who could have come at that hour? Who except the Emperor? And, in fact, it was he, who, without word to any one, had just arrived unexpectedly in a wretched carriage, and had found great difficulty in getting the palace doors opened. He had travelled incognito from the Beresina, like a fugitive, like a criminal. As he passed through Warsaw he had exclaimed bitterly and in amazement at his defeat, "There is but one step from the sublime to the ridiculous." When he burst into his wife's bedroom in his long fur coat, Marie Louise could not believe her eyes. He kissed her affectionately, and promised her that all the disasters recounted in the twenty-ninth bulletin should be soon repaired; he added that he had been beaten, not by the Russians, but by the elements. Nevertheless, the decadence had begun; his glory was dimmed; Marie Louise began to have doubts of Napoleon. His courtiers continued to flatter him, but they ceased to worship him. A dark cloud lay over the Tuileries. The Empress had but a few days to pass with her husband. He had been away for nearly six months, from May 29 till December 12, 1812, and he was to leave again April 15, 1813, to return only November 9. The European sovereigns could not have continued in alliance with him even if they had wished it, so irresistible was the movement of their subjects against him. After Leipsic everything was lost; that was the signal of the death struggle, which was to be long, terrible, and full of anguish. Europe listened in terror to the cries of the dying Empire. But it was all over. The sacred soil of France was invaded. January 25, 1814, at three in the morning, the hero left the Tuileries to oppose the invaders. He kissed his wife and his son for the last time. He was never to see them again. In all, Napoleon had passed only two years and eight months with Marie Louise; she had had hardly time enough to become attached to him. Napoleon's sword was broken; he arrived before Paris too late to save the city, which had just capitulated, and the foreigners were about to make their triumphal entrance. Could a woman of twenty-two be strong enough to withstand the tempest? Would she be brave enough, could she indeed remain in Paris without disobeying Napoleon? Was not flight a duty for the hapless sovereign? The Emperor had written to his brother, King Joseph: "In no case must you let the Empress and the King of Rome fall into the enemy's hands. Do not abandon my son, and remember that I had rather see him in the Seine than in the hands of the enemies of France. The lot of Astyanax, a prisoner among the Greeks, has always seemed to me the unhappiest in history." But, alas! in spite of the great Emperor's precautions, the King of Rome was condemned by fate to be the modern Astyanax, and Marie Louise was not as constant as Andromache.

The allied forces drew near, and there was no more time for flight. March 29, 1814, horses and carriages had been stationed in the Carrousel since the morning. At seven o'clock Marie Louise was dressed and ready to leave, but they could not abandon hope; they wished still to await some possible bit of good news which should prevent their leaving, — an envoy from Napoleon, a messenger from King Joseph. The officers of the National Guard were anxious to have the Empress stay. "Remain," they urged; "we swear to defend you." Marie Louise thanked them through her tears, but the Emperor's orders were positive; on no account were the Empress and the King of Rome to fall into the enemy's hands. The peril grew. Ever since four o'clock Marie Louise had kept putting off the moment of leaving, in expectation that something would turn up. Eleven struck, and the Minister of War came, declaring there was not a moment to lose. One would have thought that the little King of Rome, who was just three years old, knew that he was about to go, never to return. "Don't go to Rambouillet," he cried to his mother; "that's a gloomy castle; let us stay here." And he clung to the banisters, struggling with the equerry who was carrying him, weeping and shouting, "I don't want to leave my house; I don't want to go away; since papa is away, I am the master." Marie Louise was impressed by this childish opposition; a secret voice told her that her son was right; that by abandoning the capital, they surrendered it to the Royalists. But the lot was cast, and they had to leave. A mere handful of indifferent spectators, attracted by no other feeling than curiosity, watched the flight of the sovereign who, four years before, had made her formal entrance into this same palace of the Tuileries under a triumphal arch, amid noisy acclamations. There was not a tear in the eyes of the few spectators; they uttered no sound, they made no movement of sympathy or regret; there was only a sullen silence. But one person wept, and that was Marie Louise. When she had reached the Champs Elyseés, she cast a last sad glance at the palace she was never to see again. It was not a flight, but a funeral.

The Empress and the King of Rome took refuge at Blois, where there appeared a faint shadow of Imperial government. On Good Friday, April 8, Count Shouvaloff reached Blois with a detachment of Cossacks, and carried Marie Louise and her son to Rambouillet, where the Emperor of Austria was to join them. What Napoleon had feared was soon realized.

April 16, the Emperor of Austria was at Blois. Marie Louise, who two years before had left her father, starting on her triumphal journey to Prague, amid all form of splendor and devotion, was much moved at seeing him again, and placed the King of Rome in his arms, as if to reproach him for deserting the child's cause. The grandfather relented, but the monarch was stern: did he not soon say to Marie Louise: "As my daughter, everything that I have is yours, even my blood and my life; as a sovereign, I do not know you"? The Russian sentinels at the entrance of the castle of Rambouillet were relieved by Austrian grenadiers. The Empress of the French changed captors; she was the prisoner no longer of the Czar's soldiers, but of her own father. Her conjugal affection was not yet wholly extinct, and she reproached herself with not having joined Napoleon at Fontainebleau; but her scruples were soon allayed by the promise that she should soon see her husband again at Elba. She was told that the treaty which had just been signed gave her, and after her, her son, the duchies of Parma, Piacenza, and Guastalla; that the King of Rome was henceforth the hereditary Duke of Parma; that if she had duties as a wife, she also had duties as a mother; that she ought to gain the good-will of the powers, and assure her child's future. They added that she ought to give her husband time to establish himself at Elba, and that meanwhile she would find in Vienna, near her loving parents, a few weeks of moral and physical rest, which must be very necessary after so many emotions and sufferings. Marie Louise, who had been brought up to give her father strict obedience, regarded the advice of the Emperor of Austria as commands which were not to be questioned, and April 23 she left Rambouillet with her son for Vienna.

Did the dethroned Empress carry away with her a pleasant memory of France and the French people? We do not think so; and, to be frank, was what had just happened likely to give her a favorable idea of the country she was leaving? Could she have much love for the people who were fastening a rope to pull down the statue of the hero of Austerlitz from its pedestal, the Vendôme column? When her father, the Emperor Francis I., had been defeated, driven from his capital, overwhelmed with the blows of fate, his misfortunes had only augmented his popularity; the more he suffered, the more he was loved. But for Napoleon, who was so adored in the day of triumph, how was he treated in adversity? What was the language of the Senate, lately so obsequious and servile? The men on whom the Emperor had literally showered favors, called him contemptuously Monsieur de Bonaparte. What did they do to save the crown of the King of Rome, whose cradle they had saluted with such noisy acclamations? Were not the Cossacks who went to Blois after the Empress rapturously applauded by the French, in Paris itself, upon the very boulevards? Did not the marshals of the Empire now serve as an escort to Louis XVIII.? Where were the eagles, the flags, and the tricolored cockades? When Napoleon was passing through Provence on his way to take possession of his ridiculous realm of Elba, he was compelled to wear an Austrian officer's uniform to escape being put to death by Frenchmen; the imperial mantle was exchanged for a disguise. It is true that Marie Louise abandoned the French; but did not the French abandon her and her son after the abdication of Fontainebleau; and if this child did not become Napoleon II., is not the fault theirs? And did she not do all that could be demanded of her as regent? Can she be accused of intriguing with the Allies; and if at the last moment she left Paris, was it not in obedience to her husband's express command? She might well have said what fifty-six years later the second Emperor said so sadly when he was a prisoner in Germany: "In France one must never be unfortunate." What was then left for her to do in that volcano, that land which swallows all greatness and glory, amid that fickle people who change their opinions and passions as an actress changes her dress? Where Napoleon, with all his genius, had made a complete failure, could a young, ignorant woman be reasonably expected to succeed in the face of all Europe? Were her hands strong enough to rebuild the colossal edifice that lay in ruins upon the ground?

Such were the reflections of Marie Louise as she was leaving France. The moment she touched German soil, all the ideas, impressions, feelings of her girlhood, came back to her, and naturally enough; for were there not many instances in the last war, of German women, married to Frenchmen, who rejoiced in the German successes, and of French women, married to Germans, who deplored them? Marriage is but an incident; one's nature is determined at one's birth. In Austria, Marie Louise found again the same sympathy and affection that she had left there. There was a sort of conspiracy to make her forget France and love Germany. The Emperor Francis persuaded her that he was her sole protector, and controlled her with the twofold authority of a father and a sovereign. She who a few days before had been the Empress of the French, the Queen of Italy, the Regent of a vast empire, was in her father's presence merely a humble and docile daughter, who told him everything, obeyed him in everything, who abdicated her own free will, and promised, even swore, to entertain no other ideas or wishes than such as agreed with his.

Nevertheless, when she arrived at Vienna, Marie Louise had by no means completely forgotten France and Napoleon. She still had Frenchmen in her suite; she wrote to her husband and imagined that she would be allowed to visit him at Elba, but she perfectly understood all the difficulties of the double part she was henceforth called upon to play. She felt that whatever she might do she would be severely criticised; that it would be almost impossible to secure the approval of both her father and her husband. Since she was intelligent enough to foresee that she would be blamed by her contemporaries and by posterity, was she not justified in lamenting her unhappy lot? She, who under any other conditions would have been an excellent wife and mother, was compelled by extraordinary circumstances to appear as a heartless wife and an indifferent mother. This thought distressed Marie Louise, who at heart was not thoroughly contented with herself. She wrote, under date of August 9, 1814: "I am in a very unhappy and critical position; I must be very prudent in my conduct. There are moments when that thought so distracts me that I think that the best thing I could do would be to die."

When Napoleon returned from Elba, the situation of Marie Louise, so far from improving, became only more difficult. She had no illusions about the fate that awaited her audacious husband, who was unable to contend, single-handed, against all Europe. She knew better than any one, not only that he had nothing to hope from the Emperor of Austria, his father-in-law, but that in this sovereign he would find a bitter, implacable foe. As to the Emperor Alexander, he swore that he would sacrifice his last ruble, his last soldier, before he would consent to let Napoleon reign in France. Marie Louise knew too well the feeling that animated the Congress at Vienna, to imagine that her husband had the slightest chance of success. She was convinced that by returning from Elba, he was only preparing for France a new invasion, and for himself chains. Since she was a prisoner of the Coalition, she was condemned to widowhood, even in the lifetime of her husband. She cannot then be blamed for remaining at Vienna, whence escape was absolutely impossible.

Marie Louise committed one great error; that, namely, of writing that inasmuch as she was entirely without part in the plans of the Emperor Napoleon, she placed herself under the protection of the Allies,—Allies who at that very moment were urging the assassination of her husband, in the famous declaration of March 13, 1815, in which they said: "By breaking the convention, which established him on the island of Elba, Bonaparte has destroyed the only legal title on which his existence depended. By reappearing in France, with plans of disturbance and turmoil, he has, by his own act, forfeited the protection of the laws, and has shown to the world that there can be no peace or truce with him as a party. The Powers consequently declare that Napoleon Bonaparte has placed himself outside of all civil and social relations, and that as an enemy and disturber of the world's peace, he exposes himself to public vengeance." April 16, at the moment when the processions designed to pray for the success of the Austrian armies, were going through the streets of Vienna to visit the Cathedral and the principal churches, the Empress of Austria dared to ask the former Empress of the French to accompany the processions with the rest of the court; but Marie Louise rejected the insulting proposal. The 6th of May next, when M. de Méneval, who was about to return to France, came to bid farewell and to receive her commands, she spoke to this effect to the faithful subject who was soon to see Napoleon: "I am aware that all relations between me and France are coming to an end, but I shall always cherish the memory of my adopted home.... Convince the Emperor of all the good I wish him. I hope that he will understand the misery of my position.... I shall never assent to a divorce, but I flatter myself that he will not oppose an amicable separation, and that he will not bear any ill feeling towards me.... This separation has become imperative; it will in no way affect the feelings of esteem and gratitude that I preserve." Then she gave to M. de Méneval a gold snuff-box, bearing his initials in diamonds, as a memento, and left him, to hide the emotion by which she was overcome. Her emotion was not very deep, and her tears soon dried. In 1814 she had met the man who was to make her forget her duty towards her illustrious husband. He was twenty years older than she, and always wore a large black band to hide the scar of a wound by which he had lost an eye. As diplomatist and as a soldier he had been one of the most persistent and one of the most skilful of Napoleon's enemies. General the Count of Neipperg, as he called himself, had been especially active in persuading two Frenchmen, Bernadotte and Murat, to take up arms against France. Since 1814 he had been most devoted to Marie Louise, and he felt or pretended to feel for her an affection on which she did not fear to smile. She admitted him to her table; he became her chamberlain, her advocate at the Congress of Vienna, her prime minister in the Duchy of Parma, and after Napoleon's death, her morganatic husband. He had three children by her,— two daughters (one of whom died young; the other married the son of the Count San Vitale, Grand Chamberlain of Parma) and one son (who took the title of Count of Montenuovo and served in the Austrian army). Until his death in 1829 the Count of Neipperg completely controlled Marie Louise, as Napoleon had never done.

After Waterloo, every day dimmed Marie Louise's recollections of France. The four years of her reign—two spent in the splendor of perpetual adoration, two in the gloom of disasters culminating in final ruin—were like a distant dream, half a golden vision, half a hideous nightmare. It was all but a brief episode in her life. She thoroughly deserved the name of "the Austrian," which had been given unjustly to Marie Antoinette; for Marie Antoinette really became a Frenchwoman. The Duchess of Parma—for that was the title of the woman who had worn the two crowns of France and of Italy—lived more in her principality than in Vienna, more interested in the Count of Neipperg than in the Duke of Reichstadt. While her son never left the Emperor Francis, she reigned in her little duchy. But the title was to expire at her death; for the Coalition had feared to permit a son of Napoleon to have an hereditary claim to rule over Parma. Yet Marie Louise cannot properly be called a bad mother. She went to close the eyes of her son, who died in his twenty-second year, of consumption and disappointment.

By this event was broken the last bond which attached Napoleon's widow to the imperial traditions. In 1833 she was married, for the third time, to a Frenchman, the son of an émigré in the Austrian service. He was a M. de Bombelles, whose mother had been a Miss Mackan, an intimate friend of Madame Elisabeth, and had married the Count of Bombelles, ambassador of Louis XVI. in Portugal, and later in Venice, who took orders after his wife's death and became Bishop of Amiens under the Restoration. Marie Louise, who died December 17, 1847, aged fifty-six, lived in surroundings directly hostile to Napoleon's glory. Her ideas in her last years grew to resemble those of her childhood, and she was perpetually denouncing the principles of the French Revolution and of the liberalism which pursued her even in the Duchy of Parma. France has reproached her with abandoning Napoleon, and still more perhaps for having given two obscure successors to the most famous man of modern times.

If Marie Louise is not a very sympathetic figure, no story is more touching and more melancholy than that of her son's life and death. It is a tale of hope deceived by reality; of youth and beauty cut down in their flower; of the innocent paying for the guilty; of the victim marked by fate as the expiation for others. One might say that he came into the world only to give a lasting example of the instability of human greatness. When he was at the point of death, worn out with suffering, he said sadly, "My birth and my death comprise my whole history." But this short story is perhaps richer in instruction than the longest reigns. The Emperor's son will be known for many ages by his three titles, — the King of Rome, Napoleon II., and the Duke of Reichstadt. He had already inspired great poets, and given to philosophers and Christians occasion for profound thoughts. His memory is indissolubly bound up with that of his father, and posterity will never forget him. Even those who are most virulent against Napoleon's memory, feel their wrath melt when they think of his son; and when at the Church of the Capuchins, in Vienna, a monk lights with a flickering torch the dark tomb of the great captain's son, who lies by the side of his grandfather, Francis II., who was at once his protector and his jailer, deep thoughts arise as one considers the vanity of political calculations, the emptiness of glory, of power, and of genius.

Poor boy! His birth was greeted with countless thanksgivings, celebrations, and joyous applause. Paris was beside itself when in the morning of March 20, 1811, there sounded the twenty-second report of a cannon, announcing that the Emperor had, not a daughter, but a son. He lay in a costly cradle of mother-of-pearl and gold, surmounted by a winged Victory which seemed to protect the slumbers of the King of Rome. The Imperial heir in his gilded baby-carriage drawn by two snow-white sheep beneath the trees at Saint Cloud was a charming object. He was but a year old when Gérard painted him in his cradle, playing with a cup and ball, as if the cup were a sceptre and the ball were the world, with which his childish hands were playing. When on the eve of the battle of Moskowa, Napoleon was giving his final orders for the tremendous struggle of the next day, a courier, M. de Bausset, arrived suddenly from Paris, bringing with him this masterpiece of Gérard's; at once the General forgot his anxieties in his paternal joy. "Gentlemen," said Napoleon to his officers, "if my son were fifteen years old, you may be sure that he would be here among this multitude of brave men, and not merely in a picture." Then he had the portrait of the King of Rome set out in front of his tent, on a chair, that the sight of it might be an added excitement to victory. And the old grenadiers of the Imperial Guard, the veterans with their grizzly moustaches,—the men who were never to abandon their Emperor, who followed him to Elba, and died at Waterloo,—heroes, as kind as they were brave, actually cried with joy as they gazed at the portrait of this boy whose glorious future they hoped to make sure by their brave deeds.

But what a sad future it was! Within less than two years Cossacks were the escort of the King of Rome. When the Coalition made him a prisoner, he was forever torn from his father. Napoleon, March 20, 1815, on this return from Elba, re-entered triumphantly the Palace of the Tuileries as if by miracle, but his joy was incomplete. March 20 was his son's birthday, the day he was four years old, and the boy was not there; his father never saw him again. At Vienna the little prince seemed the victim of an untimely gloom; he missed his young playmates. "Any one can see that I am not a king," he said; "I haven't any pages now."

The King of Rome had lost the childish merriment and the talkativeness which had made him very captivating. So far from growing familiar with those among whom he was thrown, he seemed rather to be suspicious and distrustful of them. During the Hundred Days the private secretary of Marie Louise left her at Vienna to return to Napoleon in France. "Have you any message for your father?" he asked of the little prince. The boy thought for a moment, and then, as if he were watched, led the faithful officer up to the window and whispered to him, very low, "You will tell him that I always love him dearly."

In spite of the many miles that separated them, the son was to be a consolation to his father. In 1816 the prisoner at Saint Helena received a lock of the young prince's hair, and a letter which he had written with his hand held by some one else. Napoleon was filled with joy, and forgot his chains. It was a renewal of the happiness he had felt on the eve of Moskowa, when he had received the portrait of the son he loved so warmly. Once again he summoned those who were about him and, deeply moved, showed to them the lock of hair and the letter of his child.

For his part, the boy did not forget his father. In vain they gave him a German title and a German name, and removed the Imperial arms with their eagle; in vain they expunged the Napoleon from his name,—Napoleon, which was an object of terror to the enemies of France. His Highness, Prince Francis Charles Joseph, Duke of Reichstadt, knew very well that his title was the King of Rome and Napoleon II. He knew that in his veins there flowed the blood of the greatest warrior of modern times. He had scarcely left the cradle when he began to show military tastes. When only five, he said to Hummel, the artist, who was painting his portrait: "I want to be a soldier. I shall fight well. I shall be in the charge." "But," urged the artist, "you will find the bayonets of the grenadiers in your way, and they will kill you perhaps." And the boy answered, "But shan't I have a sword to beat down the bayonets?" Before he was seven he wore a uniform. He learned eagerly the manual of arms; and when he was rewarded by promotion to the grade of sergeant, he was as proud of his stripes as he would have been of a throne. His father's career continually occupied his thoughts and filled his imagination with a sort of ecstasy.

At Paris the fickle multitude soon forgot the son of the Emperor. In 1820 the capital saluted the birth of the Duke of Bordeaux as it had saluted that of the King of Rome. A close relationship united the two children who represented two such distinct parties; their mothers were first-cousins on both their fathers' and their mothers' side. The Duchess of Berry, mother of the Duke of Bordeaux, was the daughter of the King of Naples, Francis I., son of King Ferdinand IV. and Queen Marie Caroline; and her mother was the Princess Marie Clementine, daughter of the Emperor Leopold II. The Emperor Francis, father of the Empress Marie Louise, was himself the son of Leopold II.; his wife was Princess Marie Thérèse of Naples, daughter of Queen Marie Caroline and aunt of the Duchess of Berry. The King of Rome and the Duke of Bordeaux were thus in two ways second-cousins. July 22, 1821, at Schoenbrunn, in the same room where, eleven years later, in the same month and on the same day of the month, he was to breathe his last, the child who had been the King of Rome learned that his father was dead. This news plunged him into deep grief. He had been forbidden the name of Bonaparte or Napoleon, but he was allowed to weep. The Duke of Reichstadt and his household were allowed to wear mourning for the exile of Saint Helena.

In justice to the Emperor Francis it must be said that he showed great affection for his grandson, whom he kept always near him, in his chamber and in his study, and that he hid from him neither Napoleon's misfortunes nor his successes. "I desire," he told Prince Metternich, "that the Duke of Reichstadt shall respect his father's memory, that he shall take example from his firm qualities and learn to recognize his faults, in order to shun them and be on his guard against their influence. Speak to the prince about his father as you should like to be spoken about to your own son. Do not hide anything from him, but teach him to honor his father's memory."

Military drill, manoeuvres, strategy, the study of great generals, especially of Napoleon, formed the young prince's favorite occupations.

So long as the elder branch of the Bourbons reigned in France, the Duke of Reichstadt never thought of seizing his father's crown and sceptre, but the Revolution of 1830 suddenly kindled all his hopes. When he learned that the tricolored flag had taken the place of the white one, and heard of the enthusiasm that had seized the French for the men and deeds of the Empire; when he heard the Austrian ministers continually saying that Louis Philippe was a mere usurper who could reign but a short time; when his grandfather, the Emperor Francis, who was the incarnation of prudence and wisdom, said to him one day, "If the French people should want you, and the Allies were to give their consent, I should not oppose your taking your place on the French throne," and, at another time, "You have only to show yourself on the bridge at Strasbourg, and it is all up with the Orléans at Paris,"—the Duke was carried away by a feeling of ambition, patriotism, and exaltation. Born to glory, he imagined himself divinely summoned to a magnificent destiny; wide and brilliant horizons opened before him. His eager imagination was kindled by a hidden flame. In his youthful dreams he saw himself resuscitating Poland, restoring the glories of the Empire. He prepared for the part he was to play by studying with Marshal Marmont the campaigns of Napoleon. These lessons lasted three months, and at their end the Duke gave his portrait to his father's fellow-soldier, and copied beneath it four lines from Racine's *Phèdre*, in which Hippolyte says to Théramène:—

"Having come to me with a sincere interest,
You told to me my father's story;
You know how my soul, attentive to your words,
Kindled at the recital of his noble exploits."

He was as enthusiastic for poetry as for the military profession. One day his physician, Dr. Malfatti, quoted to him two lines from the author of the *Meditations*:—

"Limited in his nature, infinite in his desires,
Man is a fallen god who remembers heaven."

"That's a fine thought," said the young prince; "it is as pleasing as it is striking. I am sorry that I don't know Lamartine's poetry." The physician promised to send him the *Meditations*. The next day the Duke read the volume aloud; his eyes moistened and his voice broke when he came to these lines in which the poet seemed to be addressing him:—

"Courage, fallen scion of a divine race;
You carry your celestial origin on your brow;

> Every one who sees you, sees in your eyes
> A darkened ray of heavenly splendor."

And, indeed, every one recognized in him a really extraordinary being; his face, his gestures, his bearing, all had an imperial air. He seemed born to rule in a drawing-room as well as in a barracks. He was admired as well as loved; he was a true son of Caesar, born for success in love as well as for glory. When he appeared in the ball-room, his pale coloring, his lively expression, his military bearing, his proud but quiet manners, the mingled energy and gentleness of his face, attracted every woman's eye. When he appeared before his soldiers, he filled them with the wildest enthusiasm. One day when he happened to be riding a fiery horse at the review of his battalion, his superb appearance made such an impression on the troops that, although they were accustomed to maintain a profound silence in the ranks, they suddenly broke out into shouts of admiration.

Yet in spite of all his ardor it was only at intervals that Napoleon's son felt hopeful. If at one time he had confidence in his star, this feeling soon yielded to deep depression. The brilliant prospects evoked by the events in Poland and in France shone for but a moment, and then vanished. The court of Vienna recognized the monarchy of July. One day some one was urging him to go to a ball given by Marshal Maison, the French minister at the Austrian court. "What should I do," he asked, "at the house of Louis Philippe's ambassador? Has not his government exiled and outlawed me? No one there could see me without blushing; and then, too, what would my feelings be?" He became restless and silent, and distrusted even his best friends. "Answer me, my friend," he said to his confidant, Count Prokesch-Osten, "answer me this question,—which is one of great importance to me just now: What do people think of me? Do they see in me any justification for the caricatures which are forever presenting me as a creature of the feeblest intelligence?" Count Prokesch answered him: "Don't worry. Don't you appear in public every day? Can even the most ignorant see you and place the slightest confidence in such fables, which are invented by charlatans without the least care for truth?" But the young Duke was not consoled, and every day he lost confidence in his future. Once Count Prokesch-Osten found him meditating upon his father's will. "The fourth paragraph of the first article," he said, "contains the guiding principle of my life. There my father bids me not to forget that I was born a French prince." And we may be sure that he never forgot it; and if he was so uneasy, if he suffered keenly, and grief drove him with startling rapidity to the tomb, it was because he felt that fate condemned him to live and die an Austrian prince.

His overwrought mind and body soon made him ill. He sought by violent emotions and excessive fatigue to escape from the thoughts which were persecuting him like spectres, and driving him to his death. In vain the physicians commanded rest and quiet. When attacked by an incurable lung trouble, he required absolute repose: but repose was torture; he preferred death as a deliverance. Dr. Malfatti, who took the keenest interest in him, and who was much disturbed by his many imprudences, entreated him not to throw away wantonly a life which might be so well and usefully employed. "It is a great pity, sir, that Your Highness," he said, "can't change bodies as you change horses, when they are tired. I beg of you to notice that you have a soul of steel in a crystal body, and that the abuse of your will can only be pernicious to you."

The young invalid did not listen to him: he scarcely slept; his appetite failed him; he made no account of the weather; he rode the wildest horses the longest distances. His chest and throat became seriously affected, but it made no difference; he still wanted to command at the reviews. His voice was lost: soon he could not even speak; but his illness did not depress, it only annoyed him. His energetic character could not accustom itself to the idea of abandoning the struggle. He fought against suffering as he had fought against fate. "Oh!" he said, "how I despise this wretched body which cannot obey my soul!" Dr. Malfatti said, "There seems to be in this unfortunate young man an active principle impelling him to a sort of suicide; reasoning and precaution are of no avail against the fatality which urges him on."

The end drew near; the completion of the sacrifice approached. The victim did not pray that the cup might pass from his lips. He ceased to struggle against the inevitable, and submitted to his fate, becoming as gentle and peaceful as a child. As the earth left him, he turned to heaven. "I understood and felt," said Count Prokesch-Osten, "all the sublimity there is in religion, which alone could throw a light on this man's path, through the uncertainty and darkness that surrounded him…. Religion is our staff. We can find no surer support in our journey through the darkness of our life on earth." He had received from the Emperor and Empress of Austria a book of prayers, called *Divine Harmonies*, which he read over and over on his bed of suffering. It contained these words written by his grandfather's hand: "In every incident of your life, in every struggle of your soul, may God aid you with His light and strength; this is the most ardent wish of your loving grandparents." "This book is very dear to me," the prince said to his friend, after a serious talk on religious matters; "those words, written by relatives whom I sincerely respect and thoroughly love, have an inestimable value for me, and yet I give it to you. I want what I most value to go to you, in memory of what seems to me the most important of our conversations."

When he was dying, he wanted to gaze at the crucifix, in order not to complain of his sad lot, dying thus at the very threshold of a career which promised to be brilliant and glorious; to go down so early to the gloomy tomb of the Hapsburgs! To exchange his glowing visions for this untimely end; to find an Austrian tomb instead of the throne of France! He accepted his fate, but he wished as few witnesses as possible of his last sufferings. He did not want to show to the world a son of Napoleon so weak and broken. He could scarcely lift the weak, worn hand which should have wielded Charlemagne's sword and sceptre. "I am so weak," he said; "I beg of you not to let any one see me in my misery!" His sumptuous cradle he had given to the Imperial Treasury of Vienna, which is near the Church of the Capuchins, where he was to be buried. "My cradle and my grave will be near each other," he said. "My birth and my death—that's my whole story." In the overthrow, by lightning, of one of the eagles surmounting the palace of Schoenbrunn, the populace saw a prophecy of the death there of Napoleon's son, and in fact it was there that he died, in the room which his father had occupied in 1809, when possibly for the first time he thought of this Austrian marriage, which should—such at least was his dream—guarantee to the Napoleonic dynasty unlimited power and glory. The prince desired only one thing,— to see his mother. She came, and he greeted her with tenderness. He had also near him his young and beautiful relative, the Archduchess Sophia, the mother of the present Emperor of Austria. This charming princess, who was very fond of the young man who was approaching his end, told him that the time had come for him to receive the last sacraments. "We will pray together," she said; "I will pray for you, and you shall pray for me and for my unborn child." The prince, consoled and strengthened by the aid of religion, died in the enjoyment of a firm faith and thorough piety. "Mother, mother!" were his last words. General Hartmann said: "Having passed my life on battle-fields, I have often seen death, but I never saw a soldier die more bravely." The 22d of July was a very momentous date in the career of this young prince. It was July 22, 1818, that the title of Duke of Reichstadt was substituted for his name of Napoleon Bonaparte; July 22, 1821, he heard of his father's death; and July 22, 1832, he died at the age of twenty-one years four months and two days.

We desire to make five studies of the second wife and the son of Napoleon I. The first, which we are now beginning, covers a period of brilliancy of infatuation, of fairy-like splendor, which in all its glow forms a striking contrast with the dreadful shadows that follow. With the aid of eye-witnesses whose memoirs abound with most valuable recollections—such as Prince Metternich, who had the principal charge of the Archduchess's marriage; M. de Bausset and General de Ségur, both attached to the Emperor Napoleon's household, so that they saw him nearly every day; Madame Durand, the Empress's first lady-in-waiting; Baron de Méneval, his private secretary—with their aid we shall try to recall the brilliant past, taking for our motto that phrase of Michelet: "History is a resurrection." An excellent work, which deserves translation, Von Helfert's *Marie Louise, Empress of the French*, throws a great deal of light on the early years of the mother of the King of Rome. In the archives of the Ministers of Foreign Affairs—thanks to the intelligent and liberal control which facilitates historic research—we have found a great number of curious documents which had never been published, such as letters written to Napoleon by the Emperor and Empress of Austria, and despatches from his ambassador at Vienna, Count Otto. This first study will carry us to the beginning of the Russian campaign, that glorious period when the unheard-of prosperity promised to be eternal. No darker night was ever preceded by a more brilliant sun. Napoleon said on the rock of Saint Helena: "Marie Louise had a short reign; but she must have enjoyed it; the world was at her feet."

I
EARLY YEARS

Marie Louise, Archduchess of Austria, Empress of the French, Queen of Italy, afterwards Duchess of Parma, Piacenza, and Guastalla, was born in Vienna, December 12, 1791, the daughter of Archduke Francis, Prince Imperial, who a year later became Emperor of Germany under the name of Francis II., and of Marie Thérèse, Princess of Naples, daughter of King Ferdinand IV. and Queen Marie Caroline.

Marie Louise's father was born February 12, 1768, a year and a half earlier than the Emperor Napoleon. He was the grandson of the great Empress Marie Thérèse, and son of the Emperor Leopold II., who was the brother of the Queen of France, Marie Antoinette, and whom he succeeded March 1, 1792; his mother was a Spanish princess, a daughter of Charles III. of Spain. He had four wives. He was an excellent husband, but his family affections were so strong that he could not remain a widower. In 1788 he married his first wife, Princess Elizabeth Wilhelmina Louisa of Wurtemberg, who died February 17, 1790, in giving birth to a daughter who lived but six months. The same year he married by proxy at Naples, August 15, and September 19 in person at Vienna, the young Neapolitan princess Marie Thérèse, daughter of Ferdinand IV. and of Marie Caroline, who ruled over the Two Sicilies.

The young princess, who was born June 6, 1772, was then eighteen years old. She was kind, virtuous, and well educated, and her influence at the court of Vienna was most excellent. Her mother, who during her reign of thirty-six years endured many trials and exhibited great qualities as well as great faults, was a remarkable woman.

Marie Caroline, the Queen of Naples, was energetic to excess, courageous to the point of heroism; she believed that severity and sometimes even cruelty was demanded of a sovereign; her religion amounted to superstition, her love of authority to despotism; she alternated between passionate devotion to pleasure and earnest zeal for her duty; she was ardent in her affections and implacable in resentment, intense in her joys and in her sorrows; she was often an unwise queen, but as a mother she was beyond reproach. Like the matrons of antiquity and her illustrious mother, the Empress Marie Thérèse, she was proud of her large family; she had no fewer than seventeen children, and political cares never prevented her actively and intelligently caring for their moral and physical welfare. If she had not the happiness of seeing them all grow up, those who survived were yet the constant object of her tender solicitude. She took a prominent part in the education of her two sons, the Duke of Calabria and the Prince of Salerno, and still more in that of her five daughters: Marie Thérèse, the wife of the Emperor Francis II.; Marie Louise, who married the Archduke Ferdinand, Grand Duke of Tuscany; Marie Christine, wife of Charles Felix, Duke of Genoa, later King of Sardinia; Marie Amélie, Duchess of Orleans, then Queen of France; Marie Antoinette, first wife of the Prince of Asturias, later Ferdinand VII., King of Spain.

Marie Caroline was very fond of her eldest daughter, Marie Thérèse; and when the princess had, in 1790, married the Archduke Francis, two years later Emperor of Germany, the mother and daughter kept up an active and affectionate correspondence in French. They were forever consulting each other about their babies, which were born at about the same time. When the daughter had given birth to her first child, the future French Empress, the Queen congratulated her most warmly: "I congratulate you on your courage. I am sure that when you look at your baby, which I hear is large, sturdy, and strong, that you forget all that you have been through." Scarcely was this child born than the Queen, who was most anxious to have a number of descendants, besought her daughter to give the Archduchess Marie Louise a little brother. April 17, 1793, there was born an Archduke Ferdinand, later Emperor of Germany; and his grandmother, Queen Marie Caroline, wrote: "I wept for joy! Thank Heaven for the birth of this boy!" Indeed, the wife of the Emperor Francis II. followed her mother's example with regard to her own children. Her eldest daughter, the Archduchess Marie Louise, she educated most carefully. The little princess, who had a most amiable disposition, was an eager student, and acquired a good knowledge of French, English, Italian, drawing, and music. She was brought up to respect religion and to detest revolutionary ideas.

Her grandmother, Queen Marie Caroline, who in 1800 came to visit the Austrian court and stayed there two years, had many conversations with Marie Louise, which certainly were unlikely to inspire her with any taste for the French Revolution or for General Bonaparte. It is easy to understand how extremely the high-spirited and haughty Queen of the Two Sicilies must have been distressed and revolted by the sufferings and death of her sister, Marie Antoinette. There was something very solemn in the way in which she told her children what took place in Paris October 16, 1793. She had them all summoned. They found her dressed in deep black, with tears in her eyes; and she led them without a word to the chapel in the royal palace of Naples, and there, before the altar, she told them that the people of regicides had just put their aunt to death upon the scaffold. Then she bade them all to pray together for the peace of the victim's soul, and probably there mingled with Marie Caroline's prayer thoughts of wrath and vengeance. From that time she waged against the principles and the spread of the Revolution a relentless, implacable war, of varying result, which filled her more and more with detestation of the new France. On the occasion of Bonaparte's expedition to Egypt, she deemed the time ripe for a general uprising in Italy against the French. But Championnet had taken possession of Naples when the Parthenopean Republic had been proclaimed, and the Queen had been obliged, with her family, to take refuge at Palermo.

In the next year, 1799, the conditions of things changed; and while Milan was recovered by Austria, and the Russian army, led by Suwarow, completed the expulsion of the French from Northern and Southern Italy, the Parthenopean Republic expired, and the Bourbon flag waved once more over the walls of Naples.

Early in 1800 the French cause seemed forever lost in Italy; General Masséna alone held out at Genoa. Queen Marie Caroline had triumphed; and she conceived the plan of going to Austria to visit her daughter, the Empress, and to make the acquaintance of her grandchildren, whom she had never seen, and at the same time to demand an enlargement of her territory in return for the sacrifices of the Kingdom of the Two Sicilies in behalf of the common cause of the crowned heads and the Pope. She set sail from Palermo, June 9, 1800, with her second son, the Prince of Salerno, and her three unmarried daughters, Marie Christine, Marie Amélie, and Marie Antoinette.

The ideas, the feelings, the principles, the prejudices, the hates, the hopes, the interests, of Queen Marie Caroline were the same as those of her son-in-law, the Emperor, of her daughter, the Empress, and of her other daughter, the Grand Duchess of Tuscany. At Vienna she found the same political feelings as at Naples. On her way thither she had a great joy,—the news of the surrender of the French at Genoa, which caused her to utter cries of delight; and a great sorrow,—the tidings of the Austrian defeat at Marengo, which was such a blow that she fell unconscious and narrowly escaped dying of apoplexy. We may readily understand the influence which a woman of this character must have had on the mind of her daughter, the Empress of Germany, and of her granddaughter, the future Empress of the French. Doubtless the young Marie Louise would have been much astonished if any one had prophesied to her that she would marry this Bonaparte who was represented to her as a monster. Marie Caroline did not leave Schoenbrunn to return to her own kingdom until July 29, 1802. For two years she had worked persistently and not without success, to augment, if that was possible, the detestation which the court, the aristocracy, and the whole Austrian people felt for France and French ideas. When Marie Louise was a child, and with her little brothers and sisters used to play with toy-soldiers, the ugliest, blackest, and most repulsive of them was always picked out and called Bonaparte, and this one they used to prick with pins and denounce in every way.

The war of 1805, which brought Austria to the brink of ruin, added to the Archduchess's instinctive repulsion for Napoleon. At Vienna the panic was extreme; the Imperial family was obliged to flee in different directions. Marie Louise was only fourteen years old, and she was already learning bitter lessons at the school of experience. Seeking shelter in Hungary, and afterwards in Galicia, she prayed most warmly for the success of the Austrians. She wrote: "Papa must be finally successful, and the time must come when the usurper will lose heart. Perhaps God has let him go so far to make his ruin more complete when He shall have abandoned him." November 21, 1805, a few days before the battle of Austerlitz, she wrote a letter to her governess's husband, Count Colloredo, in which she said: "God must be very wroth with us, since He punishes us so sorely. Perhaps at this very moment there is living in one of our rooms at Schoenbrunn one of those generals who are as treacherous as cats. Our family is all scattered: my dear parents are at Olmütz; we are at Kaschan; there is a third colony at Ofen."

Every sort of misfortune combined to smite this suffering family. While the Emperor Francis was losing the battle of Austerlitz, his wife, who was in Silesia, with only one of her children, the little Archduchess Leopoldine, who was born in 1797 and was not yet eight years old, fell seriously ill with the measles, and dreaded giving the disease to her little girl. "The only thing which would make death terrible," she wrote to her husband, "would be to die without seeing you again…. Do not take a step that will injure you or the country. Only don't let me be taken to France." Nothing disturbed her so much as the dread of falling into the hands of the enemy. The details which her husband wrote to her about his interview with Napoleon did not allay her uneasiness. "I have been as happy," he wrote, "as I could hope to be with a conqueror who holds possession of a large part of my kingdom. With regard to his treatment of me and mine, he has been very kind. It is easy to see that he is not a Frenchman." Thus the Emperor Francis ascribed to Napoleon's Italian birth the politeness with which the hero of Austerlitz treated him. Does not this simple statement suffice to show in what esteem the German sovereign held France and the French character?

The Imperial family was at last reunited in Vienna, after many vicissitudes, early in 1806. But a new misfortune awaited them the following year. The Empress, whose health was already delicate, had a miscarriage April 9, 1807, and a pleurisy which seized her carried her off in four days, in due odor of sanctity, after she had given her blessing to Marie Louise and the rest of her children. She was only thirty-five. The untimely death of the amiable and virtuous princess, whose gayety and kindness had been the life and delight of the court, plunged her whole family into deep grief.

The Emperor Francis was an excellent husband, but he was not an inconsolable widower. April 13, 1807, he lost his second wife; but less than nine months afterwards, January 6, 1808, he married his young cousin, Marie Louise Beatrice of Este, daughter of the late Archduke Ferdinand of Modena. This princess, who was born December 14, 1787, was very short, but attractive in appearance and of an excellent character. Her disposition was pleasant and her intelligence acute, but she was not the woman to give Marie Louise any taste for France or the French; for if in all Europe there was a princess who utterly detested the French Revolution and all its works, it was the third wife of Francis II.

The new Empress was but four years older than her step-daughter, Marie Louise, and at the age of twenty-one, she looked much more like the sister than the step-mother of the young Archduchess, who was then in her seventeenth year. Nevertheless, the Empress took hold of the princess's education with a high hand, and displayed as much solicitude as if she had been her real mother.

II
1809

The Emperor Francis was not without distractions during his honeymoon with his third wife, the young Empress, Marie Louise Beatrice. It was evident to every one that the Peace of Presbourg, like that of Lunéville, could be nothing more than a truce. Austria could never be reconciled to its loss, between 1792 and 1806, of the Low Countries, Suabia, Milan, the Venetian States, Tyrol, Dalmatia, and finally of the Imperial crown of Germany; for the heir of the Germanic Caesars now styled himself simply the Emperor of Austria, and a great part of Germany had become the humble vassal of Napoleon. Of all the Austrians, it was perhaps the Emperor who felt the least hatred of France. His whole family and his whole people—nobles, priests, the middle classes, and the peasantry—nourished an angry resentment against the nation that was overturning Europe. The new Empress, whose family had been deprived of the Duchy of Modena, was conspicuous for the bitterness of her indignation and of her political feelings. In the eyes of all the Austrians, great or small, poor or rich, the French were the hereditary enemies, the invaders, the destroyers of the throne and the Church, impious, sacrilegious, revolutionary,—the authors of every evil. It was they who, for years, destroyed the harvests, shed torrents of blood, smote with the sword or the axe of the guillotine, crowded war upon war, heaped ruins upon ruins, bringing misery and disgrace to all mankind. The old nobility, once so proud of its coats-of-arms and of its sovereign rights, now enslaved, humiliated, shorn of its independence, knew no limit to its abuse of the "Corsican savage," who had cut the roots of the old Germanic tree, previously so majestic. The priests denounced the nation which had dared to confiscate the patrimony of Saint Peter, and they cursed in Napoleon the persecutor of the Holy Vicar of Christ. Women who had lost their husbands or sons in the war held France responsible for their afflictions. The Frenchmen, overthrowing and despoiling everything, foes of the human race, the enemies of morality and religion, brought suffering to princes in their palaces, to workmen in their factories, to tradespeople in their shops, to the priests in their churches, to the soldiers in their camps, to the peasants in their huts. The war of wrath was irresistible. Every one lamented the mistake that had been made in abandoning the struggle; all felt that they should have fought to the end, at the cost of every man and every florin; that a mistake had been made in not assisting Prussia at the time of the campaign of Jena; and that the moment had come for all the powers to combine against the common foe and to crush him. Did he make any pretence of concealing his intention to overthrow every throne, and to make himself the oldest sovereign? Had he not had the insolence to say at Milan in 1805, to the Prince of Cardito, the Neapolitan envoy extraordinary, "Tell your Queen that I shall leave to her and her family only enough land for their graves"? Had he not recently, under the walls of Madrid, uttered these significant words to the Spaniards, "If you don't want my brother Joseph for king, I shall not force him upon you. I have another throne for him; and as for you, I shall treat you as a conquered country"? This other throne, it was said at Vienna, this throne which Napoleon did not name, must be the throne of the Emperor Francis II. himself. Already the Imperial crown of Germany had been lost, and the Austrian crown was threatened. But, added all the archdukes and officers, that would not be so easy as the French imagined, and they would get a good lesson. The Hapsburgs were not so compliant as the Spanish Bourbons, and the Bayonne ambush could not be repeated. All Europe was thrilling with indignation; only a signal was needed for it to rise, and this signal Austria would give. This time there was every chance of success. Their cry was "Victory or Death!" but victory was certain. The French army, scattered from the Oder to the Tagus, from the mountains of Bohemia to the Sierra Morena, would not be able to withstand so many people eager to break their yoke. Were not Russia and Prussia as desirous as Austria of revenge? Was not the whole of Germany ready for the fray? Napoleon boasted that he was the Protector of the Confederation of the Rhine; but if the Confederate Princes were under his command, in his pay, the people, more patriotic, more truly German than their rulers, burned with a longing to expel the French. Let Napoleon suffer but a single defeat, and then on which one of his vassals would he be able to count? Could he even rely on his own subjects? Were there not already in his overgrown Empire many germs of decay and death? In Vienna in 1809 the same things were said as in Berlin in 1806; the same feelings prevailed. The military ardor had grown so intense that the greatest soldier of Austria, the Archduke Charles, was looked upon as too cool, too moderate, and those who were eager to begin the fight called this bold warrior, this famous general, the "Prince of Peace." Even if he had wished it, the Emperor Francis would not have been able to calm the warlike fever of his army and his people.

The musketry and the cannon would have fired themselves without waiting for war to be declared. The Landwehr, which had been organized only a few months, was impatient to cross swords with the veterans of the French army. Volunteers enlisted in crowds; patriotic gifts abounded. A story was told of a cobbler who, in despair at not being permitted to join the army, blew out his brains. Youths wished to leave school in order to serve. All classes of society rivalled one another in zeal, courage, and self-sacrifice. When it was known that the Archduke Charles had been appointed commander-in-chief, February 20, 1809, there was an outburst of confidence from one end of the Empire to the other. March 9, the Archbishop of Vienna solemnly blessed in the Cathedral the flags of the Viennese Landwehr. Together with the other members of the Imperial family, the young Archduchess Marie Louise was present at this patriotic and religious ceremony. Could she have imagined that one year later, to the delight of the vast majority of this same populace of Vienna, she was to become the wife of this Napoleon who then was calling forth such violent wrath and deep hatred?

Never was there such a terrible war; never perhaps had the world seen such slaughter. April 8, 1809, the Emperor Francis left his capital, leaving there his wife and children, who were not able to stay there after the fifth of May. From Vienna the Archduchess Marie Louise wrote frequently to her father. A rumor had spread that the battle of Eckmühl had been a brilliant victory for the Austrians, and Marie Louise wrote to her father, April 25: "We have heard with delight that Napoleon was present at the great battle which the French lost. May he lose his head as well! There are a great many prophecies about his speedy end, and people say that the Apocalypse applies to him. They maintain that he is going to die this year at Cologne, in an inn called the 'Red Crawfish.' I do not attach much importance to these prophecies, but how glad I should be to see them come true!" These sentiments, it must be confessed, are a singular preparation for the next year's wedding.

When the Empress of Austria was compelled to leave Vienna with her children at the approach of the enemy, she had more the appearance of an exile than of a sovereign. She was very ill at the time, and scarcely able to support the jolting of her carriage, and she groaned continually, as much from her moral as from her physical sufferings. "It is horrible," said Marie Louise, "to see her suffer so." It rained in torrents, and the thunder roared as if to foretell all the misfortunes which were about to overwhelm the country. The roads, made still worse by the bad weather, were abominable. When the fugitives reached Buda, after a long and difficult journey, they were wet through, and nearly worn out with fatigue.

The illusions of the Imperial family were speedily destroyed by the harsh reality. Vienna surrendered May 12, after suffering severely. In a few hours eighteen hundred shells had fallen in the city. The streets were narrow, the houses high, and the populace crowded within the narrow fortifications were terrified and infuriated at the sight of the damage caused by the shells, which started fires in every direction. Who would have said to the Viennese who were then hurling all manner of imprecations at Napoleon, the author of their woes, that in ten months later they would be singing the praise of this detested Emperor, and would be voluntarily setting French flags in their windows as symbols of friendship? May 13, 1809, the French, under the command of General Oudinot, entered Vienna, amid the curses and execrations of the populace beside itself with grief; and ten months later to a day, March 13, 1810, the same populace, joyous and peaceful, with bells ringing and cannon saluting, blessed and applauded an archduchess who was leaving Vienna to share this same Napoleon's throne!

But meanwhile there were many horrors, and much blood was shed. The artillery duel was most formidable; there was no limit to the fury and obstinacy of the two combatants. It was a war of giants in which all the infernal powers appeared to be let loose at once. Napoleon himself, familiar as he was with scenes of carnage, was surprised by the bitterness of the struggle. Never had he defied fortune with such audacity. Neglecting the usual laws of military science, he fought for twenty-four hours without cessation, on a line only three leagues long, having in his rear one of the largest rivers in Europe. Wagram was a victory, but a victory hotly disputed. When at the opening of the campaign it was thought that events would take a turn favorable to Austria, a thrill of hope, a movement of joy, ran through all the European nations, which showed the conqueror what would have happened if he had been beaten. He began to long for peace as ardently as he had longed for war. He no longer thought of making Austria, Hungary, and Bohemia three separate kingdoms, or of dethroning the Emperor Francis, and putting in his place his brother, the Grand Duke of Würzburg, formerly the Grand Duke of Tuscany. The Austrians, for whom he had felt a certain contempt, now inspired him with profound esteem; he admired their bravery, and especially the fidelity, of which they had given many touching proofs, to their unfortunate ruler. The hero of Wagram said to himself that if instead of gaining this battle he had lost it, he would not have gone back to the Tuileries as easily as Francis was going back to his palace in Vienna. An Emperor of Austria could be beaten and retain his popularity; but he, the great Napoleon, could not. That was the reflection which was made one day by his successor, himself a prisoner of Prussia, "In France one cannot be unfortunate."

When the negotiations began to arrange peace, Napoleon treated the two distinguished officers, Prince John of Lichtenstein and General von Bubna, with the utmost courtesy. He spared no pains to show his personal esteem and to flatter their national pride; he spoke in the highest terms of the Austrian army and of the bravery it had displayed in the last campaign. He said to them: "You will always remain the first continental power, after France; you are deucedly strong. Allied as I was with Russia, I never expected to have on my hands a serious continental war, and what a war!" Then to console them for the conditions imposed on mutilated Austria, he added: "Why distress yourselves about a few scraps of territory which must come back to you some day? All this can only last during my lifetime. France ought never to fight beyond the Rhine. I have been able to; but when I'm gone, it's all over." Perhaps he was thinking of marrying Marie Louise; at any rate, he showed a consideration for Prince John of Lichtenstein and General Bubna which amazed all who saw it. M. de Bausset, who accompanied him as a gentleman-in-waiting, says in his Memoirs: "I watched attentively the two Austrian commissioners while they were breakfasting with the Emperor: I tried to read their expressions, and I fancied that I saw harmony and a good understanding growing day by day…. Napoleon's politeness and graciousness towards these gentlemen never relaxed for a moment. He seemed anxious to give them a favorable idea of his manners and his person." Nevertheless there were many patriotic men and women in Austria who were inconsolable. Princess Charles of Schwarzenberg—the wife of the brilliant general who had just fought like a hero, and, in the next year, as Austrian ambassador at the court of the Tuileries Avas to negotiate the marriage of Napoleon and Marie Louise—wrote a most despairing letter to her husband, in which she said: "I shall bury myself in the past in order to escape the present and the future. I have heard that you were to be chosen to negotiate this so-called peace; it was a heavenly grace by which you escaped sullying your name. To conclude, I have only one earthly wish: it is that the ruin which we are cowardly enough to call a peace, may become complete, that our political existence may end. I pray for the calm of death."

Napoleon was about leaving Schoenbrunn, to return to France, when, October 12, 1809, just as he was about to review his troops, he saw approaching him a young German, of suspicious appearance, who was at once arrested. This young man, whose name was Staaps, was the son of a Protestant pastor at Erfurt, and under his coat was found a large, sharp dagger, with which he said he had intended to kill the Emperor, in order to deliver Germany. The cool, calm replies of this determined fanatic, whom Napoleon himself examined, made a deep impression upon him. Might not this young German be the forerunner of numberless volunteers who were about to organize against France what they would consider a holy war? At the sight of this youth, who gave calm expression to unrelenting hatred, Napoleon—who did not venture to spare his life, although no criminal act had been committed—was moved by a painful feeling in which pity was mingled with surprise. He who had cost Germany such torrents of blood and tears was singularly astonished when at last he saw that Germany did not love him. Nothing is so repugnant to the great of the earth, and especially to conquerors, as the thought of death,—death, the only unconquerable foe! What, the first comer, a fool, a vulgar fanatic, can with a kitchen knife lay low the greatest hero, the most illustrious warrior, the mightiest king! At Regensberg, when he was wounded for the first time since he had begun his military career, the hero of so many battles perceived, and not without a pang, that he was not invulnerable. Before the corpse of the brave Marshal Lannes, who had had his two legs carried off by a cannon-ball at Esoling, he wrote very sadly to the Empress Josephine: "So everything ends!" And now he might himself have fallen by the hand of a poor, unknown student! As the Duchess of Abrantès wrote: "Death, which was always prowling about the Emperor in various forms, yet never daring to seize him, but always appearing to say, Take care! ... was a prophecy, and a prophecy of evil." Napoleon began to reflect seriously. To audacity and the spirit of adventure there suddenly succeeded prudence and the need of self-preservation. The all-powerful Emperor said to himself at the moment of his triumph, that if he were to die without a direct heir, his vast Empire would fall to pieces, like that of Alexander the Great, and the unrivalled edifice, built at the price of so much toil and sacrifice, would be shattered.

The national historian has said: "In proportion as he lost the support of the public, Napoleon took pleasure in thinking that it was the lack of a future and not his own misdeeds that threatened his proud throne with premature fragility. The desire to make firm what he felt trembling beneath his feet, became his dominant passion, as if, with a new wife in the Tuileries, the mother of a male heir, the faults which had armed the whole world against him would be only causes without effects." And Thiers adds this reflection: "It would doubtless have been to his advantage to have had an undoubted heir; it would have been better, a hundred times better, to have been prudent and wise. Napoleon, who, despite his need of a son, could not, after Tilsit, at the very climax of his power and glory, make up his mind to sacrifice Josephine, at last came to a decision because he felt the Empire threatened, and he tried in a new marriage to secure the solidity which he should have tried to obtain by wise and moderate conduct."

Possibly even when at Schoenbrunn the conqueror already thought of asking for the hand of the young archduchess whose home this palace was. At any rate, it never crossed his mind that in the very room where he wove such proud visions, such far-reaching plans, his heir would die so sadly, the heir whom the daughter of the Germanic Caesars was to give to him. When he reappeared crowned with victory at Fontainebleau, October 26, 1809, Josephine felt that her fate was sealed. The immediate result of the battle of Wagram was the divorce.

III
THE PRELIMINARIES OF THE WEDDING

Austria had known terrible fears during the campaign of Wagram; it had asked anxiously, whether the Hapsburgs might not disappear from the list of crowned heads, like the Spanish Bourbons, or might not, like the Neapolitan Bourbons, be left to enjoy only part of their States. The peace which was signed at Vienna, October 14, 1809, had somewhat allayed these serious apprehensions, but the situation of Austria remained no less anxious and painful. As Prince Metternich has said in his curious Memoirs: "The so-called Peace of Vienna had enclosed the Empire in an iron circle, cutting off its communication with the Adriatic, and surrounding it from Brody, on the extreme northeast, towards Russia, to the southeastern frontiers toward the Ottoman Empire, with a row of states under Napoleon's rule, or under his direct influence. The Empire, as if caught in a vice, was not free to move in any direction; moreover, the conqueror had done all he could to prevent the defeated nation from renewing its strength; a secret article of the treaty of peace established one hundred and fifty thousand men as the maximum force of the Austrian army."

A still darker danger threatened the throne of the Hapsburgs; namely, the marriage, which was thought very probable and very near, of Napoleon with the sister of the Czar. Thus imprisoned between two vast empires, between that of the East and that of the West, as if between hammer and anvil, what would become of Austria, shorn of its territory and its strength?

There was but one chance, and a very faint one, of any defence against the dangers that threatened Austria, and that was, that the Viennese court might make the match which the Russian court was contemplating. Already, its matrimonial alliances had brought the country good fortune more than once, and it could not forget the famous maxim expressed in a Latin line—

"*Bella gerant alii; tu felix Austria, nube!*"
"Let others wage war; do you, happy Austria, marry!"

The last campaigns had been unfavorable to the Hapsburg dynasty; a marriage would set things to right.

At Vienna a party which may be called the peace party had come to power. Mr. von Stadion, a statesman of warlike tendencies, had been succeeded in the Ministry of Foreign Affairs by a young and brilliant diplomatist, Count Metternich. The new minister had been ambassador to Paris before the campaign of Wagram, and, while he had been unable to prevent the war, he had left a very favorable impression at Napoleon's court, where his success as a man of the world, as a great nobleman, had been very brilliant. He then, in the lifetime of his father, Prince Metternich, bore only the title of Count. In his desire to attest his belief in the possibility of a reconciliation between Austria and Napoleon, he had left his wife, Countess Metternich, in France during the war. When he came to power, he conceived a political plan which was founded, temporarily at least, if not finally, on a French alliance. But to secure all the benefits which he hoped to get from it, Napoleon's marriage with an Austrian princess was necessary; and Metternich, who was aware of the negotiations between the French and Russian courts, was not inclined to believe in the possibility of a marriage between an Austrian Archduchess and the hero of Wagram. Neither before nor after the conclusion of the Treaty of Vienna was a word spoken about this plan, either by Napoleon or by the Austrian court.

The Emperor of the French had absolutely decided on a divorce; but he still thought that it was the Grand Duchess Anne, sister of the Emperor Alexander of Russia, who was going to succeed Josephine. On the occasion of the interview at Erfurt he had spoken of this marriage, and the Czar appeared to be most favorable to the plan. November 22, 1809, the Duke of Cadore, Minister of Foreign Affairs, forwarded this despatch to the Duke of Vicenza, French Ambassador at Saint Petersburg: "Rumors of the divorce reached the ears of the Emperor Alexander at Erfurt, and he spoke to the Emperor on the subject, saying that his, sister Anne was at his disposition. His Majesty desires you to broach the subject frankly and simply with the Emperor Alexander, and to address him in these terms: 'Sire, I have reason to think that the Emperor, urged by the whole of France, is making ready for a divorce. May I ask what may be counted on in regard of your sister? Will not Your Majesty consider the question for two days and then give me a frank reply, not as to the French Ambassador, but as to a person interested in the two families? I am not making a formal demand, but rather requesting the expression of your intentions. I venture, Sire, upon this step, because I am so accustomed to say what I think to Your Majesty that I have no fear of compromising myself.'

"You will not mention the subject to M. de Romanzoff on any pretext whatsoever, and when you shall have had this conversation with the Emperor Alexander, and shall have received his answer two days later, you will entirely forget this communication that I am making. You will, in addition, inform me concerning the qualities of the young Princess, and especially when she may be expected to become a mother; for in the present state of affairs, six months' difference is of great importance. I need not recommend to Your Excellency the most complete secrecy; you know what you owe to the Emperor in this respect."

At that time couriers took two weeks to go from Paris to Saint Petersburg, and the answer to the despatch of November 22 had not yet arrived when Napoleon, who did not yet know who his second wife was to be, announced to Josephine, November 30, that divorce was inevitable. The unhappy Empress received for the last time at the Tuileries, which she was to leave forever, in the morning of December 16. The reception was drawing to an end. Among those who were waiting on the grand staircase or in the vestibule for their carriages to be announced, there happened to be standing together M. de Sémonville, a young man of some prominence in the court, and M. de Floret, a young secretary of the Austrian legation. Everybody imagined then that the marriage with the Grand Duchess of Russia was settled. Suddenly, in this crowd of great personages, M. de Sémonville began the following conversation with the Austrian diplomatist:—

"Well, that's fixed. Why didn't *you* do it?"

"Who says that we didn't want to?"

"People think so. Are they wrong?"

"Perhaps."

"What? It would be possible? You may think so; but the Ambassador?"

"I will answer for Prince Schwarzenberg."

"But Count Metternich?"

"There is no difficulty about him."

"But the Emperor?"

"Or about him, either."

"And the Empress, who hates us?"

"You don't know her; she is ambitious, and could be persuaded."

M. de Sémonville started at once to report this curious conversation to his friend, the Duke of Bassano, who at once hastened to speak of it to the Emperor. Napoleon appeared pleased, but not astonished. He said that he had just heard the same thing from Vienna.

This is what had happened in the Austrian capital: the Count of Narbonne had been passing through before going to Munich, where he was to represent France as Minister Plenipotentiary. This amiable and distinguished man, of whom M. Villemain has written an excellent life, had succeeded in attracting Napoleon's favor, and after receiving an appointment as general in the French army, he had been made ambassador and one of the Emperor's aides-de-camp. M. de Narbonne, who was a model of refinement and bravery, had been one of the ornaments of the court of Versailles and of the Constituent Assembly. He had been a Knight of Honor of Madame Adelaide, the daughter of Louis XV.; Minister of War under Louis XVI., in 1792; a friend of Madame de Staël; an émigré in England, Switzerland, and Germany; and in 1809, thanks to Napoleon's good-will, he had once more resumed his military career, after an interruption of seventeen years. Towards the end of the campaign the Emperor had sent him as governor to Raab, to keep an eye on Hungary and Bohemia, and in case Austria should refuse to accept the conditions imposed by her conqueror, to proclaim the independence of those two countries. The peace once signed, General the Count of Narbonne went to Vienna, where he met two of his best friends,— the Prince of Ligne, who had been one of the favorites of Marie Antoinette, and the Count of Lamarck, who had been a confidant of Mirabeau. One day when he was dining with them, and Prince Metternich and a few other intimate friends, the conversation turned to politics. The Austrian Minister congratulated himself on the peace, which, he said, made the future sure, and cut short all danger of trouble and anarchy. The Prince of Ligne expressed similar views. Then M. de Narbonne spoke out somewhat as follows: "Gentlemen, I am surprised by your recent astonishment and your present confidence. Is it possible that you are too blind to see that every peace, easy or hard, is nothing more than a brief truce? that for a long time we are hastening to one conclusion, of which peace is but one of the stations? This conclusion is the subjugation of the whole of Europe under two mighty empires. You have seen the swift growth and progress of one of these empires since 1800. As to the other, it is not yet determined. It will be either Austria or Russia, according to the results of the Peace of Vienna; for this peace is a danger if it is not the foundation of a closer alliance, of a family alliance, and does not finally restore more than its beginning took away; in a word, you are ill advised if you hesitate in your leaning towards France."

The next morning the Count of Narbonne was summoned to the Emperor Francis II., and the Austrian monarch indicated the possibility of a marriage between Napoleon and the Archduchess Marie Louise. The Count of Narbonne approved, and eloquently expressed his conviction that such a happy result as confiding once more an Archduchess to France would at last decide Napoleon to remain at peace, instead of forever hazarding his glory, and to work for the welfare of the people in harmony with the wise and virtuous monarch whose adopted son he would become. M. de Narbonne sent a note of this conversation to Fouché, to be shown to the Emperor, who thus had knowledge of the secret plans of the Viennese court six weeks before the meeting over which he presided at the Tuileries, to ask his councillors their opinion on the choice of an Empress.

Since the resumption of diplomatic relations between the two powers, the Austrian Ambassador in Paris had been Prince Charles of Schwarzenberg, the warrior and statesman who later, as commander-in-chief of the Austrian forces, was to deal such heavy blows to France. In 1810 he was all for peace, and his sole aim was to undermine, for the good of his country, the influence of his Russian colleague, Prince Kourakine. The Austrian Ambassador was very anxious that the Archduchess Marie Louise should become Empress of the French; for he was convinced that such an event would be of as much benefit to him as to his country. Yet he was still afraid to hope for the realization of his dream, when one of his friends, Count Alexandra de Laborde—who, after serving as an émigré, in the Austrian army, had returned to France and been appointed Master of Requests in the Council of State, encouraged him in his ideas which might at first have seemed fanciful, M. de Laborde, whose father had been court-banker before the Revolution, and had most generously aided Marie Antoinette, was well known and much liked in Vienna. In this matter of the marriage of Marie Louise he was the secret agent between Napoleon's Minister of Foreign Affairs and the Prince of Schwarzenberg, in whom he kindled so much zeal in behalf of the French alliance that the Ambassador, as we shall soon see, signed the marriage contract of the Archduchess with Napoleon, even before he had received the authorization of his government.

December 17, 1809, nothing had been decided. Indeed, what seemed probable, if not certain, was the Russian marriage. That day—the day when there appeared in the *Moniteur* the decree of the Senate relative to the divorce—a new despatch had been sent from Paris to Saint Petersburg by the Duke of Cadore, to demand a speedy reply from the Russian court, yes or no. The answer of the Duke of Vicenza to the first despatch, that of November 22, 1809, did not reach Paris until December 28. The Ambassador said that the Czar had received his overtures very amiably, but that the affair needed much discretion and a little patience. The Emperor Alexander, he went on to say, was personally favorable; but his mother, whom he did not wish to offend, refused her consent, and the Czar asked for a few days before giving a final answer. This delay vexed Napoleon, who nevertheless resolved to wait, although waiting suited neither his tastes nor his character.

In short, at the beginning of 1810, the matrimonial alliance with Austria was not settled. The initiative steps had not been taken by the monarch, the ministers of Foreign Affairs, or by the ambassadors. It is a curious and characteristic detail, that it was the divorced Empress, Josephine, who gave the signal. She summoned the Countess Metternich to Malmaison, January 2, 1810, and said to her: "I have a plan which interests me to the exclusion of everything else, and nothing but its success can make me feel that the sacrifice I have just made is not wholly thrown away: it is that the Emperor shall marry your Archduchess; I spoke to him about it yesterday, and he said that his choice was not yet made. But I think it would be made, if he were sure of being accepted by you." Madame de Metternich was much surprised by this overture, which she hastened to communicate to her husband in a letter dated January 3, 1810, which began thus: "To-day I have some very extraordinary things to tell you, and I am almost sure that my letter will make a very important part of your despatches. In the first place, I must tell you that I was presented to the Emperor last Sunday. I had only mentioned the matter in conversation with Champagny when I received a letter from M. de Ségur, telling me that the Emperor had appointed Sunday, and that I was to choose a lady-in-waiting to present me. In my wisdom I selected the Duchess of Bassano, and after waiting in company with twenty other women, among whom were the Princess of Isenburg, Madame de Tyskiewitz and others, from two till half-past six in the evening, I was introduced first, and the Emperor received me in a way I could not have expected. He seemed really glad to see me again, and glad that I had stayed here during the war; he spoke about you and said, 'M. de Metternich holds the first place in the Empire; he knows the country well and can be of service to it.'"

Then the Countess went on to narrate what the Empress Josephine and Queen Hortense had said the evening before at Malmaison. She had been received by Hortense while waiting in the drawing-room for Josephine to come down, and she had been much astounded to hear the Queen of Holland say with much warmth: "You know that we are all Austrians at heart, but you would never guess that my brother has had the courage to advise the Emperor to ask for the hand of your Archduchess." Josephine frequently referred to this projected marriage, on which she seemed to have set her heart. "Yes," she said, "we must try to arrange it." Then she expressed her regret that M. de Metternich was not in Paris; for if he had been, doubtless he would bring the affair to a happy conclusion. "Your Emperor must be made to see," she went on, "that his ruin and the ruin of his country are certain if he does not give his consent to this marriage. It is perhaps the only way of preventing Napoleon from breaking with the Holy See."

The letter of the Countess Metternich ended thus: "I have not seen the Queen of Holland again, because she is ill. Hence I have nothing positive to tell you concerning the matter in question; but if I wanted to tell you all the honors that have been showered upon me, I should not stop so soon. At the last levee I played with the Emperor; you may imagine that it was a serious matter for me, but I managed to come off with glory. He began by praising my diamond headband, and that everlasting gold dress, then he asked me a number of questions about my family and all my relatives; he insisted, in spite of all I could say, that Louis von Kaunitz was my brother. You can't imagine what effect that little game of cards had. When it was over, I was surrounded and paid court to by all the great dignitaries, marshals, ministers, etc. I had abundant material for philosophical reflections on the vicissitude of human affairs."

Nevertheless, in spite of the overtures which Josephine had made to the Countess Metternich, Napoleon had come to no decision about his new wife. One day when he had been working with M. Daru, whom he highly esteemed, he had the following conversation with him:—

"In your opinion which would be the better for me, to marry the Russian or the Austrian?"

"Neither."

"The devil! You are very hard to please."

"Neither, I say, but a Frenchwoman; and provided the new Empress does not have too many relatives who will have to be made princes and given a large fortune, France will approve your choice. The throne you occupy is like no other; you have erected it with your own hands. You are at the head of a generous nation; your glory and its glory ought to be shared in common. It is not by imitating other monarchs, it is by distinguishing yourself, that you find your real greatness. You do not rule by the same title that they do; you ought not to marry as they do. The nation would be flattered by your looking at home for an Empress, and it would always see in your line a thoroughly French family."

"Come, come! that's nonsense! If M. de Talleyrand should hear you, he would form a very poor idea of your political sagacity. You don't treat this question like a statesman. I must unite in defence of my crown those at home and abroad who are still hostile to it; and my marriage furnishes a chance. Do you imagine that monarchs' marriages are matters of sentiment? No; they are matters of politics. Mine cannot be decided by motives of internal policy; I must try to establish my influence outside, and to extend it by a close alliance with a powerful neighbor."

No answer had come from Russia, no official overture had been made to or by Austria; still Napoleon continued to believe, or at least pretended to believe, that his only difficulty was to make the best choice. The idea that two emperors and a king—without counting the other sovereigns on whom he did not deign to cast a glance—were simultaneously disputing the honor of allying their family with him, greatly flattered his pride. In fact, what he desired was the Austrian marriage; but he was anxious to keep his preferences secret, in order to prolong in the eyes of his principal councillors, an uncertainty in which his pride did not suffer. He convoked them to an extraordinary session, at the Tuileries, after mass, Sunday, January 21, 1810. The great dignitaries of the Empire,— Champagny, Minister of Foreign Affairs; the Duke of Cadore; Maret, the Secretary of State; the Duke of Bassano; M. Gamier, the President of the Senate; and M. de Fontanes, President of the Corps Législatif,—all took part in this solemn council. The relative advantages and disadvantages of the Russian, the Saxon, and the Austrian marriage were considered at great length. The Archtreasurer Lebrun and M. Gamier favored the daughter of the King of Saxony; the Archchancellor Cambacérès and King Murat, the Grand Duchess of Russia; M. de Champagny, Prince Talleyrand, Prince Eugene, the Prince of Neufchâtel and the Duke of Bassano, the Archduchess Marie Louise. Murat especially distinguished himself by his violent opposition to the Austrian alliance. Doubtless he was averse to the selection for Empress of the French of the granddaughter of Queen Marie Caroline of Naples, whose throne he was occupying. Napoleon remained calm and impassive. When the meeting was over, he dismissed the councillors, simply saying: "I shall weigh in my mind the arguments that you have submitted to me. In any case, I remain convinced that whatever difference may exist in your views, each one has formed his opinion only from a desire for the good of the country and devotion to my person." Thus it was that seventeen years to a day after a king of France who had married an Austrian archduchess had died on the scaffold, there was discussed the alliance of a new French ruler with another archduchess, the grandniece of the other.

Some time later, Cambacérè's, in the course of a conversation with M. Pasquier, then Counsellor of State, gave utterance to his regret at having failed to impress upon his hearers the superior advantages of the Russian alliance. "I am not surprised," he said; "when a man has only one argument to give, and it is impossible to give it, he must expect to be beaten…. And you will see that my argument is so good that a single sentence will show you all its weight. I am morally sure that in less than two years we shall be at war with the Emperor whose relative we do not marry. Now war with Austria causes me no anxiety; but I dread war with Russia; its consequences are incalculable. I know that the Emperor is familiar with the road to Vienna, but I am not so sure that he will find the road to St. Petersburg."

After quoting this conversation between Cambacérès and M. Pasquier in his admirable book, *The Church of Rome and the First Empire*, the Count d'Haussonville indulges in some philosophic reflections: "If it is curious to come upon this profound and accurate summary, compressed into a few clear and precise words by a man of remarkable sagacity dealing with a future still completely hidden, it is no less strange to think that the prospect of the Austrian marriage, destined to be so fatal to the Empire, should be suddenly discussed in a five minutes' talk between two men who met by chance on the steps of the Tuileries, at the very moment when the unhappy Josephine was about to leave this spot which had been so long her home. When we reflect on the course of all the following events, we may perhaps say that the fate of the Empire was settled in this eventful quarter of an hour; for if the Emperor had married the Grand Duchess instead of Marie Louise, probably the campaign of 1812, which Cambacérès foresaw, would not have taken place, and Heaven knows what part this unhappy expedition played in the fall of the First Empire!"

How insufficient is human wisdom, how false its calculations! This Austrian marriage which discouraged the bitterest enemies of the hero of Austerlitz, of Jena, of Wagram, this magnificent marriage which was to have been the safeguard of the Empire, proved its ruin. This great event which called forth abundant congratulations and outbursts of noisy delight was the main cause of the most tremendous and most disastrous war of modern times. If he had not blindly counted on his father-in-law's friendship, would Napoleon, in spite of all his audacity, have ventured to march to the Russian steppes, without even taking the precaution of reviving Poland? He himself has said it: his marriage with the Austrian Archduchess was an abyss covered with flowers.

January was drawing to a close; and while in Paris many people were beginning to regard Napoleon's marriage with Marie Louise as very probable, the young princess herself had no suspicion of his intentions. Count Metternich who, like his sovereign, had maintained secrecy about this delicate matter, wrote to his wife, January 27, 1810: "The Archduchess is still ignorant, as indeed is proper, of the plans concerning her, and it is not from the Empress Josephine, who gives us so many proofs of her confidence, who with so many noble qualities combines those of a tender mother, that I shall conceal the many considerations which necessarily present themselves to the Archduchess Marie Louise when the matter is laid before her. But our princesses are little accustomed to choose their husbands according to their own inclinations, and the respect which so fond and so well-trained a daughter feels for her father's wishes, makes me confident that she will make no opposition."

The same day, January 27, 1810, the Count Metternich wrote to Prince Charles of Schwarzenberg, the Austrian Ambassador in Paris, a despatch which proves that the negotiations concerning the marriage had not yet begun: "It is with great interest that his Imperial Majesty has heard the details which Your Highness has communicated to him in his last despatches, on the question of the marriage of the Emperor of the French. It would be difficult to form any definite conclusion from the different data that reach us. It is impossible not to see a certain official character in the explanations, vague as they are, which the Minister of Foreign Affairs has had with Your Highness. M. de Laborde's uninterrupted zeal, the remarks of so many persons connected with the government, all tending in one direction, and especially the very direct overtures made by the Empress and the Queen of Holland to Madame de Metternich, would incline us to suppose that Napoleon's mind was made up, as the Emperor said, if our August master should consent to give him Madame the Archduchess. On the other hand, the demands commonly reported to have been addressed to Russia conflict with this supposition. The question must, at any rate, become clearer shortly after the arrival of the next courier, if indeed not before then. So much has been said, that it is impossible to deny that an alliance with the Imperial House of Austria has entered into the designs of the French court. By following a very simple calculation and comparing the great publicity given to the alleged demand on Russia with the secrecy exercised towards us in this matter, we may possibly be authorized to suppose that at present their views tend in our direction; but probability is of very little account in a transaction of this sort to which Napoleon is a party, and we can only go on in our usual course, and the result, in one way or another, must inure to our advantage."

While the court of Vienna thus maintained a position of prudent and dignified reserve, Napoleon, annoyed by the delays of the Russian court, and now only anxious to have nothing more to do with it, impatiently awaited the despatches from Saint Petersburg. These arrived February 6, but they brought no satisfactory news. The first delay of ten days which the Czar had asked of the Duke of Vicenza came to an end January 6, but on the 21st the Emperor Alexander had not yet replied. He said, to be sure, that his mother had withdrawn her opposition; but he combined the affairs of the marriage with the political negotiations concerning Poland, and doubtless in the desire of affecting Napoleon's decision, he let the matter drag, as if he wanted to be urged. The Duke of Vicenza also said in his despatches that, according to the physicians, the Grand Duchess was yet too young to bear children, and that since she was averse to changing her religion, she insisted on having a Greek chapel and Greek priests at the Tuileries.

Napoleon hesitated no longer. That same day he sent word to the Russian Ambassador, Prince Kourakine, that, being unable to accept a longer delay, he broke off the negotiation; and that evening he had the Austrian Ambassador, Prince Schwarzenberg, asked if the contract of his marriage with the Archduchess Marie Louise could be signed the next day.

The Austrian diplomatist had never expected that events were going to move at any such speed. He knew the favorable disposition of his court, but he had received no authorization to conclude the business. The general instructions which had been sent to him regarding the marriage were dated December 25, 1809, and they had not since been modified. These left the Ambassador free to discuss the question only in accordance with the restrictions which Count Metternich had thus formulated.

"1. Every overture is to be received by you in an unofficial capacity. Your Highness must take cognizance of it only by expressing your personal willingness to see how the land lies here.

"2. You will then make it clear, as if it were a remark of your own, that if no secondary consideration, no prejudice, influence the Emperor's decision, there are laws which he will always obey. His Majesty will never force a beloved daughter to a marriage which she might abhor, and will never consent to a marriage not in conformity with the principles of our religion.

"3. You will endeavor, moreover, to get a definite statement of the advantages which France would offer to Austria in the case of a family alliance."

When, in the evening of February 6, 1810, Napoleon's Minister of Foreign Affairs asked Prince Schwarzenberg if he was ready to sign the marriage contract at the Tuileries the next morning, the Ambassador was delighted, but surprised, and perhaps, for a moment, perplexed. If he regarded the instructions conveyed in the despatch of December 25, 1809, he certainly had no authority to sign anything. In fact, not merely did he not know whether the Archduchess had given her consent, he did not know whether she had ever been informed of the projected marriage. Besides, he had no information as to the way in which the Austrian court looked on the annulment of the religious marriage of Napoleon and Josephine by the officials of the diocese of Paris, who had acted independently of the Pope. Finally, he was not in condition to stipulate for any political advantage to his government as the price of the alliance. A timid diplomatist would have hesitated. But might not there arrive the next moment a courier from Saint Petersburg, bringing a definite answer from the Czar? Would Napoleon, impatient as he was and unused to delay—would he accept the slightest postponement on the part of Austria? Prince Schwarzenberg burned his ships; he said to himself that if his action were disavowed, he could go and raise cabbages on his estate; but if it were approved, he would be at the top of the wave. Abandoning then the customary slowness and scruples of diplomacy, he answered without hesitation that he was ready, and made an engagement with the Duke of Cadore, Minister of Foreign Affairs, for the next day, at the Tuileries, to sign the marriage contract of the Emperor of the French, King of Italy, and of Marie Louise, Archduchess of Austria. IV.

∴

IV
THE BETROTHAL

February 7, 1810, M. Champagny, Duke of Cadore, the French Minister of Foreign Affairs, and Prince Charles of Schwarzenberg, met at the Tuileries, and signed, without the slightest hitch, the marriage contract of Napoleon and the Archduchess Marie Louise. The text was a copy almost word for word of Marie Antoinette's marriage contract, which had been signed forty years before.

On leaving the Tuileries, Prince Schwarzenberg despatched a messenger to Vienna to announce the momentous news, which possibly would arouse more surprise than delight. "Count," he wrote to M. de Metternich, "in signing the marriage contract, while protesting that I was in no way clothed with power *ad hoc*, I believe that I have merely signed a paper which can guarantee to the Emperor Napoleon the determination already formed by my August Sovereign of meeting him half-way in negotiation on this subject. The despatches with which you have honored me made the course that I was to follow perfectly clear. His Majesty, as Your Excellency assures me, approves of my conduct by bidding me follow the same course; hence the marriage is an affair which my government naturally regards as one of the greatest interest, and one which it desires to see arranged. It will be evident to those who know the character of Emperor Napoleon that if I had shown the slightest hesitation, he would have abandoned this plan and have formed another. If this affair was hurried, it was because that is the way in which Napoleon acts, and it seemed to me best to seize the favorable moment. I have the most profound conviction of having been of service to my sovereign on this occasion; and if by any possibility I have had the misfortune to displease him by the course that I took in perfect sincerity, His Majesty can disavow it, but in that case I shall instantly demand my recall."

The next day Prince Schwarzenberg sent to Vienna one of his secretaries, M. de Floret, with this letter to M. de Metternich: "Paris, February 8, 1810. I send to you, dear Count, M. de Floret, who will give you an account of everything that has happened. You will soon see that I could not have acted otherwise without spoiling the whole business. If I had insisted on not signing, he would have broken the affair off, to treat with Russia or Saxony. I formally declared that I had full power to give the most positive assurances that the propositions of marriage would be favorably received by my court; but that if I was not ready to sign a contract, it was only on account of the impossibility in which my minister found himself of supposing that a matter scarcely touched upon should so soon come to a head. I beg of you, my dear friend, to arrange that there shall be no obstacle to this important business, and that it be arranged with a good grace.... I pity the Princess, it is true; but yet she must not forget that it is a noble deed to give peace to such good nations, and to give a guarantee of general peace and tranquillity. Floret will give you our records, and will explain it to you by word of mouth; we have not had time to have it copied. You will not object to this, inasmuch as we wish Floret to leave at once. Conclude this matter nobly, and you will render an incalculable service to our country."

At the diplomatic reception which was held at the Tuileries, February 8, Napoleon walked up to the Austrian Ambassador and said to him, in the most friendly way, "You have been very busy lately, and I think you have done a good piece of work." Prince Kourakine, the Russian Ambassador, was much annoyed at the turn events had taken, and did not attend the reception, under the pretext that he was not well. The evening before Prince Schwarzenberg had dined at the house of Napoleon's mother with the King of Holland, Louis Bonaparte, who was loudspoken in his praise of the Emperor Francis and the Imperial house of Austria. At the court of the Tuileries there was general satisfaction. Napoleon thought that he had never achieved a greater triumph. The messenger whom Prince Schwarzenberg had despatched on the day he had signed the contract, reached Vienna February 14. The populace had not the faintest idea of the possibility of a marriage between the Archduchess Marie Louise and the Emperor of the French; the Austrian monarch and M. de Metternich, in their anxiety to keep their secret, lest some opposition should manifest itself, had not breathed a word about the overtures made at Vienna by Count Alexandre de Laborde, and at Malmaison by the Empress Josephine. Neither the Viennese nor the Diplomatic Body suspected anything. As M. de Metternich put it, Count Shouvaloff, the Russian Ambassador at the Austrian court, was literally petrified. The English breathed fire and flame. The sudden outburst of a volcano would not have been more startling than this piece of news which came from a clear sky. The impression made upon the populace was one of surprise which amounted to disbelief. People stopped in the streets to ask one another if the thing was possible.

Marie Louise had given her consent more with resignation than with pleasure. Metternich recounts in his Memoirs his speech to Francis II.: "In the life of a state, as in that of a private citizen, there are cases in which a third person cannot put himself in the place of one who is responsible for the resolutions he has to take. These cases are especially such as cannot be decided by calculation. Your Majesty is a monarch and a father; and Your Majesty alone can weigh his duties as father and emperor." "It is my daughter who must decide," answered Francis II. "Since I shall never compel her, I am anxious, before I consider my duties as a sovereign, to know what she means to do. Go find the Archduchess, and then let me know what she says. I am unwilling to speak to her of the demand of the French Emperor, lest I should seem to be trying to influence her decision."

M. de Metternich betook himself at once to the Archduchess Marie Louise, and set the matter before her very simply and briefly, without beating about the bush, without a word for or against the proposition. The Archduchess listened with her usual calmness, and, after a moment's reflection, asked him, "What are my father's wishes?" "The Emperor," the minister answered, "has commissioned me to ask Your Imperial Highness what decision she means to take in a matter concerning her whole life. Do not ask what the Emperor wishes; tell me what you yourself wish." "I wish only what my duty commands me to wish," answered Marie Louise. "When the interests of the Empire are at stake, they must be consulted, not my feelings. Beg of my father to regard only his duty as a sovereign, without subordinating it to my personal interests."

When M. de Metternich had reported to Francis II. the result of his interview, the Emperor said: "What you tell me does not surprise me. I know my daughter too well not to expect just such an answer. While you were with her, I have been considering what I have to do. My consent to this marriage will assure to the kingdom a few years of political peace, which I can devote to healing its wounds. I owe myself solely to the happiness of my people; I cannot hesitate."

We shall now make some extracts from the despatches of Count Otto, the French Ambassador at Vienna in 1810, which we have found in the archives of the Ministry of Foreign Affairs. The documents, which have never been published, are well worthy of our readers' attention, and they throw a full light on the Emperor Napoleon's relations with the Austrian court. M. Otto wrote to the Duke of Cadore, February 16, 1810, that the news of the marriage was beginning to spread through the city: "Business people are much excited. Merchants are entreating me to tell them what I know. Couriers are despatched in every direction. In short, I have never had occasion to use more reserve than at this moment, when the real feeling of this nation, which has long been compelled to be our enemy, reveals itself in a way most flattering to us. The French officers who are returning from different missions assure me that they have found the same spirit in the army. 'Arrange,' they say, 'that we can fight on your side; you will find us worthy.' Every one agrees that this alliance will insure lasting tranquillity to Europe, and compel England to make peace; that it will give the Emperor all the leisure he requires for organizing, in accordance with his lofty plans, the vast empire he has created; that it cannot fail to have an influence on the destiny of Poland, Turkey, and Sweden; and finally, that it cannot fail to give lasting glory to Your Excellency's ministry. The news of the conclusion of this marriage will be received with tumultuous joy throughout the Austrian dominions. France and the greater part of Europe will share this joy. As to the English government, I do not think it possible for it to avert the blow which this important event will deal it; the national party will finally triumph over the avarice of usurers, the rancorous passions of the ministry, and the bellicose and constitutional fury of their king. All humanity will find repose beneath the laurels of our August Emperor and, after having conquered half of Europe, he will add to his long list of victories the most difficult and most consolatory of all,—the conquest of general peace."

The first feeling that prevailed in all classes of Viennese society, on hearing of the Archduchess's marriage, was, as has been said, one of surprise, which soon gave way to almost universal joy. Count Metternich wrote to Prince Schwarzenberg under date of February 19, 1810: "It would be difficult to judge at a distance the emotion that the news of the marriage has aroused here. The secret of the negotiations had been so well kept, that it was not till the day of M. de Floret's arrival that any word of it came to the ears of the public. The first effect on 'Change was such that the currency would be to-day at three hundred and less, if the government had not been interested in keeping it higher, and it was only by buying a million of specie in two days that it succeeded in keeping it at three hundred and seventy. Seldom has anything been so warmly approved by the whole nation."

M. de Metternich was most delighted, and took especial satisfaction in the thought that it was his work. "All Vienna," he wrote to his wife, "is interested in nothing but this marriage. It would be hard to form an idea of the public feeling about it, and of its extreme popularity. If I had saved the world, I could not receive more congratulations or more homage for the part I am supposed to have played in the matter. In the promotions that are to follow I am sure to have the Golden Fleece. If it comes to me now, it will not be for nothing; but it is none the less true that it required a very extraordinary and improbable combination of circumstances to set me far beyond my most ambitious dreams, although in fact I have no ambitions. All the balls and entertainments here will be very fine, and although everything will have to be brought from the ends of the earth, everything will be here. I sent the order of arrangements a few days ago to Paris; Schwarzenberg will have shown it to you. The new Empress will please in Paris, and she ought to please with her kindness and her great gentleness and simplicity. Her face is rather plain than pretty, but she has a beautiful figure, and when she is properly dressed and put into shape, she will do very well. I have begged her to engage a dancing-master as soon as she arrives, and not to dance until she has learned how. She is very anxious to please, and that is the surest way of pleasing."

The Austrian court did everything with the best possible grace, knowing that Napoleon set great store by the details of etiquette. Everything was exhumed from the archives which bore on the weddings of Louis XIV., Louis XV., the great Dauphin, the father of Louis XVI., of Louis XVI. himself. The old gentlemen of the court of Versailles, and especially M. de Dreux-Brézé, the master of ceremonies at the end of the old régime, were consulted at every step. Napoleon was very anxious that in pomp and majesty the wedding of Marie Louise should not only be quite equal, but even superior to that of Marie Antoinette, for he thought himself of far more importance than a dauphin of France. He was given what he wanted. Speaking of the Princess's escort, Count Otto said in despatch to the Duke of Cadore, dated February 19, 1810: "In order to give the part its full importance, the Emperor of Austria has appointed to it Prince Trautmannsdorff, who on all great occasions holds the highest rank in the kingdom. The Dauphiness had been accompanied by a nobleman of no very lofty position. Moreover, the Emperor has given orders to deepen all the tints: the suite of the Dauphiness consisted of six ladies-in-waiting and six chamberlains; the future Empress will have twelve of each. The Emperor will choose the most distinguished and best-known personages of the Empire for these functionaries, and the Empress has reserved for herself the right of naming the ladies most prominent for their old families and their position in society. In a word, the Minister has assured me that no pains will be spared to make the train most brilliant."

Points of etiquette kept the French Ambassador very busy. He wrote, February 21, 1810, to the Duke of Cadore: "In reading carefully the historic summary enclosed in Your Excellency's despatch, I found but few matters requiring comment, but these seemed to me of sufficient importance to warrant my calling your attention to them. They are as follows:

"1. Since the religious ceremony is the most solemn, it seems that it is here that the distinction between the Dauphiness and the new Empress should be most distinctly marked. The first-named sat in an armchair, placed in front of the altar, but without a canopy, the Queen Marie Leczinska, daughter of King Stanislas, having a place, under a canopy, between the King and Queen of Poland.

"2. The representative and personal rank of His Highness the Prince of Neufchâtel being much higher than that of the Marquis de Durfort, who held a similar position in 1770, it has seemed to me desirable to make the reception more formal. Count Metternich has given me complete satisfaction on both these points. He has told me that the Emperor would give the most positive orders to pay to the Empress of France the same honors that were paid to the Empress of Austria at the celebration of the last marriage. The canopy and all the paraphernalia of royalty will be assigned to the new Empress, and the Emperor will furthermore make a concession on this occasion which is without precedent in the annals of the realm: at table he will resign the first place to his daughter, and take the second place himself. Nothing will be left undone to give these ceremonies their full splendor and to show the interest with which these new ties are regarded here. The Emperor is so well pleased with this alliance that he speaks about it even with private persons who have the honor to be admitted to his presence. He loudly denounces those who led him into the last war, and asserts that if he had earlier known the loyalty and magnanimity of the Emperor Napoleon, he should have been on his guard against their counsels."

The Viennese, who in their amiability and fickleness closely resemble the Parisians, passed in a moment from an apparently deep-seated hatred of Napoleon, to the most unbounded confidence. The still bleeding wounds of Wagram were forgotten; every one thought of nothing but the brilliant festivals that were preparing. Smiles took the place of tears, and it seemed as if the French and the Austrians had always been brothers.

The French Ambassador wrote to the Duke of Cadore, February 21, 1810: "Since the 16th the whole city has thought of nothing but the great marriage for which the preparations are now under way. All eyes are turned on the Archduchess. Those who have the honor of being admitted to her presence are closely questioned, and every one is glad to hear that she is in the best spirits, and does not try to conceal the satisfaction she takes in this alliance. Funds continue to rise in a surprising way, and the price of food is falling in the same proportion. A great many people have found it hard to sell their gold. Never has public opinion spoken more clearly or more unanimously. A great many people who had hoarded their silver in the hope of selling it or of sending it abroad, are now carrying it to the mint, and consider the government paper which they get for it as good as gold. The stewards of great houses are ordering new silverware to take the place of that which they have had to give to the government. Every one shows a readiness to offer all his fortune, being convinced that after such an alliance the government cannot fail to meet its engagements."

The Viennese have a very lively imagination, and bounding from one extreme to another, they began to form visions of the Austrians waging wars of ambition and conquest along with the French. They fancied that their Emperor and his son-in-law would have all Europe at their feet. "The greater their enthusiasm about the French," wrote Count Otto in the same despatch, "the more evident the old animosity of the Austrians against Prussia and Russia. The coffee-house politicians are already busy with devising a thousand combinations according to which the Emperor of Austria will be able to recover Silesia and to extend his dominions towards the east. The disappointed Russians, of whom there are very many here, are much astonished at this sudden change. One of them was heard to say, 'A few days ago we were very highly thought of in Vienna, but now the French are adored, and everybody wants to make war on us.' Count Shouvaloff himself keeps very quiet. Sensible people do not share this warlike feeling; they want a general peace, and bless an alliance which seems to secure it for a few years. In their eyes even a successful war is a great calamity. Peace, too, has its triumphs, and this last negotiation is one of the finest known to history."

The official *Gazette*, which was eagerly read by a noisy multitude in the streets of Vienna, published the official announcement of the great news. The number of February 24, 1810, contained the following paragraph: "The formal betrothal of the Emperor of the French, King of Italy, and Her Imperial and Royal Highness the Archduchess Marie Louise, the oldest daughter of His Imperial and Royal Majesty, our very Gracious Sovereign, was signed at Paris, on the 7th, by the Prince Schwarzenberg, Ambassador, and the Duke of Cadore, Minister of Foreign Affairs. The exchange of ratifications of this contract took place on the 21st of this month, at Vienna, between Count Metternich Winneburg, Minister of State and of Foreign Affairs, and the Imperial Ambassador of France, Count Otto de Mesloy. All the nations of Europe see in this event a gage of peace, and look forward with delight to a happy future after so many wars." On the day that this paragraph appeared in the official journal, the French Ambassador wrote to the Duke of Cadore: "The Emperor loves the Princess, and is very happy in her brilliant good fortune. It is long since he has seemed so happy, so interested, so busy. Everything which furthers the sumptuousness of the festivals now in preparation is a matter of great interest to him, and all his subjects, with very few exceptions, share their sovereign's amiable anxiety."

The French Ambassador was beside himself with delight; he saw everything in glowing colors,—Marie Louise, the court, all Austria. His despatch of February 17 was full of enthusiasm. In it he drew with trembling hand the portrait of the August lady, and we may readily conceive the eagerness with which Napoleon must have devoured it: "Every one agrees that the Archduchess combines with a very amiable disposition sound sense and all the qualities that can be given by a careful education. She is liked by all at court, and is spoken of as a model of gentleness and kindness. She has a fine bearing, yet it is perfectly simple; she is modest without shyness; she can converse very well in many languages, and combines affability with dignity. As she acquires familiarity with the world, which is all very new to her, her fine qualities will doubtless develop further, and endow her whole being with even more grace and interest. She is tall and well made, and her health is excellent. Her features seemed to me regular and full of sweetness."

Even the Empress of Austria, who recently had been conspicuous for her dislike of the French, so that there had been felt some dread of her dissatisfaction, if not of direct opposition, thoroughly shared her husband's joy. On this subject, Count Otto, in a despatch of February 19, expressed himself as follows: "The Empress shows herself extremely favorable to this marriage. In spite of her wretched health she has expressed her desire to be present at all the festivities, and she takes every occasion to speak of them with delight."

The Ambassador carried his optimism so far as to look upon Marie Antoinette's marriage as a happy precedent. In the same despatch he wrote to the Duke of Cadore: "The names of Kaunitz and Choiseul are on every one's lips, and every one hopes to see a renewal of the peaceful days that followed the alliance concluded by those two ministers. They had both been ambassadors, in France, and in Austria, exactly like Your Excellency and Count Metternich." The French diplomatist's satisfaction was only equalled by the vexation of the Russian Ambassador. "The Russian coteries," added Count Otto, "are the only ones that take no part in the general rejoicing. When the news reached a ball at a Russian house, the violins were stopped at once, and a great many of the guests left before supper. I must observe that Count Shouvaloff has not come to offer his congratulations." The good humor of the Viennese grew from day to day, especially in business circles. The French Ambassador concluded his letter thus: "It is at the Bourse that public opinion has declared itself in the most amazing way. In less than two hours funds went up thirty per cent. A feeling of security established itself and at once affected the price of imported provisions, which immediately began to fall. Yesterday there was a large crowd gathered at the palace to see the Archduchess go to mass. The populace was delighted to see her radiant with health and happiness. Two artists are painting her portrait. The better one will be sent to Paris." Everything had moved smoothly without the slightest jar. "In the whole course of the negotiation," Count Otto had written, February 17, "I have not heard a word about any pecuniary consideration, or the slightest objection except as to the legality of the divorce. A mere word from me was sufficient to overcome that." Consequently nothing troubled the composure of the happy Ambassador.

V
THE RELIGIOUS DIFFICULTY

The marriage was officially announced, when suddenly an incident arose which caused the greatest anxiety to Napoleon's ambassador, and threatened, if not to prevent, at least to delay, the wedding. The unexpected difficulty which arose at the last moment was of a religious nature, and in a court as pious as that of Austria it could not fail to make a very deep impression.

Even in Paris, the annulment of the religious marriage ceremony of Napoleon and Josephine had aroused serious objections, and the Emperor had shown much surprise when he was told by his uncle, Cardinal Fesch, the Grand Almoner, that there were obstacles in the way. In a matter of this sort, which concerns crowned heads, and is inspired by reasons of state, it is the Pope who must make the decision. Louis XII. had secured the dissolution of his marriage with Jane of France from Pope Alexander VI. Henry IV. had applied to Pope Clement VIII. to annul his marriage with Margaret of Valois. Napoleon himself had likewise had recourse, though without success, to Pope Pius VII., in the matter of his brother Jerome's marriage with Miss Paterson. Now, when the Pope was his prisoner, Napoleon could not apply to him; and since the sovereign pontiff had taken part in the coronation of the Empress Josephine, and profoundly sympathized with her, could he dare to say, like the diocesan officials of Paris, that she, from the religious point of view, was only the Emperor's mistress?

At the beginning of 1810 there was an ecclesiastic commission, consisting of Cardinal Fesch, President; Cardinal Maury, famous at the time of the Constituent Assembly, and later, one of the Imperial courtiers; the Archbishop of Tours; the bishops of Nantes, Trèves, Évreux, and Verceil; and the Abbé Emery, Superior of the Seminary of Saint Sulpice. The Emperor put to this committee the question whether the diocesan officials were competent to proceed to the canonical dissolution of his marriage with Josephine.

January 2, 1810, the committee decided that the diocesan officials were competent, but neither Cardinal Fesch nor the Abbé Emery signed the report. The Cardinal could not forget that it was he who, by the special authorization of Pius VII., had, on the night of December 1-2, 1804, given to the couple the nuptial blessing.

The very day that the Ecclesiastical Committee had affirmed the competence of the diocesan officials, it received from the Archchancellor Cambacérès a petition stating that the nuptial blessing given to Napoleon and Josephine had not been preceded, accompanied, or followed by the formalities prescribed by the Canon laws; that is to say, it lacked the presence of the proper priest—as the parish priest was termed—and of witnesses. To these two grounds for annulment a third was added, a new one, which could not fail to surprise the officials. It was one which in general is applicable only to a minor, wrought upon by surprise and violence; namely, lack of consent,—yes, lack of the Emperor's consent. Napoleon saw very clearly that the first two points were mere quibbles, and that the moment when he intended that his uncle, the Grand Almoner, should bless his marriage with Marie Louise, was, to say the least, a singular one to choose for denouncing his incapacity for consecrating his union with Josephine. As to the absence of witnesses, that is to be explained as due to a special dispensation of the Pope, who wished to avoid the scandal of announcing to the whole world that Napoleon, who had been married by civil, but not by religious rites, had in the eyes of the Church been living for eight years in concubinage, in spite of the entreaties of the Empress to put an end to a state of things which pained her conscience and filled her with constant dread of divorce. The Emperor consequently laid the chief weight on his lack of consent. Count d'Haussonville in his remarkable book, *The Church of Rome and the First Empire*, says on this subject: "Setting aside the religious feeling with regard to the sanctity of marriage, it is hard to understand how such a man could have been willing to represent himself as having desired, on the eve of this great ceremony of consecration, to deceive at the same time his uncle who married him, his wife whom he seemed pleased to associate with his glory, and the venerable pontiff who, in spite of his age and infirmities, had come from a long distance, to call down upon him the blessing of the Most High. This argument offended not only every feeling of delicacy, but also the plainest principles of honest and fair dealing."

The officials were not moved by such scruples. They exercised a twofold jurisdiction,—as a diocesan and as a metropolitan tribunal,—and both affirmed the nullity of the marriage. The metropolitan tribunal, while admitting the first two grounds,—namely, the absence of witnesses and of the proper priest,—based its decision principally on the non-consent of the Emperor. The diocesan tribunal had declared that to atone for the infringement of the laws of the Church, Napoleon and Josephine should be compelled to bestow a sum of money to the poor of the parish of Notre Dame. The metropolitan tribunal struck this clause out as disrespectful.

This decision was sent to Count Otto, the French Ambassador at Vienna; in fact, the original draft of the two papers, that is to say, the judgment of the metropolitan tribunal, was forwarded to him. The Ambassador spoke about it to the Emperor Francis, to satisfy that monarch's scruples, but he did not show him the papers themselves, and three days after the ratification of the marriage contract he sent them back to Paris. "I confess," he wrote to the Duke of Cadore, in his despatch of February 28, 1810, "that in returning these papers so speedily to Paris, I had a presentiment of the discussion which they might cause among the foreign ecclesiastics. Everything was settled, the Emperor of Austria was satisfied, the marriage contract was ratified, the ratification of the marriage had been exchanged for three days, when the first mention was made of these documents which have aroused the curiosity and interest of some too influential prelates. I am the more authorized to say that no one had before that thought of these papers, by the fact that the Minister, when on the 15th he asked me to give him, on my honor, my personal opinion with regard to the nullity of His Majesty's first marriage, would not have failed to add that he had asked for proof from the Prince of Schwarzenberg, and that he awaited his reply. My declaration was sufficient to determine the ratification of the contract on the next day."

Whence came these tardy scruples, this unexpected delay? What had happened? The objections did not come from the Emperor Francis, or from Count Metternich, but from a priest, the Archbishop of Vienna, who was to celebrate the marriage by proxy in the Church of the Augustins in Vienna. This prelate, who shared all the opinions of the French émigrés, and had much more respect for the Pope than for Napoleon, deemed it his duty to examine for himself the judgment of the Parisian authorities, and stoutly demanded the originals. This filled the French Ambassador with despair, and he wrote to the Duke of Cadore in great distress: "For three days the Minister of Foreign Affairs has been in negotiation with the Archbishop, trying to overcome his scruples with regard to the nullity of the first marriage of His Majesty. This prelate persists in saying to-day that he cannot give the nuptial blessing until he has seen the document which I have sent back to Your Excellency, of which, too, M. de Metternich did not speak in the course of our negotiations. It is very strange that since the Archbishop was consulted some time ago, no mention was made to me of his scruples. I have every reason to believe that he did nothing until he heard that I had received documents, the validity of which he might discuss. Now the French clergy will hardly care to submit its decision to a foreign prelate. Your Excellency's intention has been to satisfy the Emperor of Austria, the only authority which, in a question of this importance, we can consider competent, because it concerns the lot of his daughter. What would happen, sir, if this prelate, adopting other principles than those which determined the judgment of our officials, should presume to invalidate them? How can we submit to a new discussion of a treaty ratified before the eyes of all Europe, and made public by the order of the Emperor of Austria himself? May we not suppose that the Archbishop, who in the first instance approved of this alliance, to-day is moved only by scruples and inspired by a foreign faction which is ready to seize any pretext to oppose the genius of peace? I am told that the former Bishop of Carcassonne is living with the Archbishop. Possibly the Nuncio, who is still here, has brought some influence to bear on this occasion. That there is something of the sort behind it all is proved by the prominence that some of the intriguers give to an alleged excommunication of His Majesty the Emperor by the Pope. Count Metternich assures me that both the Nuncio and the Archbishop disclaim all knowledge of any obstacle of this sort. The Emperor himself, who is keenly alive to the insult to crowned heads which it implies, repels the indecent objection with the scorn which it deserves.

"The Minister has had many fruitless interviews with the Archbishop, who seems to wish to lay the matter before his tribunal. The Emperor himself is very uneasy; they are trying to gain time, and are to-day very anxious lest the Prince of Neufchâtel should arrive too soon. If he should not get here till the 3d of March, they will manage to postpone the nuptial blessing till the 11th, when it is hoped that the documents will have come back again. But even in this case, the Ambassador Extraordinary will need all the firmness of his character to overrule this cabal which brings uneasiness to the Emperor's family and uses the Archbishop as a tool. I have done everything that I could to impress upon the Minister how much the present state of affairs compromises the dignity of our court. He has shown me a list of questions presented by the Archbishop, which it is impossible to answer without seeming to recognize a tribunal with which we ought to have nothing to do. Never has so important a negotiation been hampered by a stranger incident." (Despatch of Count Otto to the Duke of Cadore, February 28, 1810.)

The Ambassador was in great perplexity, and he would have been much more uneasy if the documents demanded had been in his possession. In fact, would he have been justified in submitting to a foreign ecclesiastical tribunal papers which he could only show to the Emperor of Austria, to remove that sovereign's personal objections? Count Metternich had told the Ambassador, February 24, that the ceremony would take place in spite of the Archbishop's objection, but the next day M. de Metternich was convinced that he was mistaken.

In order to gain time, Count Otto had written to Napoleon's Ambassador Extraordinary, the Prince of Neufchâtel, to ask him to delay his arrival at Vienna until March 4. The carnival would end with brilliant festivities, for which great preparations were making. Ash Wednesday and the three following days would be consecrated to devotion; and on the 11th the church ceremonies would take place, if, as was hoped, the required documents should have arrived from Paris.

After a few days of uncertainty, as painful for the court of Vienna as for the French Ambassador, the difficulties began to settle themselves. Count Otto wrote to the Duke of Cadore, March 3, 1810: "My long silence must have surprised Your Excellency, but it was caused by the strangest circumstances that I have known for many years…. It is only to-day that we are secure from the attack of the ecclesiastical committee, and from its scruples. Seven long days and nights have been spent in ransacking the volumes of the *Moniteur* and the *Official Bulletin* in order to prove the nullity of His Majesty the Emperor's first marriage. Nothing could pacify the alarmed conscience of the Archbishop. At first I refused, and held out for twenty-four hours. After protracted discussion, and insisting on a complete recasting of the paper which I was desired to sign, I to-day consented to hand in the paper, of which I have the honor to enclose a copy, but on the express condition, which I have under the minister's signature, that it is only to be shown to the Archbishop and in no case to be made public."

This is the text of the paper mentioned by Count Otto: "I, the undersigned, Ambassador of his Majesty the Emperor of the French, affirm that I have seen and read the originals of the two decisions of the two diocesan official boards, concerning the marriage between their Majesties, the Emperor and the Empress Josephine, and that it follows from these decisions that, in conformity with the Catholic ecclesiastical laws established in the French Empire, the said marriage has been declared null and void, because at the celebration of this marriage the most essential formalities required by the laws of the Church, and always regarded in France as necessary for the validity of a Catholic marriage, had been omitted. I affirm, moreover, that in conformity with the civic laws in existence at the time of the celebration of this marriage, every conjugal union was founded on the principle that it could be dissolved by the consent of the contracting parties. In testimony whereof I have signed the present declaration, and have set my seal to it."

In his despatch of March 3, 1810, the Ambassador said, in speaking of the document just cited: "The only thing that persuaded me to adopt this course was the conviction that the Archbishop would not consent to pronounce the blessing until he had seen the two decisions; and it appeared to me very dangerous to expose these two documents to the whims of an old man who was controlled by two refugee priests. At any rate, this method has proved successful, and the delay in the Prince of Neufchâtel's arrival prevents the public from forming any suspicions about this discussion which has given us so much anxiety. The Archbishop is satisfied; all the ceremonies will take place according to the programme, except the interruption due to the heavy roads. The wedding will take place March 11; and to make up the time lost, the Archduchess will travel a little faster, and can easily reach Paris by the 27th. Now the postponement of the nuptial blessing can be ascribed only to the circumstances which have prolonged the journey of the Prince of Neufchâtel. In Lent Sunday is considered the only proper day for weddings; and since Ash Wednesday is so near, the religious ceremony cannot possibly take place before the 11th."

The last difficulties had vanished, and the festivities were free to begin.

VI
THE AMBASSADOR EXTRAORDINARY

In Vienna the animation was very great. The great event which was now in preparation was the sole subject of conversation in all classes of society. "The ceremonies and the festivities," the French Ambassador wrote, March 2, 1810, "will be in every respect the same as those that took place at the marriage of the Emperor with the present Empress. Every inhabitant of Vienna is doing his utmost to testify his joy on this occasion. Painters are at work night and day on transparencies and designs. The festivities will be thoroughly national. Every morning thousands of people station themselves before the palace to see the Archduchess pass by on her way to mass. Her portraits are in constant demand. The Emperor and the archdukes never miss a ball; they are surrounded by a crowd of maskers who say a number of pleasant things to them, and it really appears as if this alliance had added to the Emperor's already great popularity." The next day, March 3, Count Otto wrote: "I to-day presented the Count of Narbonne to the Emperor, the Empress, and the Archduchess, and I profited by the occasion to strengthen my conviction of the joy which the Count feels at this happy alliance. The Empress spoke with the greatest warmth of her step-daughters, conversed with a keen interest about France, Paris, and what she hopes to cultivate in that interesting city."

It was with impatience that was awaited the arrival of the Ambassador Extraordinary, who had been chosen by the Emperor of the French to make the formal demand for the hand of the Archduchess, to attend to the celebration of the marriage which was to be celebrated by proxy at the Church of the Augustins in Vienna, and to escort the bride to France. This Ambassador Extraordinary was Marshal Berthier, sovereign Prince of Neufchâtel, the husband of the Princess Marie Elizabeth Amelia Frances of Bavaria, Vice-Constable of France, Master of the Hounds, commander of the first cohort of the Legion of Honor, etc., etc. The most brilliant reception was prepared for him. Count Otto wrote to the Duke of Cadore, February 21, 1810: "As to the honors which I have considered due to His Most Serene Highness, the Prince of Neufchâtel, Count Metternich assures me that he regarded him not merely as Ambassador Extraordinary, but as a Sovereign Prince, a great dignitary of the Empire, as a friend and fellow-soldier of the

Emperor; that there would be no more comparison between him and the Marquis of Durfort than between the future Empress and the Dauphiness; and that consequently Prince Paul Esterhazy had been designated to proceed to the frontier to congratulate His Highness; and that, moreover, an Imperial Commissary would be sent to look after his journey, and to see that proper honor was paid to him on the way; that he would be lodged and entertained by the court, and that pains would be taken to furnish him with everything he might require; for in such a severe season, at so brief a notice, he could not possibly have supplied himself with all the articles ha needed."

The Prince of Neufchâtel's formal entrance into Vienna was accompanied with great pomp. Count Otto thus describes it in his despatch of March 6, 1810: "The Prince of Neufchâtel has just made his entrance. The ceremony was most magnificent. The court had despatched their finest carriages, and the highest noblemen sent their equipages in their grandest array. The Prince lacked only couriers and footmen. I had twelve of my servants accompanying his carriage, all in the Emperor's grand livery. The sovereign himself could not have had a warmer welcome, or one more sumptuous and enthusiastic than did our Ambassador Extraordinary, and the contrast with many fresh memories made the spectacle a very touching one. To shorten the Prince's triumphal march from the summer palace of Schwarzenberg to the Kärthnerstrasse, many thousand workmen had been busily throwing a bridge over the very fortifications that our soldiers had blown up. Cheers and applause accompanied the Vice-Constable to the door of the Audience Chamber, and from there to his house. The court has given him most sumptuous quarters in the Imperial Chancellor's offices, where he is treated like the Emperor himself."

Count Otto in the same despatch thus describes the evening of that brilliant 10th of March, 1810; "That evening there was a grand ball in the Hall of Apollo; the whole city was there. The Prince was greeted as enthusiastically as in the morning. The Emperor himself was present, together with the Archdukes, and received the congratulations and blessings of a populace beside itself with joy. The Prince scarcely left the Emperor, who talked with him most amiably and most cordially. The Emperor and the Vice-Constable attracted the eyes of the whole multitude that surrounded them, and every one rejoiced to see the friend and fellow-soldier of Napoleon by the side of the ruler of Austria. It was noticed that this was the first appearance of the Archduke Charles in the Hall of Apollo along with the Emperor; he will figure in the marriage ceremony, and shows the liveliest satisfaction in the event. The Vice-Constable was charmed with the Prince's conversation, and is going to dine with him to-morrow."

General the Count of Lauriston had just arrived in Vienna, bringing letters from Napoleon to the Emperor and Empress of Austria. We have found the replies in the archives of the Ministry of Foreign Affairs. They are as follows:—

The letter of the Emperor of Austria to the Emperor of the French:—

"March 6, 1810. MY BROTHER: General the Count of Lauriston has given to me Your Imperial Majesty's letter of February 23. Entrusting to your hands, my brother, the fate of my beloved daughter, I give to Your Majesty the strongest possible proof that I could give of my confidence and esteem. There are moments when the holiest of the affections outweighs every other consideration which is foreign to it. May Your Imperial Majesty find nothing in this letter but the feelings of a father, attached, by eighteen years of pleasant intercourse, to a daughter whom Providence has endowed with all the qualities that constitute domestic happiness. Though called far away from me, she will continue to be worthy of my most enduring affections only by contributing to the felicity of the husband whose throne she is to share, and to the happiness of his subjects. You will kindly receive the assurance of my sincere friendship, as well as of the high consideration with which I am, my brother, Your Imperial and Royal Majesty's affectionate brother FRANCIS."

The letter of the Empress of Austria to the Emperor Napoleon:—

"March 6,1810. MY BROTHER: I hasten to thank Your Imperial Majesty for the many proofs of confidence contained in the letter which Your Majesty has kindly sent to me through the Count of Lauriston. The tender attachment of the best of fathers for a beloved child has had no need of counsels. Our wishes are the same. I share his confidence in the happiness of Your Majesty and of our daughter. But it is from me that Your Imperial Majesty must receive the assurance of the many qualities of mind and heart that distinguish the latter. What might seem the exaggerated affection of a father cannot be suspected from the pen of a stepmother. Be sure, my brother, that my happiest days will be those that come to you in consequence of the alliance that is about to unite us. Accept the friendship and high esteem with which I am Your Imperial Majesty's affectionate sister MARIE LOUISE."

The different provinces of the Empire sent deputations to Vienna to bear their good wishes to the Archduchess. They were received on the 6th of March, and the ceremony was thus described by Count Otto: "Yesterday's festival was very brilliant. In the morning, the deputations of the Austrian states drove, in a procession of more than thirty carriages, to the Palace to pay their compliments to the Archduchess, who received them under a canopy. In spite of the shyness natural to her youth, the Princess replied to them in a speech which amazed and touched her hearers. She is likewise to receive deputations from Hungary, Bohemia, and Moravia. It is thought that to the first she will reply in Latin. At one o'clock we went to the Palace to dine with their Majesties and the Imperial family. The only guests were the Prince Vice-Constable, the Count of Lauriston, and myself. The Empress was in better health, and more affable than I have ever seen her. The two Ambassadors took precedence of the Archduchess. The Prince Vice-Constable was placed at the Empress's left, and I sat at the Archduchess's right; the Emperor sat in the middle and took part in the conversation on both sides. This conversation was very animated. The Archduchess asked a good many questions which displayed the soundness of her tastes." According to the Ambassador's despatch, these were the questions which Marie Louise asked: "Is the Napoleon Museum near enough to the Tuileries for me to go there and study the antiques and monuments it contains?" "Does the Emperor like music?" "Shall I be able to have a teacher on the harp? It is an instrument I am very fond of." "The Emperor is so kind to me; doubtless he will let me have a botanical garden. Nothing would please me more." "I am told that the country around Fontainebleau is very wild and picturesque. I like nothing better than beautiful scenery." "I am very grateful to the Emperor for letting me take Madame Lazansky with me, and for choosing the Duchess of Montebello; they are two excellent women." "I hope the Emperor will be considerate; I don't know how to dance quadrilles; but if he desires it, I will take dancing-lessons." "Do you think Humboldt will soon finish the account of his travels? I have read all that has appeared with great interest."

Count Otto adds, in his faithful report: "I told Her Imperial Highness that the Emperor was anxious to know her tastes and ways. She told me that she was easily pleased; that her tastes were very simple; that she was able to adapt herself to anything, and would do her best to conform to His Majesty's wishes, her only desire being to please him…. I must say, that during the whole hour of my interview with Her Imperial Highness, she did not once speak of the Paris fashions or theatres."

That evening there was a ball at which the Emperor was present with his whole family, and the Ambassador thus describes the occasion: "More than six thousand persons, of all ranks, were invited by the court, and they filled two immense halls which were richly decorated and illuminated. At the end of the first hall there was a most magnificent sideboard, in the shape of a temple lit by a thousand ingeniously hidden lamps. The Genius of Victory, surmounting an altar, was placing a laurel wreath on the escutcheons of the bride and groom. The N and L were displayed in all the decoration of the columns and pediments. To the right, a tent made of French flags covered a sideboard-laden with refreshments; and on the left there was another under a tent made of Austrian flags. There were large tables in the neighboring rooms, covered with food for the citizens who regarded it as an important duty to pledge the health of the Imperial couple in Tokay. The Archduchess, who had never been to a ball before in her life, passed through every room on the Emperor's arm. She was most warmly cheered, and the crowd followed her with a joyous enthusiasm that can scarcely be described. This ball presented the most perfect combination of grandeur, wealth, and good taste; it was further remarkable for the bond of fraternity which seemed to unite the two nations." The next day but one, March 8, the formal demand for the hand of the Archduchess Marie Louise was made at the Palace, with great pomp, by Marshal Berthier, Prince of Neufchâtel. As soon as he had delivered his speech, the Archduchess entered in magnificent attire, accompanied by all the members of the household. Count Anatole de Montesquiou, an orderly officer of the Emperor Napoleon, had just arrived in Vienna, bringing a miniature portrait of his sovereign. This officer was to be present at the wedding, and to take to Paris the first news of its conclusion. As soon as the Archduchess appeared, the Prince of Neufchâtel offered her Napoleon's portrait, which she at once had fastened on the front of her dress by the Mistress of the Robes. The Ambassador Extraordinary then went to the apartments of the Empress of Austria, whence he went to visit the Archduke Charles to tell him that Napoleon wished to be represented by him at the wedding to be celebrated by proxy, March 11, by the Archbishop of Vienna, at the Church of the Augustins. The Prince of Neufchâtel continued to be treated with a consideration such as perhaps had never before fallen to the lot of an envoy in Vienna. From morning till night his quarters were surrounded by an inquisitive multitude who were anxious to see and salute Napoleon's friend and fellow-soldier. On the 9th of March he gave a grand dinner to the most distinguished gentlemen and ladies of the city. "After the dinner," Count Otto wrote to the Duke of Cadore, "other ladies came in to pay the first visit to him, a distinction which probably no foreign prince has ever before enjoyed here. At the grand performance given at the court theatre that same evening, the Prince again had precedence of the Archdukes. He was given a seat by the side of the Empress, who all the evening said the most flattering things to him.... Among the unprecedented honors which have been paid to him, I have always found it easy to distinguish such as were personal attentions. His Highness has had the greatest success here, especially with the Archdukes, who, in order to overcome his objections to take precedence of them, said in the most obliging way, 'We are all soldiers, and you are our senior.' The Archduke Charles has especially displayed a grace and delicacy that have extremely touched the Prince…. The Emperor has presented the Prince with his portrait in a costly medallion, and His Highness has taken care to wear it on various occasions."

Napoleon, who a few days before had been so hated by the Viennese, appeared to them, as if by sudden endowment, a sort of divine being. On all sides were heard outbursts of praise, allegories, and cantatas, in his honor. The poets of the city rivalled one another in celebrating the union of myrtles and laurels, of grace and strength, of beauty and genius. "Love," they sang in their dithyrambs, "weaves flowery chains to unite forever Austria and Gaul. Peoples shed tears, but tears of enthusiasm and gratitude. Long live Louise and Napoleon!" In every street, in every square, there were transparencies, mottoes, flags, mythological emblems, temples of Hymen, angels of peace and concord, Fame with her trumpet.

At that moment there happened to be in Vienna a great many French officers and soldiers, detained there to recover from the wounds they had received in the course of the last war. All those who were able to leave their beds were anxious to have the happiness of seeing their new Empress, and thronged to the Palace doors. As soon as Marie Louise heard that they were there, she made her appearance before them, and spoke to them most graciously a few kind words. Then these veterans, wild with joy, shouted at the top of their lungs, "Long live the Princess! Long live the House of Austria!" And the good people of Vienna, enchanted at the sight, both wondered and rejoiced to see their Emperor's daughter so warmly greeted by the French soldiers of Essling and Wagram.

VII
THE WEDDING AT VIENNA

Before proceeding to the account of the wedding, celebrated by proxy in Vienna, at the Church of the Augustins, March 11, 1810, it may be well to enumerate the members, at that time, of the Imperial family.

The Emperor, Francis II., head of the house of Hapsburg-Lorraine, who was born February 12, 1768, had just entered his forty-third year; consequently, he was only eighteen months older than his son-in-law, the Emperor Napoleon, who was born August 15, 1769. The Austrian monarch had taken for his third wife his cousin Marie Louise Beatrice of Este, daughter of the Archduke Ferdinand, Duke of Modena. This Princess, who had no children, was born December 14, 1787, four years, almost to a day, before her step-daughter, the Archduchess Marie Louise, Napoleon's wife, who was born December 11, 1791. The new Empress of the French, at the time of the celebration of her wedding in Vienna, was consequently eighteen years and three months old, and twenty-two years younger than her husband.

Francis II. had eight children, three boys and five girls, all by his second wife, Marie Theresa, of the Two Sicilies, and born in the following order: In 1791, Marie Louise; in 1793, Ferdinand, the Prince Imperial; in 1797, Leopoldine, who became the wife of Dom Pedro, Emperor of Brazil; in 1798, Marie Clementine, who married the Prince of Salerno, and was the mother-in-law of the Duke of Aumale, the son of Louis Philippe; in 1801, Caroline, who married Prince Frederick of Saxony; in 1802, Francis Charles Joseph; in 1804, Marie Anne, who became Abbess of the Chapter of Noble Ladies in Prague; in 1805, John.

He had one sister and eight brothers, to wit: Marie Theresa Josepha, born 1767, who married Antoine Clement, brother of Frederic Augustus, King of Saxony; Ferdinand, born 1769, who, after having been Grand Duke of Tuscany, became Grand Duke of Würzburg, and a great friend of Napoleon; Charles Louis, born 1771, the famous Archduke Charles, Napoleon's rival on the battle-field; Joseph Antoine, born 1776, Palatine of Hungary; Antoine Victor, born 1779, who became Bishop of Bamberg; John, born 1782, who presided over the parliament at Frankfort in 1848; Reinhardt, born 1783, who was Viceroy of the Kingdom of Lombardy and Venetia when it became an Austrian province; Louis, born 1784; Rudolph, born 1788, who became a Cardinal. Consequently, at the time of Marie Louise's marriage, there were eleven Archdukes, three sons and eight brothers of the Emperor. The wedding ceremony was preceded, March 10, 1810, by a rite called the renunciation. At one in the afternoon, Marshal Berthier, Prince of Neufchâtel, Ambassador Extraordinary of France, drove to the Palace with his suite, in a state carriage drawn by six horses, and was conducted to the hall of the Privy Council, to witness this ceremony. As soon as Francis II. and Marie Louise had taken their seats beneath the canopy, the Emperor, as head of the family, spoke as follows: "Inasmuch as the customs of the Imperial family require that the Imperial Princesses and Archduchesses shall before marriage recognize the Pragmatic Sanction of Austria, and the order of succession, by a solemn act of renunciation, Her Imperial Highness the Archduchess Marie Louise, who is betrothed to His Imperial Majesty the Emperor of the French, King of Italy, is about to take the usual oath, and proceed to the formal rite of renunciation." The Archduchess then went up to a table on which stood a crucifix between two lighted candles, and the holy Gospels. Count Hohenwart, Prince Archbishop of Vienna, opened the book of the Gospel according to St. John, and the Archduchess, having placed upon it two fingers of the right hand, read aloud the act of renunciation of the right of succession to the crown, and took the oath. That evening, Gluck's *Iphigenia among the Taurians* was given at the Royal opera-house. The stairway to the boxes was brilliantly lighted, and lined with orange-trees. The next day, Sunday, the wedding was celebrated with great pomp at the Church of the Augustins. The procession filed through the apartments of the Palace, which had been covered with rugs and filled with chandeliers and candelabra. Grenadiers were drawn up in a double line from the Palace to the church. This was the order of the procession: Two stewards of the court, the pages, the stewards of the chamber, the carvers, the chamberlains, the privy councillors, the ministers, the principal officers of the court, the French Ambassador Extraordinary, the Archdukes Rudolph, Louis, Reinhardt, John, Antoine, Joseph, preceded by the Archduke Charles, accompanied by the Grand Master of the Court; the Emperor and King, followed by the Captain of the Noble Hungarian Guard, the Captain of the Yeomen, and the Grand Chamberlain; the Empress Queen holding the bride by the hand. The train of the Empress's dress was carried by the grand mistresses of the court as far as the second ante-chamber, by pages to the church, and then again by the grand mistresses. On each side of the Emperor, the Empress, and the Archdukes, marched twelve archers and as many body-guards; at some distance the same number of yeomen bearing halberds. Kettledrums and trumpets announced the arrival of the Emperor and the Empress at the church, where the Prince Archbishop of Vienna, accompanied by the clergy, met them at the door and presented them with holy water; that done, he proceeded with his bishops to the foot of the altar, on the gospel-side. The Imperial family took their place in the choir. The Archduke Charles, as Napoleon's representative, and the Archduchess Marie Louise, kneeled at the prayer-desks before the altar. When the Archbishop had blessed the wedding-ring, which was presented to him in a cup, the Archduke Charles and the bride advanced to the altar, where the ceremony took place in German, according to the Viennese rite. After the exchange of rings, the bride took the one destined for Napoleon, which she was to give herself to her husband. Then while those present remained on their knees the *Te Deum* was sung. Six pages carried flaming torches; salvos of artillery were fired; the bells of the city announced to the populace the completion of the rite. After the *Te Deum* the Archbishop pronounced the benediction. Then the procession returned to the Palace in the order of its going forth.

The French Ambassador wrote to the Duke of Cadore: "The marriage of His Majesty the Emperor with the Archduchess Marie Louise was celebrated with a magnificence that it would be hard to surpass, by the side of which even the brilliant festivities that have preceded it are not to be mentioned. The vast multitude of spectators, who had gathered from all quarters of the realm and from foreign parts, so packed the church, and the halls and passage-ways of the Palace, that the Emperor and Empress of Austria were often crowded. The really prodigious display of pearls and diamonds; the richness of the dresses and the uniforms; the numberless lights that illuminated the whole Palace; the joy of the participants, gave to the ceremony a splendor worthy of this grand and majestic solemnity. The richest noblemen of the country made a most brilliant display, and seemed to rival even with the Emperor. The ladies who accompanied the two Empresses, who were for the most part Princesses and women of the highest rank, seemed borne down by the weight of the diamonds and pearls they wore. But all eyes were fixed on the principal person of the solemnity, on this adored Princess who soon will make the happiness of our Sovereign."

When the procession had re-entered the Palace, the Imperial family and the court assembled in the room called the Room of the Mirror. The Emperor of Austria and the two Empresses received the congratulations of all the nobility. By the side of Marie Louise stood the grand mistress of the household and twelve ladies-in-waiting. "Her modesty," Count Otto continues in the same report, "the nobility of her bearing, the ease with which she replied to the speeches addressed to her, enchanted every one.... I was the first to be introduced to her. She answered my congratulations by saying that she would spare no pains to please His Majesty the Emperor Napoleon and to contribute to the happiness of the French nation which had now become her own. Her Majesty then received all the noblemen of the court, and spoke to them with an affability that delighted them. When the reception was over, I was presented to the Emperor, who spoke to me most amiably and most cordially. He told me that, in spite of his delicate health, he was unwilling to lose any opportunity of testifying his high esteem of my master, the Emperor. 'He will always find in me,' he went on, 'the loyalty and zeal which you must have noticed in this last negotiation. I give to your Emperor my beloved daughter. She deserves to be happy. You see joy on every face. We have neglected nothing to show our satisfaction with this alliance. Our nations require rest; they applaud what we have done. I am sure that the best intelligence will reign between us, and that our union will become only closer.' All these gratifying things that the Emperor said to me were made even more marked by the voice and the smile which accompanied them. This monarch, in fact, has a charm of manner which accounts for his great popularity. During and after the ceremony, the Empress held her stepdaughter by her right hand, leading her in this way in the church and through the halls and rooms. The large crowd of spectators, which almost blocked the inside of the Palace and all the approaches, seemed to belong to the Imperial family, so great was its emotion on seeing the new Empress pass by. All the Frenchmen who were near me confessed that they had never seen a grander or more touching sight. The court has had a large number of medals struck off in memory of this event. Many hundred of these have been sent to the Prince of Neufchâtel, who, to the last, has been treated with the most marked consideration."

After the wedding and the reception a grand state dinner was given at the Palace. A splendid table was set upon a platform covered with costly carpets, over which there was a canopy in the shape of a horseshoe. The Grand Master of the Court announced to their Majesties that the dinner was served. Carvers and pages brought in the meats. After the *lavabo* the Archbishop asked the blessing, and the Imperial family took their places in the following order; in the middle, the Empress of the French; on her right, the Emperor of Austria; on her left, the Empress; on the two sides the Archdukes Charles, Joseph, Antoine, John, Reinhardt, Louis, Rudolph, the Prince of Neufchâtel, the Ambassador Extraordinary. The Grand Master of the Court sat on the right, behind the Emperor's chair; near him were the Captain of the Yeomen, and on the left the Captain of the Noble Hungarian Guard. The ministers of state and the representatives of foreign courts sat on the right, and the two grand mistresses of the court on the left below the platform. The rest were opposite the table, next to the body-guard. The Emperor's children had a place assigned to them in the gallery from which they could look down on the feast. A concert, vocal and instrumental, accompanied the dinner. At the end the officiating bishop said grace in a low voice.

There was much comment on the presence of the Prince of Neufchâtel at the Imperial table, where he sat from the beginning to the end of the dinner. This was a modification of the ceremonial of the Viennese court, which admitted Ambassadors to the monarch's table only on very rare occasions, as at the marriage of an Archduchess; but even in this case, required that they should leave the table when the dessert was served, to move about among the noblemen admitted to the banquet-hall. It was recalled that at the marriage of the French Dauphin to the Archduchess Marie Antoinette, the Marquis of Durfort, the Ambassador of Louis XV., was not invited to the dinner in order to avoid the question of precedence between him and Duke Albert of Saxe-Teschen, who was present at the banquet. This same Duke, as well as the brothers of the young Empress of the French, did not attend the state dinner of March 11, 1810; and the reason given was the desire to show a particular honor to Napoleon's Ambassador Extraordinary.

The same day, the Archduke Charles who had just represented the French Emperor at the wedding, wrote to him this letter:—

"March 11, 1810. SIRE: The functions which Your Imperial Majesty has been kind enough to impose on me have been infinitely agreeable. Flattered at being chosen to represent a sovereign who, by his exploits, will live eternally in the annals of history, and convinced of the mutual happiness which must ensue from the union of Your Imperial Majesty with a Princess endowed with so many qualities as my dear niece, I have felt happy at being called on to cement this bond. I beg Your Imperial Majesty to receive the most earnest assurances of this feeling, as well as of the profound consideration with which I shall never cease to be, sire, Your Majesty's very humble and very obedient servant and cousin, CHARLES."

That evening there were free performances at every theatre. The Emperor and Empress drove through the city with the bride, who had that day sent one gold napoleon to every wounded Frenchman, and five napoleons to every one who had lost a limb. The same thing had been done for the wounded German allies of France in the last war. This exhibition of generosity produced the most favorable impression, and much gratitude was felt towards the new Empress, who in the hours of her triumph had thought of the suffering soldiers. She was everywhere cheered. The city and suburbs were rivals in the brilliancy of the illuminations. In front of the Chancellor's office, where the Prince of Neufchâtel was staying, were shown the initials of Napoleon and Marie Louise amid a circle of lights. On one window was this motto, *Ex unione pax, opes, tranquillitas populorum,*

"This union brings to the people peace, wealth, tranquillity." The dwelling of the Superintendent of Public Buildings represented a temple with this illuminated inscription, *Vota publica fausto hymeneo*, "The wishes of the public for the happy marriage."

The famous engineer Melzel had devised an ingenious decoration. Above an excellent portrait of the new Empress there appeared a rainbow; on one side, his happiest invention, an automaton, which the Viennese called the War Trumpet. But a Genius was silencing it by pointing to this motto, *Tace, mundus concors*, "Silence, the world is at peace."

To be sure there were a few satires, and some insulting placards posted secretly, but the police took pains to remove them. Unfortunately the weather was unfavorable, and scarcely one light out of ten held out to burn. Was not this a token of the enthusiasm of the Viennese for Napoleon, an enthusiasm which had succeeded hatred as if by magic, and which, after flaring up so speedily, was soon to expire?

VIII
THE DEPARTURE

Marie Louise was to pass but one day more in Vienna. The ceremony had taken place March 11, 1810, and on the 13th the new Empress of the French was to leave the Austrian capital to join her husband in France. After all these festivities and great excitement, the 12th was devoted to peace and quiet. The Emperor Francis profited by it to write to Napoleon the following letter:—

"March 12, 1810. MY BROTHER AND MY DEAR SON-IN-LAW: I appoint my Chamberlain, the Count of Clary, the bearer of this letter to Your Imperial Majesty. The great bond which forever unites our two thrones was completed yesterday. I wish to be the first to congratulate Your Majesty on an event which it has deserved, and which my wishes in harmony with your own, my brother, have crowned, for I regard it as the most precious as well as the surest pledge of our common happiness, and consequently of that of our subjects. If the sacrifice I make is very great, if my heart is bleeding at the loss of this beloved daughter, the thought, and, I do not hesitate to say, the firmest conviction of her happiness, is alone able to console me. Count Metternich, who in a few days will follow Count Clary, will be commissioned to express by word of mouth to Your Imperial Majesty the attachment which I consecrated to the monarch who yesterday became one of the members of my family. Now I confine myself to begging him to receive the assurances of my esteem and unalterable friendship. Your Imperial and Royal Majesty's affectionate brother and father-in-law,

"Francis."

March 12, the Marshal Berthier, Prince of Neufchâtel, left Vienna for Braunan, on the Austrian and Bavarian frontier. There he was to join the Empress of the French, who was to be conducted thither by the Austrian escort and then be entrusted to the French escort with which she was to continue her journey. "Before the Prince of Neufchâtel left," wrote Count Otto, March 10, "a great many Archdukes called on him, including even the high officers of the crown. His Highness started at two o'clock, amid the acclamations of a large multitude. No embassy has ever been more warmly received or filled with more dignity and nobility. The Prince left sixty thousand francs to be divided among the household where he had stayed. He was most discreet in everything that he did, and in spite of the various honors heaped upon him, I do not think that there is a single person at the court whose pride has been wounded." As the moment drew near when the young Empress was to leave her beloved family and country, to plunge into the unknown future that was awaiting her, various emotions crowded upon her. At heart a German and an Austrian, she could not accustom herself to the thought that probably she would never see again her revered and beloved father; the family who adored her; the good people of Vienna, who had always shown the kindest interest in her; the Burg and Schoenbrunn, where had been spent so many happy years of her infancy; the dear Church of the Augustins, where she had so often earnestly offered up her prayers. Could all the praise of Napoleon which she had been hearing for the last few days wipe out the memory of the abuse she had so often heard? She had been promised wealth, grandeur, power; but do those constitute happiness?

The 13th of March came; the hour of her departure struck. That same day the French Ambassador wrote: "Her Majesty the Empress of the French left this morning with a large suite. On leaving her loved family and the land she will never see again, she for the first time felt all the anguish of the cruel separation. At eight o'clock in the morning the whole court was assembled in the reception-rooms. About nine, the Austrian Empress appeared, again leading her step-daughter by her right hand. She tried to speak to me, but her voice was choked by sobs. The young Empress was accompanied to her carriage by her step-mother and the Archdukes, and there they kissed her for the last time. Here the affectionate mother broke down, and she was supported to her own room by two chamberlains. The young Empress burst into tears, and her distress moved even foreigners who witnessed it."

The procession started in the following order: a division of cuirassiers, a squadron of mounted militia, three postilions, the Prince of Paar, Director of the Posts, in a carriage with six horses; following came four carriages, each with six horses, containing Count Edelinck, Grand Master of the Court, and the chamberlains; Counts Eugene of Hangevitz; Domenic of Urbua; Joseph Metternich, Landgrave of Fürstenberg; Counts Ernest of Hoyes and Felix of Mier; Count Haddick, Field-Marshal; the Count of Wurmbrand; Count Francis Zichy; Prince Zinzendorf; Prince Paul Esterhazy; Count Antony Bathiani; then the Prince of Trautmannsdorf, First Grand Master of the Court, and Quartermaster, in a carriage with six horses; then, in one with eight horses, the Empress of the French, having with her the Countess of Lazansky, grand mistress of her household; finally, in three carriages with six horses each, her ladies-in-waiting,—the Princess of Trautmannsdorf, Countesses O'Donnell, of Sauran, d'Appony, of Blumeyers, of Traun, of Podstalzky, of Kaunitz, of Hunyady, of Chotek, of Palfy, of Zichy. A detachment of cavalry brought up the rear. The procession passed slowly through Saint Michael's Place, the Kohlmarkt, the Graben, Kärthnerstrasse, the Glacis, and the Mariahülfestrasse. The troops and national guard lined both sides of the way.

"The Empress," wrote Count Otto, in his despatch of March 13, "passed through the main streets of the city and the suburbs, amid the ringing of bells and the roar of cannon, followed by an immense concourse of persons who uttered affectionate wishes and farewells. The inhabitants had decorated their houses and even the palace gate with tricolored flags. The regimental bands played French marches for the first time. A general salvo from the ramparts finally announced that the Empress had crossed the bridge. Her Majesty will be received with the same honors in all the Austrian cities she passes through. The procession, which consists of eighty-three carriages, will probably be delayed by the bad roads, and the rain which fell heavily last night."

The Ambassador thus concluded his despatch: "The tumultuous joy which has prevailed in Vienna during this last week, which has gratified Her Majesty as much as any one, has been dimmed for a moment by a feeling which does honor to the kindness of her heart, and can only endear her the more to us. She has a great affection for her parents, and this feeling they return. She has been called Louise the Pious, and it has been said to be only right that she should share the throne of Saint Louis. The Emperor started an hour before Her Majesty for Linz, where he will embrace his beloved daughter for the last time. During these last few days it has been very obvious that his feelings as a father have had more weight with him than his position as a sovereign. This monarch's amiable disposition has appeared in the most favorable light on this occasion, and everything promises the happiest results from this alliance."

On leaving Vienna, Marie Louise doubtless thought that she would never see it again; but she was to return to it very soon and in very different circumstances. In four years the Viennese were to see her again, but how changed the condition of things! Events cruelly disappointed the hopes of peace and happiness evoked by her marriage. It was a bitter deception. The hatred of the Austrians for Napoleon, whom in 1810 they had so much admired, became once more as intense as in the days of Austerlitz and Wagram. They ceased to greet Marie Louise with applause; they simply pitied her. Her father himself ceased to regard her as a sovereign. "As my daughter," he said to her, "everything that I possess is yours, my blood and my life; I do not know you as a sovereign." The time seemed very remote when she had precedence of the Empress of Austria, and her father, the head of the house of Hapsburg, respectfully gave her place at his right hand. After losing the double Imperial and Royal crown, that of France and that of Italy, she was obliged to beg of the implacable Coalition a petty duchy, the possession of which had been promised her by a treaty signed after the fall of the great Empire. There were again festivities in Vienna, but not for her, the dethroned sovereign. Once she was curious to see one, and she watched it hiding behind a curtain. On the evening of a court ball given by her father in honor of the members of the Congress of Vienna, she concealed herself near an opening made in the attic of the great hall of the palace,—where the festivities of her wedding had been celebrated,—and from there the wife of the prisoner of Elba watched the men dancing who were condemning her to widowhood even in the lifetime of her husband.

IX
THE TRANSFER

Marie Louise's journey was one long ovation; in every town and in every village she passed through the young Empress received the homage of the authorities. Groups of girls, dressed in white, offered her flowers; bells were rung; and the enthusiasm of the country people was quite as warm as that of the Viennese. Marie Louise spent the night at Saint Pölten, where she met her father, who had gone thither incognito, in order to embrace her for the last time. The Empress, the bride's stepmother, went there also unexpectedly, and threw herself for the last time into the arms of the Empress of the French. Ried she reached the 15th of March, 1810, and thence Marie Louise started on the 16th, at eight in the morning, after hearing mass. By eleven she had reached Altheim, close to the Bavarian frontier, and here she made a stop for the purpose of exchanging her travelling-dress for a finer one. Bavaria, as part of the Confederation of the Rhine, could be regarded as a province of the French Emperor, since Napoleon was the Protector of the Confederation. It had hence been decided that on the frontier, between Austria and Bavaria, close to Braunau, should take place the ceremony of handing her over to her French escort with all formality. The scene was a close imitation of what had taken place forty years before, on the occasion of the marriage of Marie Antoinette. On the frontier line between Austria and Bavaria three pavilions were set up, opening from one to the other: the first of these was regarded as Austrian; the second, as neutral; and the third, as French. These three connected buildings formed a wooden edifice in three compartments, and was placed between Altheim and Braunau. It was furnished with care, and provided with fireplaces. The central pavilion, or hall, which was destined for the ceremony, was adorned with a canopy, beneath which, on a platform, there was an armchair for the Empress, covered with a cloth of gold. To the left of the canopy, on the Bavarian side, towards Braunau, was set a large table with a velvet cloth, on which the plenipotentiaries were to write their signatures. Two lines of young green trees had been set out, one leading to the French hall, the other to the Austrian. On the side of the first, towards Braunau, were drawn three regiments, in full uniform, two of infantry and one of cavalry, under the command of Generals Friant and Pajol. On the other, the Austrian, side, towards Altheim, there were neither troops nor sentinels, in token of the temporary neutrality of the territory. The French

Commissioner was Marshal Berthier, the Prince of Neufchâtel, and his secretary, Count Alexandre de La Borde. The Austrian Commissioner was the Prince of Trautmannsdorf: M. Thedelitz was his secretary. The French party, which was to meet Marshal Berthier at Braunau, and to serve as an escort to the Empress for the rest of the journey, was composed of the following people: Caroline, Queen of Naples, Murat's wife and Napoleon's sister; the Duchess of Montebello, lady of honor, the widow of Marshal Lannes; the Countess of Luçay, lady of the bed-chamber; the Duchess of Bassano, the Countesses of Montmorency, of Mortemart, and of Bouillé, maids of honor; the Bishop of Metz, Monsignor Jauffret, almoner; the Count of Beauharnais, lord-in-waiting; the Prince Aldobrandini Borghese, chief equerry; the Counts d'Aubusson, of Béarn, d'Angosse, and of Barol, chamberlains; Philip de Ségur, lord steward; the Baron of Saluces and the Baron d'Audenarde, equerries; the Count of Seyssel, master of ceremonies; M. de Bausset, steward.

March 16, at half-past one, the Prince of Neufchâtel, with the rest of his company, made their way to the French division of the building; they were all, men and women, in full dress. Towards two o'clock Marie Louise entered the Austrian room, and after resting a moment she was ushered into the middle room, the neutral one, by the Austrian master of ceremonies; there a throne had been set, and the formal ceremony was to take place. Marie Louise seated herself on the throne. The Prince of Trautmannsdorf took his station before the table where the papers were to be signed, with the Aulic Counsellor, Hudelitz, the secretary, behind him. The men and women of the Austrian party ranged themselves around the Empress. At the back and on the two sides of the hall were twelve Noble Hungarian Guards and twelve German guardsmen, armed and in full uniform.

While the Austrians were thus getting ready, the French were waiting in the next room, and displayed great impatience to get a sight of their new sovereign. M. de Bausset, an eye-witness of the ceremony, tells us in his Memoirs: "I was naturally anxious to see the Empress as soon as she should reach the middle room to take a place on the throne, and give her courtiers time to arrange themselves about her, before we were introduced. I had brought a gimlet, and with this I had bored a good many holes in the door of our room. This little indiscretion, which was not mentioned in our report, gave us an opportunity to inspect the appearance of our young sovereign at our ease. I need not say that it was the ladies of our party who were most anxious to make use of the little holes I had provided. The impression produced by the grace and majesty of the Empress upon these inquisitive peepers was very favorable. Marie Louise," M. de Bausset goes on, "sat straight on the throne. Her erect figure was fine; her hair was blond and very pretty; her blue eyes beamed with all the candor and innocence of her soul. Her face was soft and kindly. She wore a dress of gold brocade, caught up with large flowers of different colors, which must have tired her by its weight. Hanging from her neck was a portrait of Napoleon surrounded by sixteen magnificent solitaire diamonds, which together had cost five hundred thousand francs."

Baron von Lohr, the Austrian master of ceremonies, having knocked at the door of the next room, where were the Prince of Neufchâtel and the Empress's French court, announced to the Count of Seyssel, the French master of ceremonies, that the ceremony might begin; thereupon the Prince of Neufchâtel entered the neutral room, followed by Count de Laborde, his secretary for this occasion. After them entered the Duchess of Montebello, the Count of Beauharnais, and the rest of the French party, who stationed themselves at the end of the hall opposite the Austrians. The two commissioners, the Prince of Neufchâtel and the Prince of Trautmannsdorf, after an exchange of compliments, signed and sealed the two documents, each retaining one of the copies. Then the Prince of Trautmannsdorf approached the Empress, bowing, and asked permission to kiss her hand in bidding her farewell. This permission was readily granted to him, and to all the ladies and gentlemen who had accompanied her from Vienna.

While the French and Austrian secretaries were counting the dowry—five hundred thousand francs in new golden ducats—and verifying the Empress's jewels and precious stones, the French commissioners giving a receipt for the dowry and jewels as enumerated in an inventory attached to the document, the Austrian party drew up before the throne of Marie Louise, and each one, according to his or her rank, went up and kissed her hand with deep emotion. Even the humblest servants were admitted to present their respects and best wishes. "Her Majesty's eyes were filled with tears," M. de Bausset tells us, "and this emotion touched every heart."

When they had all regained their places, Prince Trautmannsdorf offered his hand to the Empress, to help her down from the platform and to lead her to the Prince of Neufchâtel, who took her by the hand and led her towards the French courtiers. He named them all to the Empress; then the door of the French room was opened, and the Queen of Naples, who had been standing there during the whole ceremony, went up to her, and the two sisters-in-law kissed each other and chatted for a few moments. Then the Archduke Antoine was announced; he had been sent by the Emperor of Austria to present his compliments to the Queen of Naples, and was to return at once to Vienna to bring tidings of the Empress Marie Louise. After the Queen had welcomed and thanked the Archduke, the two sisters-in-law got into a carriage and drove to Braunau, followed by the Prince of Neufchâtel and all the court. On both sides of the way troops were drawn up in order of battle, and artillery salutes were fired.

The Prince of Neufchâtel, on the suggestion of the Emperor Napoleon, invited the ladies and gentlemen of the Austrian party to spend the day at Braunau, to take part in the rejoicings which were to be celebrated there. Marie Louise also invited them in her own name. General de Ségur, who was present, thus describes the mingling of the French and Austrians: "The only thing that I remember is that the men moved about together and exchanged words very politely; but I never saw a company of women sitting more constrainedly, with less ease, than on this occasion, when the Austrian ladies were haughtily cold and silent. These ladies, who had been compelled to offer up the Princess as their part of the war indemnity, seemed to take no part in the submission which the government had forced upon them. They handed over to us the pledge of defeat with a bad grace which their husbands, who were weary of war, did not show." Generals Friant and Pajol gave a grand dinner to the Austrian officers in the citadel of Braunau, and the courtesy of both sides was worthy of note. Three toasts were drunk,—the first to the Emperor Napoleon, the second to the Empress Marie Louise, the third to the Emperor of Austria. There was a salute of thirty guns after each toast.

At Braunau the Empress occupied the house of a rich wine-merchant opposite the town-hall. The house was decorated with flags, and before it a triumphal arch was set up. Marie Louise rested there, and changed everything she had on, according to the custom, which demands that a foreign princess on entering her new country must leave behind her everything that attaches her to the country, the people and the ways she has left. The Parisian shopkeepers had made everything for her from measures and models sent from Vienna. Napoleon had had these models shown him, and taking one of the shoes, which were remarkably small, he had sportively stroked his valet's cheek with it, and said, "See there, Constant; here's a shoe that will bring good luck with it. Did you ever see feet like those?"

After the Empress had received the authorities of Braunau and the generals commanding the French troops, she sought retirement, and wrote to her father this touching letter, of which M. von Helfert has published the German text: this is the translation:—

"DEAR FATHER—Excuse me for not writing yesterday, as I should have done. The journey, which was long and very fatiguing, prevented me. It is with pleasure that I seize this occasion to give to Prince Trautmannsdorf for you the assurance that my thoughts are always with you. God has endowed me with strength to endure the cruel emotion which this separation from all my family calls forth. In Him I confide. He will sustain me and give me courage to fulfil my mission. My consolation shall be the thought that the sacrifice is in your behalf. I reached Ried very late, and I was much distressed by the thought that I was departing from you perhaps forever. At two o'clock I arrived at the French camp at Braunau. I stopped a few minutes in the Austrian pavilion, and there I had to listen to the reading of the documents about the limits of the neutral zone, in which a throne had been set. All my people then came up to kiss my hand, and I could hardly control myself. I shuddered, and I was so much moved that the Prince of Neufchâtel had tears in his eyes. Prince Trautmannsdorf delivered me to him, and my household was presented. Heavens, what a difference between the French and the Austrian ladies!... The Queen of Naples came to greet me, threw her arms about me, and was most kind; but yet I have not perfect confidence in her: I can't think she took this long journey merely to be of use to me. She came to Braunau with me, and then I had to spend two hours in arraying myself. I assure you that now I am already as much perfumed as the Frenchwomen. Napoleon sent me a superb golden dress. He has not yet written. Now that I have had to leave you, I had rather be with him than travel longer with these ladies. Heavens! how I miss the happy moments I spent with you! Now, alone, I value them at their true worth. I assure you, dear papa, that I am sad and inconsolable. I hope you have got over your cold. Every day I pray for you. Excuse my scrawl. I have so little time. I kiss your hands a thousand times, and have the honor to be, dear papa, your obedient, humble daughter,

"MARIE LOUISE.

"BRAUNAU, March 16, 1810."

That evening the Empress appeared again before the party that had accompanied her from Vienna, to take a last farewell.

"Among them," we read in the Memoirs of Madame Durand, one of the suite of the new Empress, "were many ladies who had known Marie Antoinette. They all understood with what a heavy heart Marie Louise would come to occupy a throne on which her great-aunt had suffered so sorely.... At the moment when she was getting into the carriage that was to take her to Munich, the grand master of the household, a man sixty-five years old, who had accompanied her to this point, raised his joined hands towards heaven, as if praying for a happy fate for his young mistress, and blessing her as her own father might have done. His eyes indicated a mind full of great thoughts and sad memories. His tears moistened the eyes of all who witnessed this touching sight."

The Empress, with her French escort, started from Braunau for Munich early March 17, in frightful weather; Only one of the Austrian suite remained with her, the grand mistress, Countess Lazansky. She hoped that this lady, whom she much loved, would remain another year with her. But this hope was doomed to disappointment.

X
THE JOURNEY

In the course of the 17th the Empress reached Haag, where the Bavarian Crown Prince received her, and at ten in the evening she was in Munich. The next day, M. de Boyne, the French *chargé d'affaires*, wrote to the Duke of Cadore: "Her Majesty the Empress has received all along her route, and yesterday, on her arrival in Munich, countless expressions of love and respect. This capital was illuminated with a taste and magnificence that had never been seen here. The Crown Prince went as far as Haag to pay his respects to her. The troops and the militia were under arms, and the King and Queen, with the whole court, met her at the foot of the staircase of honor." Marie Louise was not to leave Munich till the 19th of March. On the 18th she received a letter from her husband, brought by one of his equerries, the Baron of Saint Aignan. That evening there was a state dinner at the palace, a levee, and a theatrical representation. The next day, the 19th, the Empress was destined to suffer a heavy blow. She had brought with her from Vienna to Braunau, and from Braunau to Munich, her grand mistress, a confidential friend, a woman who had had faithful charge of her infancy and youth,—the Countess Lazansky. When she reached the Bavarian capital, she was sure that this woman was not to leave her. Since the Countess had not gone away at Braunau, she had every reason to suppose that she would accompany her to Paris, and Marie Louise fully intended to keep her with her at least a year. The Austrian court showed this belief, and the French Ambassador had written March 6th to the Duke of Cadore: "I shall not, even indirectly, oppose Madame Lazansky's going, since His Majesty is willing to permit her accompanying the Empress. This attention will be gratefully received." But that did not at all suit Napoleon's sister, the Queen of Naples, who had not pleased the Austrian lady, and who wished to control the new Empress without a rival.

The Queen of Naples was a very agreeable, very charming woman; but Count Otto was mistaken when he wrote that the Austrian court was flattered by hearing that Napoleon had chosen his sister Caroline to meet the new Empress; the choice was not a happy one, and the Emperor would doubtless have done better to send some other princess of his family. Could it be forgotten that there was another woman, also a queen, and also bearing the name of Caroline, Marie Louise's grandmother, whom Marie Louise tenderly loved, and whose throne was occupied by Murat's wife? It should have been remembered that in the eyes of the court of Vienna, the true, the legitimate, queen of the Two Sicilies was not Caroline, Napoleon's sister, but another Caroline, the daughter of the great Marie Thérèse, the sister of Marie Antoinette.

This is what the widow of General Durand says on the subject, in her interesting Memoirs: "Princess Caroline, Madame Murat, then Queen of Naples, had gone to Braunau to meet her sister-in-law. The Duchess of Montebello, a beautiful, sensible woman, the mother of five children, who had lost her husband in the last war, had been appointed a maid-of-honor, — a feeble compensation on the part of the Emperor for her sad bereavement. The Countess of Luçay, a gentle, kindly woman, thoroughly familiar with the customs of good society, was lady of the bedchamber. I shall speak later of the other ladies of the suite, whose functions, as established by etiquette, brought them very little into personal relations with the Empress. Each one of them had pretensions to which the presence of Madame Lazansky was an obstacle. They complained to Queen Caroline, and she decided on an act of despotism which deeply wounded her sister-in-law." This act was the dismissal of Madame Lazansky. By this course the Queen of Naples expected to add to her influence over the Empress; but, on the contrary, she only diminished it appreciably.

"Madame Murat," continues Madame Durand, "was very anxious to acquire great power over Marie Louise, and she might have been successful had she taken more precautions. Talleyrand said of her that she had the head of a Cromwell on the body of a pretty woman. Endowed by nature with a marked character, great intelligence, far-reaching ideas, a supple and crafty mind, with a grace and amiability that made her very charming, she lacked nothing but the power of hiding her love of rule; and when she missed her aim, it was because she had been too eager. The moment she saw the Austrian Princess, she imagined that she had read her character; but she was utterly mistaken. She took her timidity for weakness, her embarrassment for awkwardness; and, fancying that she needed only to give her orders, she hardened against her for all time the heart of the woman whom she expected to control."

Madame Durand thus describes the conspiracy which these women formed: "The presence of the Countess Lazansky had excited the jealousy and the fears of all the ladies of the household. They intrigued and caballed, telling the Queen of Naples that she could never win her sister-in-law's confidence or affection so long as she kept with her a person whose influence rested on so many years of devotion and intimacy. Her maid-of-honor lamented that her functions would amount to nothing, if the Princess were to keep near her this foreigner who looked after everything. Finally they persuaded the Queen to ask Marie Louise to send back her grand mistress, although she had been promised that she could keep her for a year."

The Empress might have resisted. They showed her no order from the Emperor; they merely said that the presence of the Austrian lady with a French sovereign was something anomalous,—an infringement of the laws of etiquette,—and that the best way for the Empress to please the Emperor was by this voluntary sacrifice. Marie Louise yielded for the sake of peace, and gave up her friend, as later she was to give up her husband, out of weakness. Her decision gave her great pain, and it was not without a pang that she parted from the Countess Lazansky. "How agonizing this separation is!" she wrote to her father. "I really could not make a greater sacrifice for my husband, and still I do not think that this sacrifice was intended by him."

Another thing that added to the grief of the new Empress was that she was compelled to part with a pet dog which she was very fond of: the Countess was to carry it back to Vienna. They told Marie Louise that Napoleon disliked dogs, that he could not endure Josephine's, and that they were perpetual subjects of discord. Besides, was it not her duty, on entering France, to give up everything that came from her former home? General de Ségur, who had been part of the Empress's escort since leaving Braunau, makes no mention of the Countess Lazansky, but he speaks of the dog: "The complete change of dress was simply an entertainment: that of the escort had been anticipated; it was necessary to endure it. This painful change would have taken place without too much evidence of grief, if the superfluously jealous interference of Napoleon's sister had not extended itself to a little dog from Vienna, which, it was insisted, must be sent back, though this cost Marie Louise many tears." The acquisition of a colossal empire did not console the sovereign for the loss of a little dog.

March 19, in the morning, Marie Louise and Countess Lazansky parted. "The worst thing in the conduct of the Queen of Naples," writes Madame Durand, who did not like her, "was that after having demanded the Empress's consent to Madame Lazansky's departure, she gave orders to the ladies-in-waiting not to admit that lady to the Empress if she came to say good by. This order was not obeyed; the two ladies admitted her by a secret door; she spent two hours with the Empress, and the ladies who admitted her never regretted what they had done, in spite of the many reproaches of the Queen of Naples."

While the Empress, leaving Munich March 19, continued her journey to France, her old friend was journeying back to Vienna, where she arrived

March 22. Her unexpected return made a most unfavorable impression on all classes of society.

The report that the Countess Lazansky was to accompany the Empress to Paris had spread everywhere, and it was regarded as a proof of confidence and cordiality that was most welcome to the Viennese with their devotion to the reigning family. Consequently their delight and interest, which had been fed by the festivities and all the details of the journey, made the sudden return of the mistress of the robes a cause of surprise and even of anxiety. There were riotous assemblies, and the affair was the subject of most unfavorable comment. As the Baron of Méneval has said, "The reconciliation on the part of the aristocracy and people of Austria was not sincere. Marie Louise's departure from Vienna was followed by many regrets. Instigated by English and Russian agents, the populace of Vienna gathered in the streets and public places, and began to murmur about the sacrifice which they said had been required of the Emperor. The authorities were obliged to take active measures against these assemblages." The Emperor of Austria spoke of them himself to the French Ambassador. Count Otto wrote, March 24, to the Duke of Cadore: "The Emperor having returned from Linz, I asked for a private audience to congratulate him on his happy return. Audiences of this sort are only accorded here to ambassadors of powers related by marriage, and I took advantage of this occasion to enjoy this honorable distinction. His Majesty received with his wonted kindness; he had been thoroughly satisfied with all that took place at Braunau, and with the delicate attentions paid to Her Majesty the Empress from the moment of her arrival. 'But what have you done to Madame Lazansky?' the Emperor went on, 'Why is she sent back? Your master had given my daughter leave to take a companion with her; and if an exception was to be made, Madame Lazansky deserved to be the object of it, for she has always been well disposed towards France. But I must assure you that I attach no importance to the matter, although the public amuses itself with a thousand absurd conjectures; last night there were tumults in the city and the suburbs.' I told His Majesty, in reply, that these disturbances of the public peace were doubtless the last efforts of a few foreign intriguers who are always on hand in this city; that since the escorts were changed at Braunau, nothing was simpler or more natural than Madame Lazansky's return; and that to allay the excitement, nothing more was necessary than to spread abroad the rumor that orders had been received from here recalling that lady as soon as the Empress was accustomed to her new court. 'That's just what I have already done,' resumed the Emperor, 'and it is to be hoped that the same things will be said in France, as the best way of silencing discontent.'"

A few hours later Prince Metternich, the father of the celebrated minister, who in his son's absence had charge of the Ministry, had an interview with the Ambassador about this painful incident. "Prince Metternich," Count Otto adds in the same despatch, "came to see me to give me some fuller details about the events of the previous night. He had been kept up until three in the morning, receiving the reports of the police, and having the ringleaders arrested. They had gone about in the coffee-houses, and had carried their effrontery so far as to say that the French army was again in motion, and that Napoleon's sole aim had been to distract the attention of this court."

Meanwhile Marie Louise was continuing her triumphal journey. At Stuttgart she found the court and the population as enthusiastic as at Munich; there, too, even illuminations, a state dinner, a levee, a theatrical representation. At Stuttgart the Empress received a letter from Napoleon, brought by the Count of Beauvau. Another letter from the Emperor was delivered to her by the Count of Bondy at Carlsruhe, where her reception was no less brilliant than at Munich and Stuttgart.

March 23, Marie Louise was at Rastadt, where the Hereditary Grand Duke of Baden, who had married Stéphanie de Beauharnais, Napoleon's adopted daughter, gave her a breakfast. At the bridge over the Rhine, which the Empress reached at five in the evening, she was met by twenty French generals and several divisions under arms. The bridge was decorated with flags; bells were pealing; salvos of artillery were roaring. At the entrance of the bridge the sovereign was welcomed by the Prefect of the Lower Rhine, and at the city gates by the Mayor. "It was at Strasbourg," says General de Ségur, "that France, in its turn, greeted Marie Louise. The enthusiasm on this German and military frontier was all the more lively, sincere, and widespread, because the Archduchess was regarded as the most brilliant trophy of the success of our arms, and it was thought that after eighteen years of warfare they had in her a pledge of certain peace."

March 23, Marie Louise wrote to her father, from Strasbourg, a long letter, in which she apologized for her long silence, pleading the excessive fatigue of a long journey, during which she had to get up every morning at five, travel all day, and spend every evening at receptions and theatrical performances. She added that the programme of the festivities at Strasbourg had just been submitted to her for her orders. "I can't tell you, dear papa," she said, "how funny it seems to me, who have never had any will of my own, to have to give orders." At Strasbourg she had the pleasure of meeting Count Metternich, who had left Vienna March 12, and after stopping at many German courts, was about to push on to Paris. The festivities there were very brilliant. A newspaper of the town said, March 24, "Among the guests was the Austrian general, Count Neipperg, who was here on a mission from his government, as also many officers." Who could have foreseen that this unknown general would one day be Marie Louise's consort, Napoleon's successor?

It was at Strasbourg that the Empress received her first letter from her father since her departure from Vienna. She answered it at once: "I beg of you, dear father, pray for me most warmly. Be sure that I shall try with all my strength to perform the duty you have assigned to me. I am easy about my fate. I am sure that I shall be happy. I wish you could read Napoleon's letter: it is full of kindness." With every step she made on French soil, Marie Louise became reconciled with her lot. For his part, the Emperor awaited his new companion with all the impatience of a youth of twenty, "Every day," says his valet Constant, "he sent a letter, and she answered regularly. Her first letters were very short and probably very cool, for the Emperor never mentioned them; but the later ones were longer and gradually more affectionate, and the Emperor used to read them with transports of delight.... He complained that his couriers were lazy though they killed their horses. One day he came back from hunting, carrying two pheasants in his hand, and followed by some footmen bearing the rarest flowers from the conservatory at Saint Cloud. He wrote a note, summoned his first page, and said to him: 'Be ready to start in ten minutes, by coach. In it you will find these things, which you will deliver to the Empress with your own hands. And above all, don't spare the horses. Go as fast as you can, and fear nothing.' The young man asked nothing better than to obey His Majesty. Thus authorized, he hurried at full speed, giving his postilions double pay, and in twenty-four hours he had reached Strasbourg." According to Madame Durand, "It was evident that Marie Louise read the Emperor's letters with ever-increasing interest. She awaited them with impatience; and if the courier was behind time, she asked frequently if he had not come, and what could have delayed him. This correspondence must have been charming, since it evoked a feeling destined to acquire great strength. Napoleon, on his side, was burning with desire to see his young wife; he was more flattered by this marriage than he would have been by the conquest of an empire. What most delighted him was to know that she had given her consent of her own free will."

The Baron de Méneval also tells about Napoleon's correspondence with this new wife, whom he had not seen and was so impatient to know: "He wrote to her every day as soon as she had set foot on French soil; he sent bouquets of the most beautiful flowers along with the letters, and sometimes game. He was delighted with the answers, some of which were long, that he received. These replies were written in good French; the Empress expressed herself with delicacy and decorum: perhaps the Queen of Naples aided her. She wrote many details, which interested the Emperor very much."

The Empress left Strasbourg, March 25, in the direction of Nancy. She dined at Bar-le-Duc, and at Vitry-le-Francois received the Prince of Schwarzenberg, the Austrian Ambassador, and the Countess Metternich. She had just made up her mind to hurry her journey, and thus to hasten the moment set by etiquette for meeting her husband. The hour which Napoleon had awaited so impatiently was now drawing near.

XI
COMPIÈGNE

Since the 20th of March, Napoleon had been at Compiègne, denouncing the cumbrous machinery of etiquette which was retarding the happy moment when he should at last see his new wife and enfold her in his arms. He had had the castle repaired and richly furnished, that it might be worthy to receive a daughter of the Cæsars. The grand gallery had been decorated with gilded ceilings and stucco columns; the garden had been replanted and adorned with statues. The waters of the Oise had been carried there by a system of water-works. All the members of the Imperial family had arrived; the court was most brilliant. The Emperor wished to dazzle his young wife with unheard-of splendor.

The minutest details of the meeting of the Imperial couple had been carefully arranged beforehand; it was settled that this should take place in all formality, March 28, between Soissons and Compiègne. The Emperor was to leave the last-named place with the princes and princesses of his family, preceded and followed by detachments of the mounted Imperial Guard. Two leagues from Soissons they would find a pavilion composed of three tents, entered by two flights of steps, one on the side towards Compiègne, the other on that towards Soissons; the first one was for Napoleon, the other for Marie Louise. The pavilion, which was richly decorated with flags, was surrounded by trees; near it flowed a brook. The central tent, the one in which the Emperor and Empress were to meet for the first time, was decorated with purple and gold. It had been settled that Marie Louise should fall on her knees as soon as she saw her husband, that he should help her to her feet and kiss her; then that both should get into a state carriage, and both the escorts should unite and form one.

The preparations were completed March 27. Everything—horses, carriages, escort, pavilion—was ready. That morning Prince Charles of Schwarzenberg, the Austrian Ambassador, and the Countess Metternich, the Minister's wife, arrived at the castle of Compiègne from Vitry-le-François, where they had seen the Empress, of whom they could bring news to Napoleon. At noon the Emperor received a letter from Marie Louise, in which she said that in order to make greater haste she was leaving Vitry-le-François that very morning for Soissons. When this letter was handed to him, Napoleon was walking up and down in the park, as if to overcome the impatience which this interminable waiting produced. When he learned that his wife was so near, he could wait no longer, and he decided to turn his back on the etiquette which had been so laboriously prepared for the next day, and to hasten to meet Marie Louise. He summoned Murat, whom he wished to have as his sole companion, and leaving the park secretly by a hidden gate, he and his brother-in-law got into a modest, undecorated carriage, which was driven by a coachman not in livery towards Soissons as fast as the horses could carry it.

Never had the Emperor known time to drag so slowly. A double feeling—of curiosity and love—set his heart beating as if he were a youth of twenty. When he had got beyond Soissons, he judged that Marie Louise could not be far distant, and he alighted at a village called Courcelles.

The Empress meanwhile had been journeying ever since the morning in the same carriage as her sister-in-law, Queen Caroline, with no idea of what was going to happen. She had passed through Châlons and Rheims, and proposed to dine at Soissons, where she expected to pass the night; for the meeting with the Emperor was set down for the next day, March 28, at the pavilion erected two leagues from that town. It was raining in torrents when Napoleon reached there, and he got down with his brother-in-law and sought shelter under the porch of the church opposite the posting-station. No one in the village had a suspicion that the two strangers seeking refuge from the rain were the great Emperor and the King of Naples. Suddenly the clatter of wheels was heard, and a carriage, preceded by an outrider and followed by a great many vehicles, rolled up. It was she, at last,—Marie Louise, Archduchess of Austria, Empress of the French, Queen of Italy, the woman who would bring him a son and heir to the vast empire! Pride and the intoxication of triumph mingled with the conqueror's joy.

The carriage stopped, and the men began to change the horses. Napoleon hastened to the carriage-door. He did not want to be recognized for a few moments yet, but the equerry, d'Audenarde, scarcely believing his eyes, shouted, "The Emperor!" The happy husband flung himself into the arms of his wife, who was overcome with surprise and emotion. The first glance delighted him. That fine young woman, fresh and young, full of strength and health, with her blonde hair, her blue eyes, her air of innocence and candor, was the wife he wanted, the Empress of his dreams; and the words she said to him flattered and touched him, went straight to his heart! After looking at him for some time, she said timidly and gently: "You are much better-looking than your portrait."

A courier was despatched to carry the news at full speed to Compiègne, that the Emperor and Empress would arrive there at about two o'clock, and the carriage containing Napoleon and Marie Louise, with the King and Queen of Naples, started in the direction of Soissons, followed by the carriages containing the Empress's suite. They stopped but a moment at Soissons. "I had the honor," says M. de Bausset, "to be in the carriage with Mesdames de Montmorency and de Montemart and the Bishop of Metz. It seemed to me that these ladies were more contented than I was to leave the excellent dinner which was awaiting us there." Soissons, which had made many expensive preparations, had no return for its money and trouble. As to the ceremonious meeting in the pavilion two leagues off, which had been prepared for the next day at some expense, it was not to be thought of. Napoleon showed tact and courtesy by relieving his wife of this alarming formality, and especially of the necessity of kneeling before him. He was happily inspired in setting feeling before etiquette, and in yielding to his impatience to see the face and hear the voice of his long-awaited wife.

As soon as the courier, sent in advance, reached Compiègne, and announced the great news, the town was in commotion. The illuminations were got ready, the triumphal arches were decked with flags, orders were given to greet the entry of the Emperor and Empress with a salute of a hundred and one cannon. Marshal Bessières made ready the mounted guard. In spite of the rain, the inhabitants assembled in crowds to meet the sovereigns at the stone bridge where Louis XV. had met the Dauphiness, Marie Antoinette. The courts and galleries of the castle, which were open to the public, were thronged with inquisitive visitors. A hard rain was falling, and the night was so dark that nothing could be seen without torches. At ten o'clock the cannon announced the arrival of the Imperial couple, who rapidly ascended the Avenue. The princes and princesses were waiting at the foot of the staircase, and the Emperor presented them to the Empress. The town authorities were assembled in a gallery where was the Prince of Schwarzenberg; a band of young girls dressed in white paid their respects to the Empress, and offered her flowers. The Emperor then conducted her to her apartments, where she was delighted, as she was surprised, to find her little dog and her birds from Vienna, as well as a piece of tapestry which she had left unfinished at the Burg. This delicate attention of Napoleon's moved her to tears. She was also pleased to see a magnificent piano. After a quiet supper, at which the Queen of Naples was the only guest, the Emperor conducted his wife to the room of his sister Pauline, the Princess Borghese, who had been prevented by illness from taking part in the reception. Then he showed her to her own room.

The portrait of the Empress which the Baron de Méneval has drawn, is as follows: "Marie Louise had all the charm of youth; her figure was perfectly regular; the waist of her dress was rather longer than was generally worn at that time, and this added to her natural dignity and contrasted favorably with the short waists of our ladies; her coloring was deepened by her journey and her timidity; her fine and thick hair, of a light chestnut, set off a fresh, full face, to which her gentle eyes lent a very attractive expression; her lips, which were a little thick, recalled the type of the Austrian Imperial line, just as a slightly aquiline nose distinguishes the Bourbon princes; her whole appearance expressed candor and innocence, and her plumpness, which she lost after the birth of her son, indicated good health."

The next day, after breakfast, the ladies and officers of the household who had not met her at Braunau were presented to the Empress, and they took the oath of allegiance. Then followed the presentation of the Generals and Colonels of the Guards, of the Ministers and high officers of the crown, and of the officers and ladies who were to attend her on leaving Compiègne. She had the pleasure of meeting at the castle her uncle, the Grand Duke of Würzburg, her father's brother, with whom she talked for a long time about her country and her family. She also chatted with the Prince of Schwarzenberg and with the Countess Metternich. All day Napoleon was in charming humor. Contrary to his usual custom he dressed for dinner, putting on a coat which his sister Pauline, an authority on fashions, had commanded of Léger, the tailor of the King of Naples, who was fond of expensive and handsome clothes. This coat and a white tie were not becoming to Napoleon; his simple uniforms and black tie suited him much better. This was the only time he wore the coat which the Princess Pauline had ordered; on ordinary occasions he appeared in the green uniform of the Chasseurs of the Guard; and on Sundays and reception days in his blue uniform with white facings.

March 29, the Count of Praslin set out from Compiègne for Vienna, carrying two letters, one from Napoleon, the other from Marie Louise, to the Emperor Francis II. In his letter Napoleon said to his father-in-law, "Allow me to thank you for the present you have made me. May your paternal heart rejoice in your daughter's happiness!" Marie Louise, too, expressed content and joy; after telling her father with what delicacy her husband had lessened the embarrassment of the first interview, she went on: "Since that moment I feel almost at home with him; he loves me sincerely, and I return his affection. I am sure that I shall have a happy life with him. My health continues good. I am quite rested from the journey…. I assure you that the Emperor is as solicitous as you were about my health. If I have the least cold, he will not let me get up before two o'clock. I only need your presence to be perfectly happy, and my husband would also be very glad to see you. I assure you that he desires it as sincerely as I do." Five days later she wrote: "I am able to tell you, my dear father, that your prophecy has come true: I am as happy as I can be. The more friendship and confidence I give my husband, the more he heaps upon me attentions of every kind…. The whole family are very kind to me, and I can't believe all the evil that is said of them. My mother-in-law is a very amiable and most respectable princess who has welcomed me most kindly. The Queens of Naples, Holland, and Westphalia and the King of Holland are very amiable. I have also made the acquaintance of the Viceroy of Italy and his wife. She is very pretty."

The court left Compiègne March 31. At the entrance of the Bois de Boulogne the Emperor and Empress were met by Count Frochot, Prefect of the Seine, and a crowd of Parisians. The Prefect made a speech which concluded with these words: "Escorted from Vienna to this point by the love of the people, Your Majesty now knows that by the prominence of her virtues as well as by the graces of her person, her destiny is to rule over all hearts. Our own, Madame, shall be to make you find again here in your customary abode, the country that you most love, where you were most cherished, and to succeed in making worthy of Your Majesty the homage of our allegiance, of our respect, and of our love."

At half-past six in the evening Napoleon and Marie Louise arrived at Saint Cloud, where were assembled in full dress the marshals, the cardinals, the great dignitaries of the Empire, the senators and the state councillors. At the palace there was a family dinner, and after it the ladies of the Palace of the Italian Crown, Countesses Porro, Visconti, Thiene, Trivulci, and Mesdames Gonfalonieri, Trotti, de Rava, Fe, Mocenigo, Montecuculli, were presented by the Italian maid-of-honor, the Duchess Litta, and they all took the oath of allegiance. The civil marriage was appointed for the next day, April 1, at Saint Cloud, and the religious ceremony for the next but one, April 2, in the *Salon Carré* of the Louvre, between the long gallery of the Museum and the Apollo Gallery. The formal entry of the Emperor and Empress into their capital on the day of the religious marriage was to be an occasion of great pomp. Strangers had gathered from all quarters of Europe to witness this impressive sight, and as much as six hundred francs was paid for the smallest room from which the passage of the Imperial procession could be seen. Never, perhaps, in France or anywhere else, had any ceremony excited so much curiosity. The Royalists themselves had come to believe that Napoleon, the miraculous being, had forever fastened fortune to his triumphal chariot. There was a truce to recriminations. For a moment the caustic wit of the Parisians turned into profound admiration. The great conqueror, in light of his apotheosis, was more like a demigod than a man. Every one was eager to look upon him and his young Empress.

XII
THE CIVIL WEDDING

The civil wedding of Napoleon and Marie Louise was celebrated at Saint Cloud, Sunday, April 1, 1810. At the end of the Apollo Gallery, which was adorned with Mignard's frescoes, and still full of reminiscences of the great century, had been placed on a platform two armchairs, each under a canopy; the one to the right for the Emperor, the other for the Empress. Below the platform, and to one side, was a table covered with a costly cloth, on which were an inkstand and the civil registers. At two in the afternoon the Colonel of the Guard on duty and the high officers of the crown of France and Italy went to escort Their Majesties. The procession formed and made its way through the Emperor's study, the Princes' drawing-room, the throne-room, the Mars room, to the Gallery of Apollo, in the following order: ushers, heralds-at-arms, pages, assistants to the masters of ceremonies, the masters of ceremonies, the officers of the household of the King of Italy, the equerries of the Emperor, his aides-de-camp, the two equerries on duty, the aide on duty, the Governor of the Palace, the Secretary of State of the Imperial family, the high officers of the crown of Italy, the High Chamberlain of France and the one of Italy, the Grand Master of Ceremonies and the Chief Equerry of Italy, the Princes who were high dignitaries, the Princes of the family, the Emperor, the Empress; and behind Their Majesties, the Colonel of the Guard on duty, the Chief Marshal of the Palace, the Grand Master of the House of Italy, the Grand Almoner of France, the one of Italy, the Knight of Honor and the Prince Equerry of the Empress, carrying the train of her cloak, the maids-of-honor of France and Italy and the Lady of the Bedchamber, the Princesses of the family, the ladies of the palace, the maids-of-honor of the Princesses, the officers on duty of the households of the Princes and Princesses.

When the procession had reached the Apollo Gallery, the ushers, the heralds-at-arms, and the pages drew up in line to the right and left in the Mars room, near the door. The officers and high officers of France and Italy, the maids-of-honor and the Lady of the Bedchamber took their places behind Their Majesties' chairs, in order of rank. The Emperor and Empress seated themselves on the throne, the Princes and Princesses on the right and left of the platform in the following order and according to their family rank: To the right of the Emperor:

> His mother;
> Prince Louis Napoleon, King of Holland;
> Prince Jerome Napoleon, King of Westphalia;
> Prince Borghese, Duke of Guastalla;
> Prince Joachim Napoleon, King of Naples;
> Prince Eugene, Viceroy of Italy;
> The Prince Archchancellor;
> The Prince Vice-Grand Elector.

On the Empress's left:—

> Princess Julia, Queen of Spain;
> Princess Hortense, Queen of Holland;
> Princess Catherine, Queen of Westphalia;
> Princess Elisa, Grand Duchess of Tuscany;
> Princess Pauline, Duchess of Guastalla;
> Princess Caroline, Queen of Naples;
> The Grand Duke of Würzberg;
> Princess Augusta, Vice-Queen of Italy;
> Princess Stéphanie, Hereditary Grand Duchess of Baden;
> The Hereditary Grand Duke of Baden;
> The Prince Archtreasurer;
> The Prince Vice-Constable.

As soon as the Emperor was seated, the Prince Archchancellor of the Empire, followed by the Secretary of State of the Imperial family, approached the throne, bowed low, and said: "In the name of the Emperor (at those words Their Majesties rose), Sire, does Your Imperial and Royal Majesty declare that he takes in marriage Her Imperial and Royal Highness Marie Louise, Archduchess of Austria, here present?" Napoleon replied: "I declare that I take in marriage Her Imperial and Royal Highness Marie Louise, Archduchess of Austria, here present." The same question was then put to Marie Louise in these terms: "Does Her Imperial Highness Marie Louise, Archduchess of Austria, declare that she takes in marriage His Majesty the Emperor and King, Napoleon, here present?" She answered: "I declare that I take in marriage His Majesty the Emperor and King, Napoleon, here present." Then the Archchancellor, Prince Cambacérès, announced the marriage in these words: "In the name of the Emperor and of the Law, I declare that His Imperial and Royal Majesty Napoleon, Emperor of the French and King of Rome, and Her Imperial and Royal Highness, the Archduchess Marie Louise, are united in marriage." At the same instant the ceremony was proclaimed by salvos of artillery fired at Saint Cloud and repeated in Paris by the cannon of the Invalides. Napoleon must have felt a thrill of pride at this moment. The Apollo Gallery, where the rite was celebrated, was full of pleasant memories; there it was that the Ancients were sitting on that eventful 19th Brumaire when the foundations of his vast power were laid, and there it was that he had uttered that ringing sentence, "Remember that I march in the company of the God of Fortune and the God of War." There it was that, May 18, 1804, he had said to the Senators who came to proclaim the Empire: "I accept the title which you deem of service to the nation's glory. I hope that France will never repent the honors with which it loads my family." And in this same gallery he was marrying in triumph the daughter of the Germanic Cæsars. The Palace of Saint Cloud brought him good luck. And yet it was from this palace that he set out two years later on the disastrous Russian campaign; and from there his successor, sixty years later, started for a still more ruinous war. And as for this Palace of Saint Cloud, so brilliant and radiant, what was to become of it? But in 1810 no one could have felt such fears for the future.

The marriage proclaimed, the document had to be signed. The Secretary of State of the Imperial family presented the pen to the Emperor and then to the Empress, who signed (without leaving their places or rising) on a table brought up before the throne. The Princes and Princesses then walked up to the table, and after bowing to Their Majesties, signed in the order fixed by the order of ceremonies. When, finally, the Archchancellor and the Secretary had affixed their signatures, the procession, in the same order as before, reconducted Their Majesties to the Empress's apartments.

Possibly only one thing gave Napoleon a vague uneasiness: fourteen of the Italian cardinals had approved as regular and satisfactory the judgment of the officials of Paris concerning the invalidity of the religious marriage with Josephine; while thirteen others, among whom was Consalvi, thought that the Pope alone was competent to decide so important a matter. The rumor had spread that these thirteen recalcitrant cardinals would not be present at the nuptial benediction to be given to Napoleon and Marie Louise the next day in the *Salon Carré* of the Louvre. But Napoleon in his wrath had exclaimed, "Bah! they will never dare to stay away!"

That evening after dinner Their Majesties went into the family drawing-room. The company that was to accompany them to the play assembled in the neighboring rooms. The orange-house, which had been converted into a court theatre, was illuminated. The piece to be given was *Iphigenia in Aulis,* one of the favorite operas of the unhappy Marie Antoinette, the new Empress's great-aunt. The choice of this piece seemed an unhappy one; for Iphigenia recalled the idea of a sacrifice, and the aristocracy of Europe thought that Marie Louise had been sacrificed. General de Ségur, in spite of his admiration for the Imperial glories, says in his Memoirs: "The feeling that prevailed in Paris, along with the general curiosity, was surprise at the presence of a princess ascending a throne reared so near the scaffold stained with the blood of one of her near relatives. This cruel memory offended the feeling of propriety peculiar to the French and especially to the Parisians. They were insensibly pained by this reminder which made too evident the sacrifice extorted from Austria, and they felt that their victory had been carried too far. They condemned the imitation of Louis XVI., whose sad fate was attributed to a similar selection." But the fickle crowd which assembled, eager for pleasure in the park of Saint Cloud, made no such reflections. "The illumination of the park," says the *Moniteur,* "had been arranged with infinite art; the fountains were rendered more brilliant by the lights which were thrown upon the cascades. The great waterfall especially produced a magical effect. Poets, in their description of enchanted gardens, have given but a feeble idea of such an appearance and of such an effect of light. Throughout the park sports of all kinds had been prepared. An immense crowd, from Paris and the suburbs, took part in the festival, which was most gay and animated. The arrangements were novel and far exceeded general expectations."

At Saint Cloud, Sunday, April 1, 1810, when the civil marriage was celebrated, the weather was pleasant, while in Paris the streets were flooded by a heavy rain. The next day, that of the religious marriage, it rained at Saint Cloud, but the weather in Paris was magnificent, so that nothing was lost of the magnificence of the procession or of the brilliancy of the illuminations. The Emperor's good fortune, it was said, had twice triumphed over the equinoctial storms. In the ever-flattering *Moniteur* it was said: "April 2 had been chosen for Their Majesties' entrance into the capital and the wedding rites. One strange circumstance aroused universal attention and called forth much favorable comment. A tempest had raged almost all of the previous night…. It was hence natural to suppose that all the preparations which for a month had excited general interest would have to be kept until a more favorable day; but such was not the case, and what has often happened occurred once more. The agreeable temperature which the sunshine produced was the more remarkable because it lasted only while the festivities were going on, beginning and ending with them, and never was one more strongly reminded of the two familiar lines of Virgil when, recalling the tempest in the night and the calm of the day appointed for a great entertainment, he represents the heavens under the divided control of Augustus and Jupiter:—

"'Nocte pluit totâ, redeunt spectacula mane,
Divisum imperium cum Jove Cæsar habet.'"

XIII
THE ENTRANCE INTO PARIS

Monday, April 2, 1810, as soon as day began to break, Paris and all the country round about set forth towards the Saint Cloud road. From eight in the morning the windows were filled with women. Everywhere scaffolding had been put up; fences, roofs, and trees were crowded with numberless spectators. At the base of the side openings of the great Arc de Triomphe de l'Étoile, steps had been set in the form of an amphitheatre, where a great many persons had taken their place by invitation of the Prefect of the Seine. Of the arch itself, which was to be built in stone, only the bases had been built to a height of about twenty feet, but the rest of the structure was raised in canvas over a framework for the Emperor's formal entry into Paris. The speed with which the work had been done seemed magical; nearly five thousand laborers had been employed, and the temporary structure, imitating the real one, had been finished in less than twenty days. At the summit was this inscription: "To Napoleon and Marie Louise, the city of Paris." The top of the arch, where the vaulting started, was decorated with bas-reliefs, and with sunk panels in the middle of which were eagles.

There were twelve medallions—six towards Passy, six on the other side; namely, the portrait of the Emperor, with this motto, "The happiness of the world is in his hands" (the address of the Senate); a laurel with many sprouts, and these words, "He has made our glory"; a roaring leopard, with this motto, "He laughed at our discords, he weeps at our reunion"; the monograms of Napoleon and Marie Louise, with this inscription, "We love her through our love for him, we shall love her for herself"; a Love placing a wreath of myrtles and roses on the helmet of Mars, with this motto, "She will charm the hero's leisure"; the sun and a rainbow, and these words, "She announces happy days to the world"; the Empress's portrait, and this inscription, "To her we owe the happiness of the August spouse who has set her so high in his thoughts"; the figure of the Danube, and this line, "He enriches us with what is most precious"; the Austrian coat-of-arms; the monogram of Their Majesties, and the motto, "She will be a true mother to the French"; the figure of the Seine, motto, "Our love will be grateful for the gift he makes to us"; and last, the French coat-of-arms.

The six bas-reliefs represented the following subjects: Legislation—the Emperor in his robes, seated upon the throne, points towards the tables on which is inscribed the Code, while Innocence, in the form of a young maiden, is sleeping at the foot of the Imperial throne; National Industry—merchants presenting to the Emperor various products from their warehouses; the Arrival of the Empress in Paris; the Decorations of the Capital; the Emperor's Clemency—Napoleon seated, with his hand on his sword, is crowned by Victory, while he generously pardons his vanquished enemies; union of the Emperor and Empress—Napoleon and Marie Louise hand-in-hand, in token of alliance, before an altar placed at the foot of the statue of Peace.

The salvos of artillery were heard, announcing the departure of the Emperor and Empress from Saint Cloud. At the same moment, as if in obedience to the signal, the sun appeared on the horizon, to shine all day, and just when the procession reached the Arc de Triomphe, it appeared with greater brilliancy. The cavalry of the Imperial Guard headed the procession, the lancers in front, then the chasseurs, followed by the dragoons, with the bands in advance; the heralds-at-arms came next; and after them the carriages, the one containing the Emperor drawn by eight horses, the others by six. Napoleon and Marie Louise were in the famous coronation coach. Its four sides consisted of four large pieces of clear glass, set in slender, gilded and wrought corner-posts, giving as unimpeded view of those within as if the coach was open. The Emperor was to be seen in his cloak of red and white velvet; the Empress, in court dress and wearing the crown diamonds. The top of this magnificent coach consisted of a sort of golden dome, upheld by four eagles with outspread wings, and surmounted by a huge crown. The Marshals of France and the colonels in command of the Guard rode on each side, near the doors of the carriage, the aides near the horses, the equerries near the hind wheels. According to the etiquette prescribed for the occasions when the Emperor used this state carriage, as many pages as possible got on the footboard and on the seat near the driver.

The procession reached the Arc de Triomphe at one o'clock. Twelve cannon had been placed on the high ground near by, twelve others in the garden of the Tuileries, on the terrace by the riverside, and their salutes were repeated by the cannon of the Invalides. Bands which had been stationed along the routes played triumphal marches. All the church bells were rung at full peal. The Imperial coach stopped beneath the arch, where the Governor of Paris, the Prefect of the Seine, the Prefect of the Police, and the twelve mayors received the sovereigns.

Count Frochot, Prefect of the Seine, then pronounced the following speech: "Sire, Your Majesty has at last interested himself in his own happiness, and has succeeded in this as in all he undertakes. If never in the world's annals did any sovereign's marriage have such grandeur, never could love and glory better unite their interests or more happily inspire Your Majesty. From the shouts of joy which have echoed beneath the arches of the monument erected in honor of your triumphs, Your Majesty may judge that the wishes of his good city of Paris, that all the wishes of his people, are satisfied. And it is not in the vast extent of your empire alone that this joy prevails; Sire, a whole continent celebrates with equal delight the alliance made by the greatest of its monarchs, and a hundred different nations bless in unison these August bonds, secretly woven by Providence, these bonds, so dear to our hearts, since they give us at once a pledge of Your Majesty's happiness, and of the fairest hopes of the country."

Then turning to the Empress, the Prefect went on: "You, Madame, will realize this double hope; and, seated on the first throne of the universe, you will adorn it for the prince; you will thus make it dearer to his subjects; you will ensure its durability for posterity. The mere presence, Madame, of Your Majesty, reveals to every eye the precious gifts of the Providence who called you to this throne. No longer, in order to admire you, are we forced to content ourself with the report of fame, and already are verified those words of your immortal spouse, that loved first on his account, you will soon be loved for yourself. May it be permitted, Madame, to apply these words to the city of Paris! May you honor it at first with your good-will, and soon love for itself this great part of the immense family of Frenchmen, which on this solemn day proudly attaches itself to Your Majesty's destiny by all the ties of its allegiance, its respect, and its love!"

The Empress replied that she loved the city of Paris because she knew how attached were its inhabitants to the Emperor. Young girls, clad in white, offered her baskets of flowers, which she accepted graciously, and the procession moved on.

Then Marie Louise, after passing between a double line of picked troops before an enthusiastic crowd, through the brilliant avenue of the Champs Élysées, reaches the fatal Place at its further end. Could all the roar of artillery, the peals of church bells, the music, so far distract the young Empress as to make her forget that here for two years stood the hideous guillotine, on which more than fifteen hundred people were murdered? Could all the happy cheers drive from her thoughts that beating of the drums which drowned the voice of Louis XVI. at the moment when that descendant of Saint Louis essayed to speak a few last words to his people? The place was full of horrid memories, haunted by gloomy ghosts. But sixteen years before, cattle would not traverse it, repelled by the smell of blood. The terraces of the Tuileries were crowded, and, as the *Moniteur* put it, the stone images of fame above the garden gates seemed ready to fly away to proclaim the glories of that great day. Well, sixteen years and a half before, the same terraces were quite as densely crowded. Yes, a huge throng gathered in the cool, foggy morning of October 16, 1793, to get a good view of the death of a woman whose grand-niece this new Empress was in two ways: on the father's side by her father, the son of Emperor Leopold II.; and again, on the maternal side, through her mother, the daughter of Marie Caroline, Queen of Naples. Yes, on the very spot over which the Imperial procession passed with so much pomp, in front of the gateway of the Tuileries, thirty metres from the middle of the Place, where stood the base on which had been set first the equestrian statue of Louis XIV. and then the statue of Liberty, there had been raised, sixteen and a half years before, the scaffold of Marie Antoinette. Could that gorgeous state carriage drive from her mind the memory of the martyred queen's tumbrel? And when Marie Louise first saw the Tuileries, must she not have thought of the last glance which that queen, her near relation, cast on that fateful palace before she bowed her August and charming head upon the block? All the flattery and homage of courtiers, the hymns of poets, the marriage songs, the whole chorus of adulation, cannot drown the inexorable lamentations of the voice of history!

XIV
THE RELIGIOUS CEREMONY

The procession reached the entrance of the Tuileries gardens, passed beneath a triumphal arch, wound around the basin of water, by the side of the flower-beds, which the crowd had respected, and drew near to the palace walls. The central pavilion had been decorated with a large orchestra, divided by a passage leading to the vestibule. In the middle of the orchestra was an arch, on top of which was set a tribune in the shape of a tent. On all the bas-reliefs the panels and other ornaments were initials surrounded with flowers and various emblems and allegories. The carriages passed under this arch; the Emperor and Empress alighted in the vestibule and ascended the grand staircase. Marie Louise entered the bedroom of the grand apartment by the great door, which was thrown wide open. The maids-of-honor of France and Italy, as well as the ladies of the bedchamber, were shown thither from the throne-room through the dressing-room. They removed the Empress's court cloak, and put on her the Imperial cloak. Meanwhile the procession was forming again in the Gallery of Diana, and as soon as Their Majesties had arrived, it started again, entered the long Gallery of the Louvre, passing through its entire length, to the *Salon Carré*, which had been turned into a chapel for the religious ceremony.

This magnificent gallery presented a fine appearance, divided, as it is, into nine unequal compartments by arches rising from columns of rare marble with gilded bases and capitals. It is the famous gallery in which are gathered the finest pictures of the masters of every school. The invited guests had been gathering there since ten o'clock. They ascended thither by two staircases, one leading from the quay, the other from the Place du Carrousel to the central pavilion. The Imperial party alone was to enter by the door of the Pavilion of Flora. Two rows of benches had been placed the whole length of the gallery for the ladies, and two rows of men were to stand behind them, so that there was room for about eight thousand persons without crowding. Bars had been placed in front of the first line of benches to leave an unencumbered passage-way for the Emperor and Empress. Thanks to the exertions of the officers of the Imperial Guard, who discharged their duty with perfect courtesy, four thousand women, in their most brilliant dresses, without trouble, without confusion, and as many men, all chosen from the highest society, took their places when the procession was to pass. They had to wait not less than five hours, but the order was so good that every one could easily leave and resume his place. The gallery was turned with a magnificent promenade in which Paris was treated to a display of the elegance and luxury of its leading men and most fashionable women. Refreshments of various kinds were handed about while orchestras played marches or pieces composed by Paër, the famous leader of the Emperor's music. The waiting was thus a long entertainment. At three in the afternoon the whole company was standing in place; the doors of the Pavilion of Flora opened, and the heralds-at-arms appeared, followed by the Imperial procession. The spectacle is thus described by the *Moniteur* with its accustomed enthusiasm: —

"The sound of the music was drowned in the roar of applause which rang through all parts of the gallery. At times the applause ceased, when the spectators silently regarded the Emperor and the Empress. This silence was eloquent; it was a respectful homage that attested the solemn thoughts which the spectacle evoked, and the deep impressions it made on every soul; this keen emotion, this silent expression of an irresistible feeling, gave way to heartfelt enthusiasm, to cries of joy, to transports of delight. Their Majesties acknowledged this enthusiasm most courteously as they passed through this long and brilliant gallery leading to the chapel, which was a sort of nave of the temple where their August union was to be consecrated anew."

The chapel was the *Salon Carré*, which lies between the picture-gallery and the Apollo gallery. Two rows of seats had been placed all around it. The altar, which was placed in front of the picture-gallery had been adorned with a large bas-relief and many rich ornaments. The six candelabra and the crucifix were masterpieces. Thirty feet from the altar, on a platform, and beneath a canopy, were the two armchairs and the prayer desks of the Emperor and the Empress. Near the altar, on two chandeliers, had been placed the two candles designed for offerings; in each one had been set twenty pieces of gold. The Cardinal, Grand Almoner of France, assisted by the Grand Almoner of Italy, went to receive the sovereigns at the door, and to offer them holy water and incense. Their Majesties then took their places on the platform, the Empress on the Emperor's left. The rest of the procession arranged themselves in the following order: on the Emperor's right, below the platform, Prince Louis Napoleon, King of Holland; Prince Jerome Napoleon, King of Westphalia; Prince Borghese, Duke of Guastalla; Prince Joachim Murat, King of Naples; Prince Eugene de Beauharnais, Viceroy of Italy; the Hereditary Grand Duke of Baden; the Prince Archchancellor Cambacérès; the Prince Archtreasurer Lebrun; the Prince Vice-

Constable Berthier; the Prince Vice-Grand Elector Talleyrand;—on the Empress's left, below the platform, Napoleon's mother; Princess Julia, Queen of Spain; Princess Hortense, Queen of Holland; Princess Catherine, Queen of Westphalia; Princess Elisa, Grand Duchess of Tuscany; Princess Pauline, Duchess of Guastalla; Princess Caroline, Queen of Naples; the Grand Duke of Würzburg; the Princess Augusta, Vice-Queen of Italy; Princess Stéphanie, Hereditary Grand Duchess of Baden. The Colonel commanding the Guard on duty, the Grand Marshal, the High Chamberlain, the First Equerry, the First Almoner of the Emperor, the high officers of Italy, the French Maid-of-Honor, the Italian Maid-of-Honor, the Lady of the Bedchamber, the Knight-of-Honor, the First Equerry and the First Almoner of the Empress, stationed themselves behind Their Majesties' chairs.

On his way through the gallery Napoleon seemed perfectly radiant with joy, but suddenly his face clouded. "Where are the cardinals?" he asked, in a tone of annoyance, of his chaplain, the Abbé de Pradt; "I don't see them." He saw them very well, but he noticed that they were not all there. "A great many of them are here," timidly replied the Abbé; "besides, many of them are old and feeble." "No, they are not there," the Emperor repeated, casting his eye on some empty benches. "Fools! fools!" he said angrily, his face growing darker. It was true! The thirteen cardinals who had declared that they would not come, had had the singular audacity to keep their word. What! they had dared to persist in a factious opposition which he, the Emperor, had defied them to exhibit! They had dared to brave him, to offer him a public insult! They were to receive one in their turn. They did not want to be present at the marriage; very well, he would expel them in disgrace from his court on the very next day!

Nevertheless, the ceremony began, but the Emperor was absorbed, and found it difficult to forget the sudden annoyance. The Grand Almoner, after a deep bow to Their Majesties, intoned the *Veni Creator*, and then proceeded to bless the thirteen pieces of gold and the ring. Napoleon and Marie Louise arose, advanced to the altar, and clasped their bared right hands. The priest then addressed the Emperor, "Sire, do you acknowledge and swear before God and His Holy Church that you now take for your lawful wife Her Imperial and Royal Highness, Madame Marie Louise, Archduchess of Austria, here present?" Napoleon answered, "Yes, sir." Then turning to the Empress, "Madame, do you acknowledge and swear before God and His Holy Church that you now take for your lawful husband the Emperor Napoleon here present?" "Yes, sir." "Do you promise and swear to show to him the fidelity in all things which a faithful wife owes to her husband, according to God's holy commandment?" "Yes, sir." The priest then gave the Emperor the pieces of gold and the ring; he presented the pieces of gold to the Empress and placed the ring on her finger, saying, "This ring I give unto you in token of the marriage we are contracting." The priest made the sign of the cross upon the hand of the Empress, and said, "*In nomine Patris et Filii et Spiritus Sancti, Amen.*" Then mass was said. After the Gospel the First Bishop carried the holy volume to Their Majesties to kiss, and waved incense before them. After the benediction, the Grand Almoner offered them holy water, and gave them the corporal kiss; then he turned towards the altar and intoned the *Te Deum*, which was sung by the chapel choir, producing a deep impression.

The procession formed anew after the ceremony, and retraced its steps. The Emperor gave the Empress his hand, and it was observed with surprise that in passing through the long gallery, his face, which had been so triumphant and joyous, no longer wore the same expression. Could the absence of the thirteen cardinals have been enough to mar this magnificent ceremony? The procession after leaving the long picture-gallery reached the Gallery of Diana by the Pavilion of Flora, and then it stopped. The sovereigns and the Imperial family entered the Emperor's drawing-room, which opened on this gallery. Marie Louise withdrew to her own room. The maid-of-honor and the Lady of the Bedchamber removed her Imperial cloak and the crown, to give them to the Chamberlain, who had carried them in ceremony to Notre Dame. Then Their Majesties appeared on the balcony of the Hall of the Marshals and watched the infantry and cavalry of the Imperial Guard march by. Officers and men waved their weapons, and filled the air with their loud cheers, which were repeated by an enthusiastic multitude. The Imperial dinner took place at seven in the theatre of the Tuileries. The stage had been decorated like the rest of the hall, so that instead of being separate divisions, there was but one huge, unbroken room. The decoration consisted of two cupolas upheld by double arches with the intermediate vaults adorned with columns. One of the two parallel divisions contained the table destined for the Imperial banquet, which stood on a platform beneath a magnificent canopy. As soon as the dinner was ready, the Grand Chamberlain offered the Emperor a basin in which to wash his hands. The First Equerry offered him a chair. The Grand Marshal of the Palace gave him a napkin. The First Prefect, the First Equerry, and the First Chamberlain of the Empress had similar duties. The Grand Almoner stood up by the table, asked a blessing, and withdrew. During the repast the Grand Marshal of the Palace offered the Emperor wine. It was an imposing sight. According to the *Moniteur:* "Here again it is impossible to do justice to the extraordinary magnificence of this imposing occasion. Pen and pencil can describe but faintly the majestic order, the admirable regularity, the blaze of diamonds, the beauty of a brilliant illumination, the gorgeous dresses, and above all the noble ease, the indefinable grace, and perfect elegance which have always characterized the court of France."

After the banquet Napoleon and Marie Louise went to the Hall of the Marshals and appeared on the balcony. A vast crowd had gathered in the garden, under the walls of the palace, around the amphitheatre which had been built for the public concert. They greeted the sovereigns with repeated calls and cheers. The following cantata was given, with words by Arnault and Méhul's music:—

WOMEN.

> "Mars himself has yielded the earth
> To the only god peace cannot disarm.
> Beneath serener skies see all revive,
> All grow tender, all take fire.
> On the oak, beneath the heather,
> See, yielding to the call of love,
> The proud eagle itself forgetting his thunder.

MEN.

> "See the many warriors mingling with the citizens,
> Hiding their old laurels beneath the new myrtles,
> For the first time forgetful of their conquests.
> See the Frenchman, see the German,
> Clasping each other's hand
> And inviting you to the same festivals.

MEN AND WOMEN.

> "Hear the voice resounding
> From the banks of the Danube to the banks of the Seine;
> Hear the voice that promises
> A long reign to the happiness which this day brings."

Then was given the chorus from *Iphigenia:* "What grace, what majesty!" a chorus which Glück, said the *Moniteur,* "could not have made more beautiful, even if he had foreseen this occasion." Alas! the same thing had been said, in the same words, for the unhappy Marie Antoinette; but away with these gloomy presentiments! After the concert the discharge of a rocket from the palace gave the signal for the fireworks. These had been arranged for the whole length of the Avenue of the Champs Élysées. The illumination brought out the impressiveness of the vast architectural lines of the Tuileries. The main avenues of the gardens were richly decorated; around the flower-beds were one hundred and twenty-eight porticoes and twenty-eight arches from which hung transparencies and garlands; and at the entrance of this enchanted garden there was a graceful triumphal arch with twenty-four columns and eight pilasters illuminated with colored lanterns. The Place de la Concorde was surrounded by pyramids of fire and lights arranged to resemble orange-trees; the Champs Élysées, the Garde Meuble, the Temple of Glory, the Tuileries, the Palace of the Corps Législatif, were all ablaze. This last-named building, with a hastily constructed front to show how it was to be finished, represented on that occasion the Temple of Hymen. A transparency represented in front Peace blessing the August couple; on each side were genii carrying bucklers on which were to be seen the arms of the two Empires. Behind this group were magistrates, soldiers, and people, offering crowns, and at the ends of the transparency, the Seine and the Danube, surrounded with children, in token of fecundity. The twelve columns in front, the steps, the stone statues of Sully, of l'Hôpital, of Colbert, of d'Aguesseau, as well as those of Themis and Minerva, were most brilliant. The bridge Louis XV., leading from the Place de la Concorde to the Temple of Hymen, resembled a triumphal avenue with its double row of lights, its colored glass, its obelisks, its hundreds of blazing columns, each one topped by a star. The calmness of a lovely spring night was favorable to the illuminations; all Paris seemed a sea of flame with waves of fire.

The festival continued till late into the night. "All the happy families," says the *Moniteur*, "returned to their peaceful homes after a long absence. Every one had had the happiness of gazing at the Emperor and his August spouse, and all could feel that they too had been seen of them, so thoroughly did the feeling of the benevolence and affability with which their homage had been received by Their Majesties, repay the most enthusiastic testimonials of love and gratitude which a great nation has ever been able to present to its rulers."

Tuesday, April 3, was the day for the presentation at the Tuileries to the Emperor and Empress, seated on their throne, of the great bodies of the State. The Emperor replied to the address of the Senate in these words, "I and the Empress merit the sentiments which you express by the love we nourish for our people." The President of the deputation from the Kingdom of Italy spoke in Italian. "Our people of Italy," replied the Emperor, "know how much we love them. As soon as possible, I and the Empress wish to go to our good cities of Milan, Venice, and Bologna, to give new pledges of our love for our Italian people."

The thirteen Italian cardinals who were unwilling to be present at the wedding the day before were in the Hall of the Marshals, where, amid a throng of prelates, officers, functionaries, and court ladies, they were waiting for the moment to pass before their formidable master. They had been there for three hours, in great anxiety, when aides appeared, bidding them depart at once, the Emperor being unwilling to receive them. Much disconcerted, they made their way with difficulty through the crowd to their carriages. When the other cardinals, who had been present at the wedding, presented themselves in the throne-room, Napoleon stood up and violently denounced their expelled colleagues. Cardinal Consalvi, formerly Secretary of State to Pius VII., was especially attacked. "The others," he said, "may perhaps be excused on the score of their theological prejudices, but he has offended me from political motives. He is my enemy, and he seeks to revenge himself for my driving him from the ministry. That is why he has made this deep plot against me, raising against my dynasty a pretext of illegitimacy, a pretext which my enemies will be sure to lay hold of when my death shall have freed them from the fear that restrains them to-day." It was in vain that the offending thirteen cardinals wrote together an apologetic letter in which they said that they had never wished to judge the validity of the Emperor's first marriage or to throw any doubts on the lawfulness of the second. Napoleon remained implacable. He turned them out of their office, stripped them of their cardinals' robes, bade them resume their attire as simple priests, so that afterwards they were known as the black cardinals, in distinction from the others, the red cardinals. He deprived them of all their estates, ecclesiastic or inherited, and placed them under sequestration. He made them live in bands of two, in various cities of France, dependent on the charity of the faithful. The contest with the Pope began: but the Pope, though defeated in the beginning, was to conquer in the end, and the persecutor of one day was himself persecuted the next. The captive of Savona and of Fontainebleau was to re-enter the eternal city in triumph, and the all-powerful Emperor, the Pope's jailer, was to die, a prisoner of the English, on the rock of Saint Helena.

XV
THE HONEYMOON

Napoleon was happy; his new wife pleased him; he found that she was what he had wanted her to be,—gentle, kindly, timid, modest. It seemed sure that she would bring him heirs. Being neither ambitious nor prone to intrigue, she did not meddle with politics. She was religious, moral, and her principles were most sound. She would never oppose her husband, whose slightest wish she regarded as a command. She would appease his few stubborn foes of the French aristocracy, and put a stop to the last surviving backbiting of the Faubourg Saint Germain. As a bond of union between the past and the present, she brought not to France alone, but to all Europe, stability and repose, and rendered the foundations of the Imperial edifice firm and indestructible. The Emperor's marriage seemed his greatest triumph. For her part, Marie Louise was pleased with her new throne. Surrounded as she was by a chosen society, having in her service the proudest names of the French, the Belgian, the Italian nobility; flattered by the attention of a court in which elegance, wit, politeness, followed all the most brilliant traditions of the old régime, the daughter of the German Cæsars could not imagine that France, with its tranquillity, its profound respect, its affection for the monarchy, in which she was treated more like a goddess than a sovereign, had, a few years earlier, been governed by the Jacobins.

Marie Louise found more luxury and pleasure at the Tuileries and at Compiègne than at the Burg or at Schoenbrunn. Modest as she was, the ingenious flattery, the delicate homage, she received from all quarters could not fail to affect her. The sympathy with which her maid-of-honor, the Duchess of Montebello, inspired her, soon grew into a warm and firm friendship.

Napoleon had particular regard for his young wife, and in his love there was a shade of fatherly protection. He was not yet forty-one. Success and glory had given to his mature face a greater beauty than it had worn in his youth. His manners, formerly harsh and almost violent, had become much softer. To the Republican general had succeeded a majestic monarch familiar with all the usages of courts, all the laws of etiquette, maintaining his rank like a Louis XIV., and playing his royal part with the ease and dignity of a great actor. Successful in everything he undertook, never exposed to contradiction, surrounded by people whose most anxious desire was to forestall his wishes, to anticipate his commands, he seldom had occasion to give way to the outbursts of anger, sometimes real, oftener assumed, in which he formerly indulged. He liked to talk, and his conversation was easy and witty, and full of an irresistible charm. His dress, which in old times he neglected, became elegant. His expression and voice acquired gentleness and an almost caressing quality. Not only did he try to fascinate the young and handsome Empress, he spared no pains to please her. Being much honored and flattered in his vanity as a Corsican gentleman,—for this man of Vendémiaire, the saviour of the Convention, always had a weakness for coats-of-arms and for titles,—he was proud as well as happy in having for his wife a woman belonging to so old and illustrious a race; and this sensation of gratified pride inspired an equability of temper, a serenity, a gayety, which delighted his courtiers, who were glad to see his happiness, for they enjoyed its agreeable results. It was in this spirit that Napoleon and Marie Louise started, April 5, 1810, from Saint Cloud for Compiègne, whence they set forth on the 27th for a triumphal progress in the departments of the North.

In short, this wedded life began under the happiest auspices. At Vienna, the Emperor Francis was perfectly satisfied. Count Otto, the French Ambassador, wrote to the Duke of Cadore, March 31, 1810, as follows: "The events of the 29th were celebrated here yesterday by a general illumination, and by a grand court levee where His Majesty received again the congratulations of the Diplomatic Body, the nobility, and of many foreigners. The Emperor seemed thoroughly contented; he spoke to me very warmly of his satisfaction, which is shared by all his subjects with but few exceptions. Both when I came in and when I was leaving, he spoke to me in the most gracious manner possible, and especially about the incomparable benefit His Majesty had rendered to European civilization by restoring France to its real basis. He praised our army, and added that he would do what he could to aid those of our soldiers who still remained in the hospitals here. 'Henceforth,' the Emperor continued, 'we have but one and the same interest, to work together for the peace of Europe and the furtherance of the arts of use for society. Everything can be made good, except the loss of so many excellent men killed or maimed in the last war.' His Majesty's example in addressing me before any one else was followed by his brother."

The Emperor Francis was very happy to learn that his daughter was pleased with Napoleon and the French. The French Ambassador wrote from Vienna to the Duke of Cadore, April 8, 1810: "The letters which the Emperor and Empress of Austria have received from Their Majesties have given them the greatest satisfaction, and especially those brought two evenings ago by the Count of Praslin. The Emperor was moved by them to tears. This sentence, 'We suit each other perfectly,' made the deepest impression, as well as two letters from Her Majesty the Empress, written in German, in which, among other things, she said, 'I am as happy as it is possible to be; my father's words have come true, I find the Emperor very lovable.' Prince Metternich wept for joy when he gave me these details, and put his arms round my neck and kissed me. The court is perfectly happy since it has heard of this meeting, and of the affection and confidence each has felt for the other."

Count Metternich sent to the Emperor Francis the minutest details about the magnificent way in which the marriage was celebrated, and the French Ambassador thus described that monarch's satisfaction: "The Emperor of Austria received to-day from Count Metternich most circumstantial accounts of what took place in Paris, April 5, and he expressed to me his great delight. The unprecedented honors paid to his daughter did not touch him so much as the delicacy displayed by His Majesty the Emperor Napoleon. I am especially bidden to convey to Your Excellency the expression of his gratitude for the consideration His Majesty showed in relieving the Empress of the ceremony of the first interview. By urging Her Majesty to talk freely with Count Metternich, the Emperor has also delighted his August father-in-law, who thoroughly appreciates his noble conduct. The Empress said that on this occasion she received from the Emperor not only the most delicate consideration, but also the attentions and instructions of an affectionate father. That report called forth many happy tears, and I cannot too strongly express to Your Excellency the happiness that exists here, and the desire that it should be known in Paris.... The Emperor of Austria is much flattered by the marked distinction with which his Minister of Foreign Affairs [Metternich] is treated in Paris, and he certainly seems to deserve it by his unflagging zeal and his unbounded devotion to the principles of the alliance." (Count Otto's despatch of April 15, 1810.)

The famous Prince Metternich, who was then only a count, and had left his father the Prince in charge of the ministry in Vienna, had intended to stay only four weeks in Paris, but he was detained there nearly six months. "I went thither," he states in his Memoirs, "not to study the past, but to try to forecast the future, and I was anxious to succeed speedily. I said one day to the Emperor Napoleon that my stay in Paris could not be a long one. 'Your Majesty,' I said to him, 'had me carried to Austria, almost like a prisoner; now I have come back to Paris of my own free will, but with great duties to perform. To-day I am recalled to Vienna and entrusted with an immense responsibility. The Emperor Francis wanted me to be present at his daughter's entry into France; I have obeyed his orders; but I tell you frankly,

Sire, that I have a loftier ambition. I am anxious to find the line to follow in politics in a remote future.' 'I understand you,' the Emperor replied; 'your wishes coincide with mine. Remain with us a few weeks longer, and you will be perfectly satisfied.'"

Metternich held a privileged position at the French court; for he was very amiable and charming, a perfect man of the world, an accomplished diplomatist, and thoroughly familiar with France and the French, moreover, very intimate with Napoleon and the whole Imperial family. "Napoleon asked me one day," he says in his Memoirs, "why I never went to see the Empress Marie Louise except on reception days and other more or less formal occasions. I answered that I had no reason for doing otherwise, and indeed had many good reasons for doing as I had done."

"By breaking the customary rule," Metternich continued, "I should arouse comment; people would say that I was intriguing; I should do harm to the Empress and injustice to my own character. 'Bah!' interrupted Napoleon, 'I want you to see the Empress; call on her to-morrow morning; I will tell her to expect you.' The next day I went to the Tuileries and found the Emperor with the Empress. We were talking commonplaces when Napoleon said to me, 'I want the Empress to talk to you freely, and to tell you what she thinks of her position; you are her friend, and she ought to have no secrets from you.' Therewith Napoleon locked the drawing-room door, put the key in his pocket, and went out by another door. I asked the Empress what this meant, and she asked me the same question. Since I saw that she had not been primed by Napoleon, I conjectured that he evidently wished me to receive from her own lips a satisfactory idea of her domestic relations, in order to give a favorable account to her father, the Emperor, The Empress was of the same opinion. We remained closeted together more than an hour. When Napoleon came back, laughing, he said, 'Well, have you had a good talk? Has the Empress been abusing me? Has she been laughing or crying? But I don't ask you to tell me; those things are your secrets, which do not concern any third person, not even if that third person is her husband.' We carried on the conversation in that vein, and I took my leave. The next day Napoleon sought for an opportunity to talk with me. 'What did the Empress say yesterday?' he asked. 'You told me,' I replied, 'that our interview did not concern any third person; let me keep my secret.' 'The Empress told you,' Napoleon interrupted, 'that she is happy with me, that she has nothing to complain of. I hope you will tell the Emperor, and that he will believe you more than any one else.'"

In fact, Metternich told the Emperor Francis, and he believed Metternich. Moreover, he had every reason to believe him; for the

Empress Marie Louise was then perfectly happy, and no clouds were yet to
be seen on the sky which was later to be torn by terrible tempests.

We will end this chapter by copying the curious letter which Marie Louise's step-mother, the Empress of Austria, wrote to Napoleon, April 10, 1810, which expresses in a tone almost of familiarity the favorable impressions of the Viennese court: "My brother,—I cannot express to Your Majesty the feeling of gratitude I have experienced on receiving your last letter, which has filled me with joy by the assurance it contains of your satisfaction with the being we have confided to you. My maternal heart was the more open to this emotion because I had felt doubtful about the result. Now, however, that I am reassured by Your Majesty, I have no further fear, and I cheerfully share my daughter's happiness. She has described it to me with touching sincerity, and is never tired of telling me how gratified she is by the many attentions she has received since your meeting. Her sole desire is to make Your Majesty happy, and I venture to flatter myself that she will succeed; for I know her character well, and it is excellent. Louise promises to write to me regularly, and this somewhat consoles me for a real loss. It is pleasant to be able to keep up one's relations with a person one loves, and I am sure that I feel for her the tenderness of a mother, so kind has she been to me, treating me like a real friend. Your Majesty is good enough to say that your wife has spoken about me. I am not surprised; for I know that she, like me, has a very loving heart. But with due regard to truth, I cannot leave Your Majesty under any mistake with regard to her obligations towards me. From what she says you may form a favorable opinion of her candor. If I can boast of anything, it is that I have tried to preserve this candor, which may at first have made her seem timid, while in fact it renders her only the more worthy of Your Majesty's esteem and friendship.

"Some may blame me because my daughter has so few ideas, such a meagre education. I acknowledge it; but as to the world and its perils, one learns them only too soon, and I will say frankly she was only eighteen, and I wanted to preserve her innocence, and cared only that she should have a loving heart, an honest nature, and clear ideas about what she did know. I have entrusted her to Your Majesty. I beg you, as her mother, to be my daughter's friend and guide, as she is your devoted wife. She will be happy if Your Majesty will always confidently appeal to her; for, I say once more, she is young and too inexperienced to face the world's dangers and to fill her position understandingly. But I perceive that I am wearying Your Majesty with this long letter. You will pardon this outpouring of a mother's heart, which knows no bounds when a beloved daughter's happiness is concerned. I must say one thing more. Your Majesty sets too high a value on my eagerness to satisfy you by letting you have the portrait of my dear Louise. I was too anxious to please you as soon as possible, not to be selfish in this matter, but I shall certainly thoroughly appreciate the portrait you promise me. It will have this advantage, that it will show me how happy she is."

It must be said that seldom has a step-mother spoken of her step-daughter in a more tender and more touching way. No letter could have better pleased Napoleon; it was not written in official style, with all the formal compliments, but rather with affectionate sincerity. When he read it, Napoleon must have felt that he had at last really entered the brotherhood of kings. Everything she had said of her step-daughter was true. The young Empress of the French had a candor, a simplicity, a freshness of mind and body, which delighted her husband. Doubtless the feeling she inspired was not a fiery, romantic passion such as he had felt for his first wife; and Marie Louise, with her northern beauty, had not the same charm as Josephine, the bewitching creole. Napoleon certainly would not have written to his second wife burning letters, in the style of the *Nouvelle Héloise,* such as he sent to Josephine during the first Italian campaign. His love for Marie Louise was less fervent, but he esteemed her more highly. He thought that the society of the Austrian court was after all a better school for a wife than the society of the Directory, and he had found in Marie Louise, a girl worthy of all regard, one invaluable blessing, one treasure which a widow, charming, it is true, but a coquette, lacked; namely, innocence.

XVI
THE TRIP IN THE NORTH

"Napoleon and Marie Louise left Compiègne April 27, 1810, at seven o'clock in the morning, to make a journey in several of the northern departments, which was one long ovation. In their suite were the Grand Duke of Würzburg, brother of the Emperor of Austria, the Queen of Naples, the King and Queen of Westphalia, Prince Eugene de Beauharnais, Prince Schwarzenberg, and Count Metternich. The last-named says in his Memoirs: 'I was an eye-witness of the enthusiasm with which the young Empress was everywhere greeted by the populace. At Saint Quentin Napoleon formally expressed his desire that I should be present at an audience to which he had summoned the authorities of the city. 'I should like to show you,' he said, 'how I am accustomed to speak to these people.' I saw that the Emperor was anxious to let me see the extent and variety of his knowledge of matters of administration.'"

Those who care to know the adulation offered to Napoleon and Marie Louise on this expedition should read the following passage from M. de Bausset's Memoirs: "Their Majesties went off to visit some of the northern departments, in order to give Paris and all the great bodies of the State the time required for preparing the festivities which circumstances made necessary. It was a triumphal march. The provinces greeted their young and beautiful Empress with enthusiasm. Amid all the brilliant tokens of respect, one attracted especial notice. It was a little hamlet, with a triumphal arch, bearing the simplest inscriptions. On the front was written *Pater Noster*; on the reverse, *Ave Maria, gratiâ plena*. The mayor and the village priest presented wild-flowers. Flattery could have devised no more delicate attention." Thus we have M. de Bausset finding it simple to compare the Emperor to the Almighty and the Empress to the Blessed Virgin. Was not this a sign of the times?

Thiers says of this journey: "The populace, glad of a break in their monotonous lives, hasten to meet their princes, whoever they may be, and are often lavish of their applause on the very brink of a catastrophe. Whenever Napoleon appeared anywhere, curiosity and admiration were strong enough to gather a multitude; and when he had rounded out his wonderful destiny by marrying an archduchess, the interest and enthusiasm were all the greater. Indeed, everywhere he appeared, their raptures were warm and unanimous."

Starting from Compiègne April 27, the Emperor and Empress reached Saint Quentin the same day. The canal connecting the Seine with the Scheldt was illuminated, and Napoleon and his court sailed over it in gondolas richly decked with flags. On the 30th of April they embarked on the canal which goes from Brussels to the Ruppel, and by the Ruppel to the Scheldt. The First Lord of the Admiralty and Admiral Missiessy were in command of the Imperial flotilla. When they arrived in sight of the squadron of Antwerp, which Napoleon had created, all the ships, frigates, corvettes, gunboats, were drawn up in line, and Marie Louise passed under the fire of a thousand cannon thundering in her honor. When the sovereigns entered the city, the throng was most dense. "It expressed," the *Moniteur* tells us, "the gratitude of the inhabitants for its second founder. It was impossible not to make a comparison between the present condition of the port and city of Antwerp with its condition seven years before, on His Majesty's first visit."

At Antwerp they made a stay of five days, which the Emperor, who was on his horse at sunrise, spent in visiting the works of the port, the arsenal, the fortifications, in holding reviews, in inspecting the fleet. May 2 there was launched a ship of eighty guns, the largest ship that had ever been built on the stocks of this port. It was blessed by the Archbishop of Mechlin. According to the Baron de Méneval, "the Empress was affable, simple, and unpretentious. Possibly the memory of Josephine's charm and earnest desire to please was a misfortune to Marie Louise. Her reserve might have been attributed to German family pride, but that would have been a mistake; no one was ever simpler or less haughty. Her natural timidity and her unfamiliarity with the part she had to play, alone gave her an air of stiffness. She was so thoroughly identified with her new position and so touched by the regard and affection with which the Emperor was treated, that when he proposed to her to stay at Antwerp while he was visiting the islands of the Zuyder Zee, she besought him to take her with him, undeterred by any fear of the fatigues of the journey." Consequently Napoleon started with her to visit Bois-le-Duc, Berg-op-Zoom, Breda, Middelburg, Flushing, and the island of Walcheren, which the English had evacuated four months before.

At Breda the Emperor soundly abused a deputation of the Catholic clergy whom he knew to be opposed to him. "Gentlemen," he broke out, "why are you not in sacerdotal garments? Are you attorneys, notaries, or physicians? ... Render unto Caesar the things which are Caesar's. The Pope is not Caesar; I am. It is not to the Pope, but to me, that God has given a sceptre and a sword.... Ah, you are unwilling to pray for me. Is it because a

Roman priest has excommunicated me? But who gave him any such power? Who has the power to release subjects from their oath of allegiance to the legally appointed ruler? No one; and you ought to know it.... Renounce the hope of putting me in a convent and of shaving my head, like Louis the Debonair, and submit yourselves; for I am Caesar! If you don't, I shall banish you from my empire, and scatter you over the surface of the earth like the Jews.... You belong to the diocese of Mechlin; go to your bishop; take your oath before him, obey the Concordat, and then I will see what commands I shall have to give you."

After visiting the towns on the frontier, as well as the islands of Tholen, Schomven, North and South Beveland, and Walcheren, Napoleon, constantly accompanied by Marie Louise, ascended the Scheldt once more, merely passed through Antwerp, made a brief stop at Brussels, spent three days at the castle of Lacken, and hastily ran through Ghent, Bruges, Ostend, Dunkirk, Lille, Calais, Dieppe, Havre, and Rouen.

June 1, 1810, they were back at Saint Cloud. The Baron de Méneval tells us that Marie Louise was extremely delighted with the way she had been greeted throughout this journey. Everywhere she had been received under arches of triumph, with countless festivities, balls, illuminations, and every token of the popular enthusiasm and affection, so that "she was able to appreciate the French character, and to decide that she would readily grow accustomed to a country where the devotion of the people to their sovereign, the enormous influence he wielded, and the affection he bore to them, as well as theirs for his cause, filled her with hopes for a happy life." Napoleon's life at that time was one long deification. Louis XIV. himself, the Sun-King, had never received more flattery in prose and verse. All the official poets had tuned their lyres to sing his marriage, and the *Moniteur* was full of dithyrambs. It also published a translation of an Italian cantata entitled, "*La Jerogamia di Creta, Inno del Cavaliere Vincenzo Monti,*" which began thus: "The silence of Olympus is broken up by the noisy neighing of coursers and by the prolonged and disturbing rattle of swift chariots. The Immortals descend to the banks of the Gnossus to celebrate with fitting rites the new marriage of the ruler of the gods." It ended thus: "The waves of two seas, in motion, though no wind blows, roar in terror, and Neptune, alarmed, feels with surprise his trident tremble in his hand. If such is the sport of the monarch of thunder when he yields to the sweets of Hymen, what will it be when he again grasps the thunderbolt? Divine nurses of Jove, bees of Mount Panacra, ah! distil upon my verses, from the summit of Dicte, one drop of the sweet-savored honey, food of the King of Heaven, that my August sovereign, whose soul is like Jupiter's, may find some pleasure in hearing them!"

Napoleon seemed to rule the present and the future. Even those who had fought against him had become his courtiers. The most illustrious of these, the Archduke Charles, to whom he had just sent the broad ribbon of the Legion of Honor, as well as a simple cross of a knight, which was more precious because he himself had worn it, wrote to him: "Sire, Your Majesty's Ambassador has transmitted to me the decorations of the Legion of Honor, and the affectionate letter with which you have honored me. Being deeply impressed by these tokens of your goodwill, I hasten to express to Your Majesty my sincere gratitude, which is only equalled by my admiration for Your Majesty's great qualities. The esteem of a great man is the fairest flower of the field of honor, and I have always jealously desired, Sire, to merit yours."

A stranger thing yet: even the Spanish Bourbons, the victims of the Bayonne treachery, the princes whom Napoleon had ousted, set no limits to their adulation. Nowhere was the Emperor's marriage with Marie Louise celebrated with greater show of enthusiasm than at the castle of Valençay, where Ferdinand III. was living. The Spanish Prince had a *Te Deum* sung in the chapel; he gave a banquet, at which he proposed this toast: "To the health of our August Sovereigns, the great Napoleon and Marie Louise, his August spouse." In the evening there were magnificent fireworks. He chose that moment when his subjects were exposing themselves to every danger, welcoming every sacrifice in their bitter war in his name, against the French, to beg Napoleon to adopt him as his son and to concede to him the honor of letting him appear at court.

XVII
THE MONTH OF JUNE, 1810

The whole month of June was filled with a succession of brilliant festivities. Under the Empire things were not done by halves; battles or balls, everything was on a vast scale. "Never," says Alfred de Musset, "were there so many sleepless nights as during this man's lifetime; never was there such a silence when any one spoke of death: and yet, never was there so much joy, so much life, so much warlike feeling in every heart; never had there been a brighter sun than that which dried so much blood. It was said that God had created it for this man, and it was called the sun of Austerlitz; but he made it himself with his ever-roaring cannon, that dispelled the clouds on the morrow of his victories."

The entertainment given to the Emperor and Empress by the city of Paris, June 10, was magnificent. There were great rejoicings in the capital on that day. In the afternoon there were public sports in the Champs Élysées, and dancing in the open places and the long walks. With nightfall the illuminations began. A troupe of mountebanks performed on a huge stage a ballet in pantomime, called the "Union of Mars and Flora." There were as many as five hundred performers. There were bands playing in every direction, and food was distributed to the contented multitude. From the Arc to the Tuileries, from the Tuileries to the Louvre, from the Louvre to the Hôtel de Ville, the spectacle was really fairy-like. Napoleon and Marie Louise, starting from Saint Cloud at eight in the evening, made their way, in torchlight, through a countless multitude. Their approach was announced to the people by the sudden ascent of a balloon, from which fireworks were discharged. At half-past nine they reached the Hôtel de Ville. Nearly a thousand persons had gathered in the concert hall, almost three thousand in the record room, the Hall of Saint John, and in the semicircular place in front, opposite the spot, on the left bank of the Seine, where the fireworks were to be set off at a signal of Napoleon and Marie Louise. These fireworks were divided into three parts, representing a military scene, the Temple of Peace, and the Temple of Hymen. In the first there were two forts which soldiers were assaulting, firing their guns amid the sound of trumpets and the rattle of drums. The forts were discharging shells and bullets, which burst into flame, and were reflected in the water before they fell into the river. When the two forts were captured, they disappeared in a great blaze. Then the ship, the symbol of the city of Paris, appeared and took its station between two columns of light. The decoration changed, and first the Temple of Peace was seen, then that of Hymen—a real pyrotechnic masterpiece. After the fireworks the Emperor and Empress went first into the record room, then into the concert hall, where was sung a cantata, with words by Arnault and music by Méhul, which began with this apostrophe to the Empress:—

> "From the throne where our homage rises to you,
> From the throne where beauty reigns by the side of courage,
> And Minerva by the side of Mars,
> On these shores of which love has made you sovereign,
> On these happy shores adorned by the Seine,
> Louise, cast thy glance."

After the cantata a ball began. Napoleon did not dance, but Marie Louise did. The first quadrille was thus made up: the Empress and the King of Westphalia, the Queen of Naples and the Viceroy of Italy, Princess Pauline Borghese and Prince Esterhazy, Mademoiselle de Saint-Gilles and M. de Nicolaï. The second quadrille: the Queen of Westphalia and Prince Borghese, the Princess of Baden and Count Metternich, the Princess Aldobrandini and M. de Montaran, Madame Blaque de Belair and M. Mallet. The Emperor descended from his throne and walked through the room, exchanging a few words with a great many people. About midnight he withdrew with the Empress. At two o'clock supper was served: at this fifteen hundred ladies were present, and the ball went on till daybreak.

Princess Pauline Borghese gave a very brilliant entertainment June 14, at the castle of Neuilly. At the end of an illuminated lawn appeared the Austrian palace of Laxenburg, and the ballet consisted of dancers arrayed like peasants of the neighborhood of Vienna. June 21, another great ball was given by the Duke of Feltre, the Minister of War. But the finest, the most original, the grandest ball, was that given by the Imperial Guard at the Champ de Mars and the Military School, at that time called the Napoleon quarter. Marie Louise was thoroughly delighted with it; she said she had never seen anything so magnificent. Never had Rome under the Caesars seen a more gorgeous spectacle. For many months the public had been watching the vast preparations for this event. Two wings had been added to the Military School, large enough to hold eight thousand persons. The main courtyard had been transformed into a garden in which were set out numberless orange-trees, shrubs, and flowers. The officers of the Guard, who were models of French politeness, received the ladies at the entrance of this garden, offering each one a bouquet, and escorted them to the galleries which led to the two newly constructed buildings, one of which was the ball-room; the other, the supper-room. The ball-room was shaped like a tent, and the ceiling was decorated with the signs of the Zodiac and allegorical representation of a triumph. A throne was set there, above seven rows of seats. All around the room hung muslin draperies, on which were embroidered gold bees and branches of myrtle and laurel. When the Emperor and Empress appeared at seven o'clock, three thousand women, each with a bouquet in her hand, rose at once. It seemed like a living flower-garden. The wives of the most illustrious officers of the Guard, the Duchess of Dalmatia, of Treviso, of Istria, Countess Walter, Dorsenne, Curial, Saint-Sulpice, Lefebore, Desnonettes, Krasenska, Baronesses Kirgener, Lubenska, Guiot, Gros, Delaistre and Lepic, had been chosen to escort the Empress. Marshal Bessières, Duke of Istria, presented her with a magnificent bouquet.

Meanwhile the Champ de Mars, which was covered with flags, was filled with three or four hundred thousand spectators, who had assembled quietly, without crowding, on the terrace, the amphitheatres, and in the walks. When Napoleon and Marie Louise showed themselves on the balcony of the Military School, there broke out loud applause. Afterwards dinner was served to the Imperial family. When that was finished, they gave the signal for the horse and chariot races. Franconi's equestrian troupe gave performances in the intervals. When all the prizes had been given, a balloon, carrying a woman, Madame Blanchard, made an ascent. She saluted the Imperial pair, waved a flag, threw down flowers, and speedily attained a great height. Then there were fireworks. Amid rockets, bombs, and shooting-stars, two pretty young women walked up and down on the tight rope, like magical apparitions, amid the encircling flames. After the fireworks a ballet was performed by the dancers from the Opera, under the direction of Gardel; it represented the different nations of Europe in their national dress. After the ballet came the ball, which was most animated. Napoleon and Marie Louise left towards midnight, escorted to their carriage by most of the guests, who cheered, and did not return to the ball-room until the Emperor and Empress had gone out of sight. This exceptional entertainment was favored by pleasant weather and a bright night; the moon and the stars seemed to rival the illuminations. The main courtyard, filled with trees and flowers, was like the enchanted garden of Armida, where one walked amid delicious music. At two in the morning the doors of the supper-room were opened, a large bower of gilded trellis work, with Corinthian columns, and a roof covered with frescoes representing groups of children sporting in the air amid flowers and garlands. About fifteen hundred people sat down to table.

The Imperial Guard had every reason to be proud of its entertainment. The officers, young, brilliant, devoted to pleasure as to glory, found their life more joyous as war threatened to make it short. They displayed the same ardor, the same enthusiasm, in the ball-room as on the battle-field. They loved the smell of flowers as much as the smell of gunpowder. Every form of conquest tempted them, and they revived the customs of chivalry. In the language of the time, there flourished the twofold reign of Mars and Venus. In those heroic days courage was set higher than wealth. The women, with few exceptions, were indifferent to money; they did not think that an honorable scar disfigured a soldier's face, and the disinterested kindness of a beauty was the reward of bravery.

XVIII
THE BALL AT THE AUSTRIAN EMBASSY

The series of grand entertainments which had been given in Paris was to be concluded by a ball, which Prince Schwarzenberg, the Austrian Ambassador, was to give at the Embassy, July 1, 1810, to the Emperor and Empress; it had been announced that this was to be a marvel of luxury, elegance, and good taste. The Ambassador lived in the rue de la Chaussée d'Antin, in a mansion formerly belonging to the Marchioness of Montesson, widow of the Duke of Orleans, to whom this lady had been united by a morganatic marriage. Great preparations had been made with extraordinary magnificence. Since the ground floor of the house was too small, a large ball-room of wood had been built, reached by a gallery, also of wood, leading from the body of the house. The ceiling of this gallery was covered with varnished paper, decorated and painted; the floor-boards, which were supported on a framework, were raised to the same height as the floors of the house. A large chandelier hung from the ceiling of the ball-room. The sides and the circuit of the gallery were lit by candelabra fastened to the walls. A high platform was reserved for the Imperial family, in the centre of the right-hand side of the ball-room, directly opposite a large door opening on the garden. Behind the platform was a small door reserved for the sovereigns. The Ambassador and his wife had staying with them his brother and sister-in-law, Prince Joseph and Princess Pauline Schwarzenberg, who were to help him in doing the honors of the ball.

Napoleon and Marie Louise, who started from Saint Cloud, reached the gates of Paris at quarter to ten; there they got into another carriage, and soon after ten were at the door of the Embassy, where the Ambassador received them. The Emperor wore over his coat the broad Austrian ribbon of Saint Stephen.

The grand ball was opened; a troupe of musicians in the court of honor sounded a flourish of trumpets at the entrance of Their Majesties, who passed through the concert hall into the garden, where they stopped a moment before the Temple of Apollo. There women, dressed to resemble the Muses, sang a joyous chorus. Napoleon and Marie Louise passed slowly along a water-walk, where hidden music issued from a subterranean grotto, to a vine-clad arbor adorned with mirrors, monograms, flowers, and wreaths, and listened to a concert of vocal and instrumental music, French and German; then they went further into the garden, stopping before a Temple of Glory, where were four handsome women representing Victory, the muse Clio, and Renown; then trumpets sounded, triumphal songs were sung, and perfumes were burning on golden tripods. Then they turned to see a delightful ballet danced on the greensward, with a view of the Palace of Laxenburg—so dear to Marie Louise—in the background; that done, they entered the wooden gallery just put up before the front of the mansion, and finally entered the ball-room, which was large enough to hold about fifteen hundred people.

It was midnight, and so far everything had gone on without a hitch. The Emperor and Empress seemed delighted; the Ambassador was radiant; every one was enchanted with the magic of the spectacle. The ball was opened with a quadrille, in which the Queen of Naples danced with Prince Esterhazy, and Prince Eugene de Beauharnais with Princess Pauline de Schwarzenberg. When that was over, the Emperor descended from his throne to walk through the room; while the Empress, the Queen of Naples, and the Vice-Queen of Italy remained in their places on the platform. Napoleon had just come up to Princess Pauline de Schwarzenberg, who had presented to him the princesses, her daughters, when suddenly the flame of a candle set fire to the curtains of a window. Count Dumanoir, the Emperor's chamberlain, and several officers tried to tear the curtains down; but the flames continued to spread, and in less than three minutes they had reached the ceiling, and all the light decorations which hung from it were ablaze. Count Metternich, who happened to be at the foot of the platform, at once ran up to tell the Empress what had happened, and to persuade her to follow him as soon as possible. As to the Emperor, who was as cool as if he were on the battle-field, he was able to reach the platform to join Marie Louise, and to escape with her to the garden, urging every one to be calm in order to avoid disorder.

Fortunately the means of exit were wide, and the greater part of the guests were able to find refuge in the garden; but, alas! there were many accidents and many victims. It so happened that just when the fire started a great many young girls had left their mothers to dance a schottische; their mothers tried to find them, and they tried to find their mothers, amid wild shrieks and the most desperate confusion. Wives called for their husbands, parents for their children. The officers of the Imperial Guard gathered about Napoleon with drawn swords, for at first they suspected treachery and waited for some further development of a malicious plot. Prince Schwarzenberg, who did not leave the Emperor, said to him: "I know how this room is built; it is doomed; but there are so many exits that every one can escape. Sire, I shall cover you with my body." Napoleon, under his protection, reached the platform with composure, took the Empress by the hand, and succeeded in going out with her. They passed through the garden, got into a carriage, and drove to the Place Louis XV., where they separated, the Empress pushing on to Saint Cloud, while the Emperor, retracing his steps, went back to the Austrian Embassy, where he hoped to be able to help extinguish the fire.

The Ambassador, who had accompanied Napoleon and Marie Louise to their carriage, went back to the house, then a hideous scene of destruction. A storm had arisen, and a violent wind had spread the ravaging flames in every direction. The Queen of Westphalia had fainted and had been rescued by Count Metternich; the Queen of Naples, Prince Eugene, and his wife, who was in a delicate condition, had remained on the platform. The Queen tried to escape by the main door, by which the Emperor and the Empress had left; but this was speedily so blocked up by the crowd that she, who was behind every one, would certainly have been caught by the flames, like many others, had it not been for the assistance of the Grand Duke of Würzburg and of Marshal Marcey, who seized her and forced a way for her. Prince Eugene saw the chandelier fall, and the passage across the room wholly blocked; but, fortunately, he noticed the little door which led into the house, and through that he escaped with his wife. The Ambassador beheld the calamity with despair. His wife was brought out senseless, but untouched by the flames. He saw his brother, Prince Joseph de Schwarzenberg, running to and fro, wild with grief and disquiet; he was looking for his wife, Princess Pauline de Schwarzenberg, and could not find her. What had become of the unhappy mother? When the fire broke out, knowing her eldest daughter, Eleonore, to be safe, she had run to the assistance of her second daughter, Pauline, who was dancing the schottische, and led her speedily to the steps of the entrance, where the crowd was surging amid the flames. A moment more, and mother and daughter were safe: they had but a few steps to take to be on the staircase and then in the garden, but suddenly a falling beam separated mother and child, and the staircase broke down beneath the weight of the struggling crowd. Missing her daughter, the courageous princess plunged once more into the ballroom. No one knew what had become of her; in the cruel, heart-wringing uncertainty the stern face of the Ambassador was wet with tears.

Napoleon returned to the Embassy, and directing everything, supervising everything as on a battlefield, there he stayed more than two hours, exposed to a heavy rain which began after the fire, and to all the heat and smoke. Alone, unguarded, evidently anxious to dispel all misinterpretation which malevolence could draw from the unhappy event, he displayed great energy and perfect self-possession.

It was not till four in the morning that he returned to Saint Cloud, where he had been most anxiously awaited. "From the time that the Empress arrived," we read in Constant's Memoirs, "we had felt the keenest anxiety; every one in the palace had been most uneasy about the Emperor. At last he arrived, unharmed, but very tired; his dress in disorder, his face scorched, his clothes and stockings all blackened and singed by the fire. He went straight to the Empress's room, to console her for the fright she had had; then he went to his own room, flung his hat on the bed, dropped into an easy-chair, saying, 'Heavens! what a festivity!' I noticed that his hands were all blackened; he had lost his gloves at the fire. He was overwhelmed with sadness, and he spoke with an emotion such as I had seen in him only two or three times in his life, and never about his own misfortunes. I remember that he expressed a fear that the terrible event of that night betokened future calamities. Three years later, in the Russian campaign, he was told one day that Prince Schwarzenberg's army corps had been destroyed, and that the Prince himself had perished. It happened that the news was false; but when it was brought to the Emperor, he said, as if in accordance with a thought that had long haunted him, 'It was he then whom that evil omen threatened!'"

The morning of the next day Napoleon sent his pages to learn the news. The accounts they brought back were most gloomy: the Princess de la Leyen had died from her injuries; General Touzart was in a desperate condition, as well as his wife and daughter, who, in fact, died the same day. Prince Kourakine, the Russian Ambassador, was seriously injured; he had made a misstep on the staircase leading to the garden, and had fallen senseless into the flames, which, fortunately, had been unable to get through his coat of cloth of gold and the decorations which covered him like a cuirass; nevertheless, it was many months before he recovered. "Prince Joseph de Schwarzenberg," says the *Moniteur* of July 3, 1810, "spent the night in looking for his wife, whom he could not find at the Embassy or at Madame Metternich's. He was still ignorant of his loss when at daybreak there was found in the ball-room a corpse which Dr. Gall thought that he recognized as that of the Princess Pauline de Schwarzenberg. Further doubt was impossible when her jewels with her children's initials, which she wore about her neck, were recognized. Princess Pauline de Schwarzenberg was the daughter of the Senator von Avenberg, and the mother of eight children. She was as renowned for her personal charms as for the distinction of her mind and heart. The act of devotion which cost her her life shows how much her loss is to be regretted, for death was certain amid the fury of the flames. Only a mother would have dared to face the danger."

The *Moniteur* adds to this pathetic account: "The Austrian Ambassador during the whole night displayed the zeal, the activity, the calmness, and the presence of mind to be expected of him. The members of the Embassy and the Austrians who were present were tireless in their courage and devotion. The public has been most grateful to the Ambassador for insisting on accompanying the Emperor and the Empress to their carriage, without regard to the dangers to which his family was exposed. The Emperor left the spot at about three in the morning. During the rest of the night he sent several times for information about the fate of the Princess Schwarzenberg. It was not until five o'clock that he received word of her death. His Majesty, who held this princess in the highest esteem, sincerely regrets her sad lot. The Empress exhibited the most perfect calmness throughout the evening. When she heard this morning of the death of Princess Pauline de Schwarzenberg, she burst into tears."

The young Princess Pauline, the daughter of the woman who had perished, was for a long time in a state that caused the utmost anxiety. Her mother's death was concealed from her, but she became uneasy at her absence, and read on her father's face the marks of the grief which he tried to conceal. At last she recovered; later she married Prince Schoenburg; but her wounds reopened, and she died a few years later, a victim, like her mother, of the fatal ball.

The day after these occurrences Marie Louise wrote a letter in German to her father, in which she said: "I did not lose my head. Prince Schwarzenberg led the Emperor and me out of the place, through the garden. I am the more grateful because he left his wife and son in the burning room. The panic and confusion were terrible. If the Grand Duke of Würzburg had not carried the Queen of Naples away, she would have been burned alive. My sister-in-law Catherine, who thought her husband was in the midst of the fire, swooned away. The Viceroy had to carry his wife off. Not a single one of my ladies or of my officers was by me. General Lauriston, who adores his wife, cried out in the most lamentable way, and impeded us in our flight. I was calmer then than when the Emperor left me again. We sat up with Caroline until four in the morning, when he came back, wet through with the rain. The Duchess of Rovigo, one of my ladies, is seriously burned. The Countesses Bucholz and Loewenstein, the Queen of Westphalia's ladies, are also injured.... Lauriston, in saving his wife, had his hair and forehead singed. Prince Kourakine was so severely injured that he lost consciousness; in the panic the crowd trampled upon him, and he was dragged out half dead. Prince Metternich is hardly hurt at all. Prince Charles Schwarzenberg, who insisted on staying until every one had got out, is badly burned. The poor Ambassador is beside himself, though he is in no way responsible for the calamity."

Marie Louise, who had been interrupted at this point, continued as follows: "I have just come from the Emperor, where I heard a terrible piece of news. Princess Pauline Schwarzenberg has been found, burned to a crisp.... Her diamonds were lying near her. She wore on her neck a heart in brilliants, on which were engraved the names of her two daughters, Eleonore and Pauline, and it was by this that she was recognized. She leaves eight children, and was expecting another. Her family is inconsolable. Kourakine is very low; so is Madame Durosnel, the general's wife. I am so distressed that I cannot stir."

The Emperor Francis wrote to his son-in-law about this distressing event: "July 15. My Brother and very dear Son-in-law,—It is with the greatest satisfaction that I have heard that Your Imperial Majesty, as well as the Empress, my beloved daughter, has escaped the melancholy accidents that occurred at the ball of my Ambassador, Prince Schwarzenberg. I cannot express to you, my brother, my gratitude for the tokens of your interest which you manifested on that occasion, and for your personal exertions, as noble as they were courageous, to arrest the progress of the disaster. Count Metternich and Prince Schwarzenberg cannot find words to express their profound gratitude for your kindness and anxiety, and I beg Your Majesty to receive this expression of all that I have experienced in reading their reports."

The calamity produced a most melancholy impression. It recalled to every one the disasters that attended the festivities given to Marie Antoinette forty years before. This ball, followed by a horrid catastrophe, this grand drawing-room, vanishing in flames, were they not omens of evil? Was not the great empire to perish in the same way? This fire, bursting forth in a night of revelry and triumph, was it not like a prophecy of a still more terrible fire, that which laid Moscow in ashes? But nations have short memories; gloomy presentiments soon vanish. The Empire was then so glorious that a passing incident could not seriously disturb it, and a few days after the catastrophe it was forgotten. Every one, even the enemies of France, felt the fascination of this most wonderful career which formed the strangest and most improbable of romances.

XIX
THE BIRTH OF THE KING OF ROME

Napoleon and Marie Louise grew fonder and fonder of each other as time went on. The Empress wrote to her father: "I assure you, dear papa, that people have done great injustice to the Emperor. The better one knows him, the better one appreciates and loves him." Napoleon's satisfaction was even greater when he learned that his young wife was to bring him an heir; he redoubled his solicitous attention and regards; he never blamed her, he uttered only words of praise and tenderness. This extract from Metternich's Memoirs will serve to show how anxious the Emperor was at this time to spare his wife every form of annoyance: "In the summer of 1810, Napoleon asked me to wait after one of his levees at Saint Cloud. When we were alone, he asked me, with some embarrassment, if I would do him a great favor. 'It's about the Empress,' he said; 'you see she is young and inexperienced, and she does not understand the ways of this country or the French character. I have given her the Duchess of Montebello for a companion; she is an excellent woman, but sometimes a little indiscreet. Yesterday, for example, when she was walking with the Empress in the park, she presented one of her cousins to her. The Empress talked with him, and that was a mistake. If she is going to have young men, and second and third cousins, presented to her, she will become the tool of intrigues. Every one in France has always some favor to ask. The Empress will be besieged, and will be exposed to a thousand annoyances, without being able to do anything for anybody.' I told Napoleon that I quite agreed with him, but that I did not see why he confided this matter to me. 'It is,' said Napoleon, 'because I want you to speak about it to the Empress.' I expressed my surprise that he did not do that himself. 'Your opinion is sound and wise, and the Empress is too intelligent not to regard it.' 'I prefer,' said Napoleon,'that you should do this. The Empress is young, and she might think that I am merely a cross husband; you are her father's minister and an old friend; what you may say will have a great deal more weight with her than any words of mine.'"

Napoleon manifested great regard, not for his wife alone, but also for his father-in-law, of whom he always spoke with warm sympathy. When Count Metternich came to bid farewell before returning to Vienna, at the end of September, 1810, Napoleon charged him to convey to the Emperor

Francis the most positive assurances of his friendship and devotion. "The Emperor must be sure," he said, "that my only wish is for his happiness and prosperity. He must reject any idea of my encroaching on his monarchy. That cannot fail to grow, and speedily too, through our alliance. Assure him that anything which he may hear to the contrary is false. I had rather have him than any one of my own brothers on the Austrian throne, and I don't see any cause for quarrel between us."

Early in July, when their hopes were still vague, Marie Louise wrote to her father: "Heaven grant that they may prove true! The Emperor would be so happy!" And later she wrote: "I can assure you, dear papa, that I look forward without dread to this event, which will be a great happiness." The official notification of her condition was not made till November, when Napoleon sent the Baron de Mesgrigny to Vienna with two letters, one from himself and one from the Empress, to the Emperor Francis. "This letter," Marie Louise wrote, "is to announce to you, dear papa, the great news. I take this opportunity to ask your blessing for me and for your grandchild. You may imagine my delight. It will be complete if the event shall bring you to Paris." The hope of seeing her father soon was continually present with her, and Napoleon encouraged it. As she wrote to her father, "My husband often speaks of you and is anxious to see you again."

The Emperor Francis answered his son-in-law, December 3, 1810, in these terms: "My Brother and very Dear Son-in-law,—The letter which M. de Mesgrigny has handed to me fills me with the liveliest joy. The happy event which it mentions arouses my fullest sympathy. My best wishes go out to you, my brother, and the present condition of things which your letter announces, is too intimately connected with our reciprocal satisfaction for me not to set the greatest store, as friend and father, by the news you give me. Everything which Your Majesty says about your domestic happiness is corroborated by my daughter; in no way can you, my brother, contribute more directly to my own. I knew the excellent traits of my daughter when I entrusted her to you, and Your Imperial Majesty must be sure that my only consolation for the separation is her happiness, which is inseparable from that of her husband."

Napoleon asked of the Bishops and Archbishops special prayers in behalf of the Empress. December 2, the anniversary of his coronation, and of the battle of Austerlitz, he gave an audience to the Senate, who came to thank him for the notification of the Empress's expectations. At the Tuileries that day was celebrated by mass a *Te Deum*, an illumination, and a play. Twelve young girls, who were dowered by the Empress, were married in the Cathedral, and there was a generous distribution of alms.

The Emperor founded a society of Maternal Charity, to aid poor women during their confinement. The Empress was appointed patroness of the society, and Mesdames de Ségur and de Pastoret Vice-Presidents; a thousand ladies joined it, and fifteen held offices; there was a Grand Council which sat in Paris, and administrative councils were appointed for the provinces. The Grand Almoner was made secretary, and there was a general treasurer. The capital of the society amounted to five hundred thousand francs, raised in part from the public funds, and in part by voluntary subscriptions, which soon furnished the required sum.

New Year's Day was approaching, and Marie Louise desired a set of Brazilian rubies, costing forty-six thousand francs. As she wanted to make some presents to her sisters, and these cost twenty-five thousand francs, she saw that only fifteen thousand francs would be left of her December allowance. Consequently she denied herself the rubies, and forbore to say anything about them to the Emperor. But Napoleon happened to hear of it, and was delighted with his wife's economy and sense of order, which he rewarded in the most delicate manner. He secretly ordered of the crown-jeweller a set of rubies like the one she had wanted, but worth between three and four hundred thousand francs, and surprised her with these, an attention by which she was highly gratified. He asked her at the same time if she had thought of sending any New Year's presents to her sisters, the Archduchesses. She answered yes, and that she had ordered for the young Princesses presents worth together something like twenty-five thousand francs. Napoleon thought that a rather small sum; but she told him that they were not so spoiled as she was, and that they would think their presents superb. Then the Emperor presented her with a hundred thousand francs.

In January, 1811, the Emperor thus thanked Napoleon for a portrait of his daughter, the Empress:—

"My Brother,—The delicate way in which Your Imperial Majesty has fulfilled my wishes by sending me the portrait of the Empress, your dear wife, lends a new value to the letter you have written to me. I hasten to give expression to the joy which I feel in seeing the features of my beloved daughter, which seem to add to a perfect likeness the merit of expressing her happiness in a congenial marriage."

The Countess of Montesquiou, a most worthy woman, was appointed Governess of the Imperial children, with two assistants, Mesdames de Mesgrigny and de Boubers, and later a third, Madame Soufflot. A nurse was chosen,—a sturdy, healthy woman, wife of a joiner at Fontainebleau; and two cribs were prepared,—a blue one for a prince, a pink one for a princess. The baby-linen, which was valued at three hundred thousand francs, aroused the admiration of all the ladies of the court.

In January and February, 1811, Marie Louise still went about. She drove to the hunt in the forest of Vincennes, in that of Saint Germain, and at Versailles. She used to walk in the Bois de Boulogne with Napoleon. Towards the middle of February great preparations began to be made for the happy event. Dr. Dubois was installed at the Tuileries, in the apartments of the Grand Marshal of the Palace, and the Duchess of Montebello, lady-in-waiting, took up her quarters in the palace. Marie Louise, who had gone to a fancy ball at the Duchess of Rovigo's, February 10, was present on the 25th at a quiet ball given at the Tuileries, at which were present only two strangers,—Prince Schwarzenberg, the Austrian Ambassador, and Prince Leopold of Coburg.

March 5 Count Frochot, Prefect of the Seine, came to the Tuileries, at the head of the Municipal Council, to present, in the name of the city of Paris, a magnificent red cradle, shaped like a ship, the emblem of the capital. This cradle, a real masterpiece, had been designed by Prudhon the artist, and is now in the Imperial Treasury of Vienna, to which it was given by the King of Rome when Duke of Reichstadt. The ornamentation, which is in mother-of-pearl and vermilion, is set on a ground of orange-red velvet. It is formed of a pillar of mother-of-pearl, on which are set gold bees, and is supported by four cornucopias, near which are set the figures of Force and Justice. At the top there is a shield with the Emperor's initials, surrounded by three rows of ivy and laurel. A figure representing Glory overhanging the world, holds a crown, in the middle of which shines Napoleon's star. A young eagle at the foot of the cradle is gazing at the conqueror's star, with wings spread as if about to take flight. A curtain of lace, covered with stars and ending in rich gold embroidery, hangs over each side.

When Marie Louise's walks were limited to the terrace of the Tuileries, by the side of the sheet of water that bounds the garden, a small doorway with an iron grating was thrown open into the first floor of the palace, to make easier her access to the spot. Around the grating the crowd used to gather to watch the Empress and respectfully to offer her their best wishes.

At nine o'clock in the evening of March 19th, 1811, the great bell of Notre Dame and all the church bells sounded, bidding the faithful spend the night in prayer and to invoke the blessings of Heaven on their Empress and the child which was about to enter the world. With Marie Louise there were M. Dubois, the Duchess of Montebello, the Countess of Luçay, Mesdames Durand and Ballant, ladies-in-waiting, ladies of the bedchamber, etc., and Madame Blaise. The Emperor, his mother and sisters, and two physicians,

Drs. Corvisart and Bourdier, were in the next room. Napoleon kept going in and out of his wife's chamber, encouraging her with kind and cheery words. At five in the morning Dubois thought that the birth was not immediate, and the Emperor sent away the princesses, and, tired out by anxiety and his prolonged watch, went to take a bath. But Dubois soon found that he was mistaken, and ran to get Napoleon. He was trembling with anxiety when he burst open the door of the Emperor's room, finding him in his bath, and told him that he feared that he should not be able to save both the mother and the child. "Come, come, Mr. Dubois," exclaimed Napoleon, "don't lose your head; save the mother; think only of the mother.... Imagine she's some shopkeeper's wife in the Rue Saint Denis, that's all I ask of you; and, in any case,—I repeat it,—save the mother.... I shall be with you in a moment." Thereupon he sprang out of his bath, threw himself into a dressing-gown, and hastened to Marie Louise's bedside. He found her in great suffering, and grew very pale. Never on the field of battle had he displayed such emotion; but he tried to hide his anguish, and kissed his wife very gently, reassuring her with tender words. But, unable to control himself, and fearful of adding to her already excessive alarm, he hurriedly went into the next room, and there, listening to every sound, as pale as death, trembling from head to foot, he passed a quarter of an hour in intense anxiety. At last, and with difficulty, the child was born; at first it was supposed to be dead, and for seven minutes it gave no sign of life. The Emperor hastened to Marie Louise and kissed her most tenderly. He thought only of her; he did not give a look to the child. He had decided to care for nothing if only the Empress was saved. A few drops of brandy were poured into the prince's mouth; he was gently slapped all over and wrapped in hot towels, and he came to life with a little cry. Napoleon, wild with joy, kissed him. The thought that he had a son filled him with rapture such as none of his triumphs had given him. "Well, gentlemen," he said, when he went back to his own room, "we have got a fine, healthy boy. We had to urge him a little, to persuade him to come, but there he is at last!" And then he added, with deep emotion: "My dear wife! What courage she has, and how she has suffered! I had rather never have any more children than see her suffer so much again."

All this while the people of Paris were in a state of expectancy, wondering whether the child was to be a boy or a girl. If a boy, he would have a fine-sounding name. According to a decree calling the Eternal City the second city of the French Empire, which had become the capital of a simple department,—the department of the Tiber,—and in accordance with old usages of the Holy German Empire, by which the prince destined to succeed the Germanic Caesar, was called King of the Romans before bearing the title of Emperor, Napoleon's son was to be called the King of Rome.

But would Napoleon have a son? Would Heaven crown his unexampled prosperity with this new favor? That was the subject of conversation everywhere, in the grandest mansions as in the humblest garrets. From daybreak of March 20th the Tuileries garden was crowded with people of all ages and conditions. The courtyards and quays were thronged. In the garden, along the terrace, in front of the palace, a rope was stretched from the grating by the Pont Royal to the Pavilion de l'Horloge. The crowd was so fearful of disturbing the Empress that this frail barrier, this simple rope, was more respected than would have been a lofty wall. The assemblage, which had been growing ever since six o'clock, remained at some distance from the rope, and only spoke in a low voice. They waited in extreme impatience, yet in perfect quiet, for the sound of the cannon of the Invalides. If it was a girl, only twenty-one guns would be fired; if a boy, there would be a hundred and one.... Every window was opened; in the squares and streets everything stood still,—foot-passengers, horses, carriages. The cannon of the Invalides was heard, and the anxious multitudes in deep emotion began to count, at first very low, but gradually louder—one, two, three, four, and so on up to twenty. Then the excitement was tremendous. Twenty-one. Is that all? No; there is the twenty-second, and the rest of the hundred and one are to follow; but there was no more need of counting: Napoleon had a son! At once the enthusiasm of the multitude broke forth like a volcano. Cheers, hats tossed in the air, loud cries of joy, universal, noisy delight, what a sight for the Emperor, as he stood at one of the Empress's windows, gazing in silence at the rapturous crowd! Tears flowed down his cheeks. "Never had his glory brought a tear to his eyes," Constant informs us; "but the happiness of fatherhood softened this soul which the most brilliant victories, the sincerest tributes of public adoration, had left untouched. Indeed, if Napoleon ever had reason to believe in his good fortune, it was on the day when the Archduchess of Austria made him the father of a king, him who had begun as the younger son of a Corsican family. In a few hours the event which France and Europe had been awaiting was a festival in every family."

At half-past ten the aeronaut, Madame Blanchard, set forth in a balloon from the Champ de Mars, to throw down papers announcing the great news to the populace. The telegraph, unimpeded by any mist,—for it was a lovely spring day,—began to work in every direction, and by two o'clock answers had been received from Lyons, Brussels, Antwerp, Brest, and other large towns of the Empire. All of course gave expression to the wildest enthusiasm. In the course of the day Napoleon wrote to his father-in-law, the Emperor of Austria, to inform him of the happy event. "These are very good letters," he said; "I have never written better ones." Officers of the

Emperor's household, pages, and couriers were despatched with letters and messages for the great bodies of the State, for the towns and cities, for the Ambassadors and Ministers of France and other powers. The Empress Josephine was not forgotten; Napoleon sent a page to her in her castle of Navarre, in Normandy.

On the very day of his birth the King of Rome was privately christened at nine o'clock in the evening, in the chapel of the Tuileries, surrounded by his family and the court; the Emperor took his place in the middle of the chapel, on a chair with a prayer desk before it, beneath a canopy. Between the altar and the rail, on a granite base covered with white velvet, had been set a superb vermilion vase which served for the baptismal font. When Napoleon approached to present his son, there was a moment of religious silence, which contrasted with the noisy gayety of the vast crowd which had gathered near the Tuileries from every quarter of the city to see the fireworks and the magnificent illumination. "The houses," Constant says in his Memoirs, "were illuminated voluntarily. Those who try to make out from the outside appearance the real thoughts of a people on occasions like this, observed that the highest stories in the remotest quarters were as bright as the most sumptuous mansions. The public buildings, which are generally most brilliant in contrast with the darkness of the neighboring houses, now were scarcely to be distinguished in the profusion of lights which the rejoicing public had set in every window. The boatmen improvised a festival which lasted nearly all night, and attracted a huge and happy crowd to the banks of the river. The populace who had been through so many emotions, had celebrated so many victories in the last thirty years, displayed as much enthusiasm as if this were the first of its festivities in honor of a happy change in its destiny,"

March 22, Napoleon received in the throne-room at the Tuileries the great bodies of the State.

"Your people," said the President of the Senate, "greet with unanimous applause this new star rising above the horizon of France, whose first ray scatters every shadow of future gloom."

When we think of the end of this matter, and reflect that this King of Rome was to be deprived not merely of his title of Prince Imperial and of King, but of the name of Napoleon and of Bonaparte, that he was destined to be known as Francis, Duke of Reichstadt, and to be buried in the Church of the Capuchins in Vienna, in Austrian uniform, is it possible to repress a sad smile at the simple optimism of courts? In 1811 illusions were universal. "Amid all our triumphs," says General de Ségur, "when even our enemies, at last resigning themselves to their fate, seemed hopeless, or had rallied to the side of our Emperor, what pretext was there for gloom, or for any foreboding of a total or partial eclipse? It was pleasanter to trust in his star, which dazzled us from its height, so many wonders had it wrought!... And how many of us, despite the ever-shifting sky of France, when we see it clear, are tempted to think that no change threatens, and are every day surprised by some sudden storm! Who, when he hears that some apparently healthy person has dropped dead, is not astonished? We were in just such case, when, March 20, 1811, Heaven, feeding our pride to make our humiliation deeper, vouchsafed the conclusion of the fairy-show and completed the illusion with the birth of the King of Rome." Napoleon, in the enjoyment of every happiness and of every triumph, had reached the lofty summit of glory and prosperity; from this he was soon to fall in a swift, giddy flight, at the end of which opened a terrible abyss, full of blood and tears.

XX
THE RECOVERY

Marie Louise made a quick recovery, and her restoration to health delighted both her husband and herself. Her father, the Emperor of Austria, sympathized with their happiness, as is shown by the following letter of his to Napoleon, dated March 27, 1811: "My Dear Brother and Son-in-Law,—It is impossible for me to express in a formal letter of this sort the satisfaction I feel at the good news you have sent to me about my daughter. Your Majesty must already know my keen interest in an event of such importance, both for her and for France, as the birth of a prince, and the fact that this is safely over only augments my joy. May Heaven preserve this new pledge of the ties uniting us! Nothing could be more precious or surer to unite firmly the happy bonds existing between the two Empires."

Napoleon, on the 20th of March, had despatched to Vienna Count Nicolai, who arrived there on the 28th. On that day Francis wrote to his son-in-law: "My Brother and Dear Son-in-Law,—Count Nicolai has this moment delivered to me the two letters of Your Majesty. Since I am unwilling to delay a courier, who is on the point of departure, and will carry to Your Majesty and to the Empress the first expressions of my delight at the happy event, I postpone my formal answer to Your Majesty's invitation to hold his son at the baptismal font, but I hasten to take this opportunity to say that I accept so agreeable a duty.

"All the details which Your Majesty gives me about the birth of the prince arouse my sincerest interest. Your letter proves your kindness towards a wife who returns it with affection as deserved as it is sincere, and for this I hereby express all my gratitude. I thank you, too, for the full details you have written to me. I know the Empress well enough to be sure that, though her sufferings were great, the happiness of satisfying the wishes of Your Majesty and of your people is an ample compensation. I am sure that Your Majesty's presence must have given her strength and her attendant confidence in difficult circumstances. Your Majesty has already so many claims upon my friendship that these details were not needed to induce me to cherish more and more the bonds that unite us, and which I charge my daughter and her son to make even closer."

The health of Marie Louise and of the King of Rome was perfect. In order to respond to the eagerness of the crowd that was ever thick at the doors of the Tuileries in search of news about the Empress and the young prince, it had been decided that one of the chamberlains should be present all day in the first drawing-room of the grand apartment, to receive all who came and report to them the bulletin issued twice a day by the physicians. But soon that was stopped, and there were no more bulletins, the mother and child being perfectly well. April 6, Marie Louise got up and wrote six lines to her father. The 17th she walked on the terrace by the water, amid the applause of the crowd. The next day Prince Clary, whom the Emperor of Austria had sent from Vienna, was received. Napoleon spoke for a long time about the courage, the virtue, the kindness, the excellent education, the exquisite tact, and the perfect dignity of the Empress. "Moreover," he added, "every one admires her." The same day, April 18, the Empress drove in the Bois de Boulogne, and was present at a reception to receive the congratulations of the Diplomatic Body. The churching took place the next day, the 19th, in the chapel of the Tuileries. Prince Rohan officiated.

April 21, Marie Louise and the Emperor went to Saint Cloud, whence, two days later, she wrote to her father the following letter, published by M. von Helfert in German: "My dear Father,—You may imagine my great bliss. I never could have imagined that I could be so happy. My love for my husband has grown, if that is possible, since my son's birth. I cannot think of his tenderness without tears. It would make me love him now, if I had never loved him before, for all his kind qualities. He tells me to speak to you about him. He often asks after you, and says, 'Your father ought to be very happy to have a grandson.' When I tell him that you already love my child, he is delighted. I am going to send you a portrait of the boy. I think you will see how much he looks like the Emperor. He is very strong for only five weeks. When he was born he weighed nine pounds. He is very well, and is in the garden all day long. The Emperor takes the greatest interest in him. He carries him about in his arms, plays with him, and tries to give him his bottle, but he does not succeed. You know from my uncle's letter how much I suffered for twenty-two hours, but my happiness in being a mother makes me forget it. The baptism is set for the month of June. I am sorry that you are too busy to come. Heaven grant that you may come soon! I was glad to hear from Prince Clary that you are well. I hope that God will hear my prayers, and that dear mamma will soon be quite recovered. You may imagine how many questions I asked about you; for talking about you, about your kindness, is my greatest pleasure."

The return of summer induced Napoleon to go to Rambouillet for a few days with the Empress, for the hunt. In this residence, which was simpler and smaller than the other Imperial castles, the Emperor had a taste of domestic life. He reached there May 13, and left on the 22d, to make a trip through Normandy. Marie Louise was so urgent that at last he decided to take her with him. The departments of Calvados and La Manche greeted them with the utmost enthusiasm. The Emperor celebrated his stay at Caen by granting favors and conferring benefits. Many young men of good family were appointed ensigns; one hundred and thirty thousand francs were distributed in charity. From Caen the Emperor and Empress went to Cherbourg to visit the works in the harbor, which had just been dug out of the granite rocks to the depth of fifty feet.

"What delight," General de Ségur writes in his Memoirs concerning this trip, "What delight, what admiration was ours! Great must have been Napoleon's pride, judging from our own satisfaction which we received as old and trusted companions of so great a man!... I saw Cherbourg for the first time. This port, which Louis XVI. had designed simply for one of refuge, had been transformed by Napoleon into one from which an attack could be made. In those days of prodigies, however incapable of amazement I might have been, this roadstead, won by superhuman exertion from the ocean, this vast basin hewn to a depth of fifty feet in the granite, with accommodations for fifty men-of-war, for their building, for their repair, for their armament, filled me with an admiration such as I had felt at the first sight of the grandeur of the Alps."

The day after his arrival at Cherbourg, Napoleon rode out early, visited the heights about the town and inspected different ships. The next day he presided at several meetings and visited the works of the navy-yard; then he went down to the bottom of the basin hewn out of the rock, which was to contain the ships-of-the-line, and to be covered by the water to a depth of fifty-five feet. "During our stay," says M. de Bausset, "the Emperor wanted to breakfast on the dyke, or jetty, which had been begun in the unhappy reign of the most virtuous of kings. I got there before Their Majesties, on a most lovely day, and had everything arranged. The table was set in view of the sea; the English ships were plainly visible on the distant horizon; certainly they were far from suspecting Napoleon's presence. There was still a strong battery on the breakwater to protect the roadstead and the harbor. I do not think that our neighbors would have ventured to salute us at closer quarters, even if they had been better informed. At a signal from the Emperor the squadron lying in the roadstead, consisting of three large ships, under the command of Admiral Tronde, put out under full sail and passed in front of the jetty on which we were…. The Admiral's ship came up as close as it could; the Rear-Admiral came in his gig to fetch Their Majesties and their suite, and took us on board, amid the cheers of the crew, who were all in full uniform. While the Empress and her ladies were resting in the ward-room, Napoleon inspected the rest of the ship. Just when we least expected it, he ordered all the cannon to be fired together; never in my life did I hear such a noise: I thought that the ship was blowing up."

Napoleon and Marie Louise were back at Saint Cloud June 4, 1811. The Empress, then in the full flower of her beauty, and radiant with happiness, had responded to the profuse manifestations of public enthusiasm by her gracious reception of the authorities and the people of the departments.

It would be hard to imagine all the homage paid at this time to the Imperial pair. Dithyrambs upon the birth of the King of Rome were composed in every language of Europe except the English. There was a real avalanche of poems, odes, epistles; in less than a week the Emperor received more than two thousand of these tributes. Probably he read very few of these extravagant compositions, which were crammed panegyrics and allegories of the Greek mythology. The sum of one hundred thousand francs was divided among the authors of these official poems. "Of all these memorials, the most curious that flattery ever elevated," Madame Durand writes, "is a collection of French and Latin verses, entitled, 'The Marriage and the Birth,' which was printed at the Imperial press, and appointed by the University to be given as a prize to the pupils of the four grammar schools of Paris, and of those in the provinces, thereby assuring a ready sale. In this heap of trash figures the names of all the authors who, when the giant had fallen, insulted his remains and burned their incense before the new deity who took his place.

> "As Béranger said about those poets:—
> "They are, like the confectioners,
> Friends of every baptism."

The *Moniteur*, in its number of June 9, 1811, the day of the King of Rome's baptism, spoke as follows: "The happy event which, at the moment of writing these lines, is throughout this vast Empire the object of the thanksgivings which a great people can offer to Heaven; which inspire songs of happiness in our temples, our public places, our peaceful cities, our fertile fields, and in the camps of our invincible warriors; which fulfils at once the wishes of the people for the happiness of their Sovereign, and those of the Sovereign for the firm establishment of the institutions he has consecrated to the prosperity of his people, ought more than any other to kindle the fervor of our poets and fill them with a lively and noble inspiration. Yet no one of them has been able to disguise the difficulty of his task; all have recognized that their greatest efforts would be required, not only to rise to the height of a subject of which its greatness is the first peril, but even to attune their lyre to the pitch of the enthusiasm that fires us, an enthusiasm of which the mighty voice, filling all France and heard in the remotest corner of Europe, is itself the grandest hymn of poetry and the most harmonious music. But no such obstacle has discouraged their muse; admiration, gratitude, love, furnish a happy inspiration, and our poets have felt it; they have faithfully transcribed the language of the populace in the language ascribed to the gods."

In proof of this we quote some of the verses inserted in the official organ:—

> "Sion, rejoice! The voice of the prophets
> Announces again the days of the Eternal One.
> Before a young child, dear hope of Israel,
> The cedars of Lebanon will bow their heads.
> Of the oppressed he will become the support:
> He will punish crime, and will brand vice;
> His words will be the voice of justice,
> And the Spirit of the Lord will march before him."

That is the Biblical style, which was used freely a few years later to celebrate the baptism of the Duke of Bordeaux. Mythology, too, was called in:—

> "Do you see the leopard, weary of carnage,
> Sated with blood, towards his savage lair
> Run roaring?
> Seized by an invincible, unknown terror,
> He announces his death, and flees at the sight
> Of a new-born Alcides."

The poet Millevoye exclaimed:—

> "With your head encircled with laurel and flowers,
> Come to reopen henceforth the progress of the year,
> Month long since consecrated to the lover of Venus!
> Triumph, and seize again thy faded garland,
> Which the friend of Egeria placed
> On the double brow of Janus."

M. Le Sur spoke about the Tiber in these terms:—

> "The Tiber, too long drowsing on its urn,
> Lets grow in its bosom the silent reed.
> It awakens at the resonant noise of brass,
> And with a proud wave washing its shore'

> Of its old heritage
> It offers the remains to the Young Sovereign."

A poet who was destined to become famous, and at that time was a scholar in the Lycée Napoléon, Casimir Delavigne, tried his muse, a youthful muse, according to the *Moniteur*:—

> "Receive, royal child, the vows of the country.
> May thy father's laurel shadow thy cradle!
> May glory and the arts, adorning thy life,
> Consecrate forever the happiest reign!
> Child beloved of heaven, awaited by the earth,
> Promised to posterity,
> May thou, under the eyes of thy August father,
> Grow to immortality!"

A professor famous for his Latin verses, M. Lemaire, was so fired by his lyrical enthusiasm that he compared Marie Louise to another Mary, the Queen of Heaven. Of the two queens,—one, he said, rules in Heaven; the other on earth:—

"Haec coelo regina micat; micat altera terris."

XXI
THE BAPTISM

The baptism of the King of Rome was celebrated with great pomp, Sunday, June 7, 1811, at Notre Dame. The festivities began the evening before, when, at seven o'clock, Napoleon and Marie Louise and their son arrived from Saint Cloud with a grand retinue. The courtyard of the palace, the garden, and the terraces were filled with applauding spectators. Free performances were given at all the theatres, at which songs referring to the event were loudly cheered. Paris was illuminated, and in all the public places food was given away to the populace. Wine flowed in the fountains, and everywhere was drunk the health of the young king and of his happy parents.

The baptism took place at seven o'clock the next evening; at two in the afternoon troops of the line and the Imperial Guard formed a double row from the Tuileries to Notre Dame. Many public buildings and private houses were decorated with tapestry, leaves, and designs.

At four the Senate started from the Luxembourg, the Council of State from the Tuileries, the Court of Appeal, the Court of Accounts, the Council of the University, from their respective places of meeting. From the Hôtel de Ville started the Prefect of the Seine, the Mayors and the Municipal Council of Paris, the Mayors and Deputies of forty-nine more or less important cities of the Empire. It was said that the Mayor of Rome and the Mayor of Hamburg happened to be placed side by side, and greeted one another with, "Good day, neighbor!"

Before the façade of Notre Dame had been built a large, tent-shaped portal, supported by columns and decorated with draperies and garlands. The interior of the Cathedral was brilliantly lit, and adorned with flags. The seats in the choir to the right had been reserved for foreign princes; those to the left, for the Diplomatic Body; the outer edge, for the wives of the ministers of the high crown officers, as well as for the households of the Imperial family; the sanctuary, for the twenty cardinals, and the hundred archbishops and bishops; the choir, for the Senate, the Council of State, the Mayors and Deputies of the forty-nine cities; the upper part of the nave, for the civil and military authorities; the rest of the nave, and the triforiums, for invited guests.

At five o'clock the mounted chasseurs of the Guard, who were at the head of the procession, began to move. But let us rather yield to the *Moniteur*, which is always lyrical and enthusiastic, whatever the Prince, imperial or royal, who is to be baptized: "At half-past five," says the official organ, "the cannon, which had been firing at a certain distance ever since the evening before, announced the departure of Their Majesties from the Palace of the Tuileries, accompanied by their suite in the order prescribed by the programme. For the first time the public was able to behold the August infant whose royal name was to be consecrated under the auspices of religion. The effect that this sight produced upon every soul defies description. 'Long live the King of Rome!' was the uninterrupted acclamation all along the route. Their Majesties were greeted in the same way; their August names united in every mouth, with accents of love, respect, and gratitude. They seemed to appreciate this double homage, which was, in fact, but one alone, and they deigned to express their feeling in the most touching way to the attendant multitude."

As the legendary grandmother says in Béranger's *Memories of the People*, the weather was perfect, the Emperor radiant:—

> "I, a poor woman,
> Being in Paris one day,
> Saw him with his court;
> He was going to Notre Dame—
> All hearts were happy;
> Every one admired the procession.
> Every one said: What fine weather!
> Heaven is always favorable to him.
> His smile was very gentle;
> God had made him father of a son."

And the little villagers all sing in chorus:—

> "What a great day for you, grandmother!
> What a great day for you!"

At a little before seven the Imperial procession reached Notre Dame. The sovereigns were met at the door by the Cardinal Grand Almoner, who gave them holy water. Then the procession advanced in the following order: ushers, heralds-at-arms, the Chief Herald, the pages, the aides, the orderly officers on duty, the masters of ceremonies, the prefects of the Palace on duty, the officers of the King of Rome, the Emperor's equerries, ordinary and extraordinary, in attendance, the chamberlains, ordinary and extraordinary, in attendance, the equerries of the day, the chamberlains of the day, the First Equerry, the grand eagles of the Legion of Honor, the high officers of the Empire, the ministers, the High Chamberlain, the First Equerry, and the Grand Master of Ceremonies;—the various objects to be used, to wit: the Prince's candle, carried by the Princess of Neufchâtel; the chrisom cloth, by the Princess Aldobrandini; the saltcellar, by the Countess of Beauvau;—then the objects belonging to the godfather and godmother, to wit: the basin, carried by the Duchess of Alborg; the ewer, by the Countess Vilain XIV.; the towel, by the Duchess of Dalmatia;—in front of the King of Rome, to the right, the Grand Duke of Würzburg, representing the Emperor of Austria, godfather; to the left, the mother of Napoleon, godmother, and Queen Hortense, representing the Queen of Naples, the second godmother; the King of Rome, carried by his governess, in a coat of silver tissue embroidered with ermine, with his two assistant governesses and nurse on each side (the train of his coat was carried by Marshal, the Duke of Valmy); the Empress, beneath a canopy upheld by canons, her First Equerry holding Her Majesty's train; the lady-in-waiting and tirewoman, the Knight of Honor and the First Almoner, to the right and left;—behind the canopy Princess Pauline, an officer of her household carrying her train; the ladies of the Palace; Cambacérès, Duke of Parma, Archchancellor of the Empire; Marshal Berthier, Prince of Neufchâtel and of Wagram, Vice-Constable; Talleyrand, Prince of Benevento, Vice Grand Elector; Prince Borghese, Duke of Guastalla; Prince Eugene, Viceroy of Italy; the Hereditary Grand Duke of Frankfort; Prince Joseph Napoleon, King of Spain; Prince Jerome Napoleon, King of Westphalia;—the Emperor under a canopy, upheld by canons: to the right and left of the canopy, his aides; behind the canopy the Colonel commanding the Guard on duty, the Grand Marshal of the Palace, and the First Almoner; the ladies-in-waiting of the Princesses, the ladies and officers of Their Imperial Highnesses on duty.

When the procession had taken their places according to their rank, the Grand Almoner intoned the *Veni Creator*, and the governess having carried the child to the railing of the choir, he went through the preliminary rites, and then took place the baptism. As soon as the Imperial child had been baptized, the governess placed him in the hands of the Empress; the First Herald-at-Arms advanced to the middle of the choir and called out three times, "Long live the King of Rome!" Cheers and applause, which till that moment had been restrained by the sanctity of the ceremony and the solemnity of the place, then broke forth on all sides. While they lasted, Marie Louise stood with the child in her arms; the Emperor then took him and held him aloft, that all might see him.

Thiers thus comments in a page of real eloquence on this imposing spectacle: "What a solemn mystery surrounds human life! What a painful surprise it would have been, if beyond this scene of power and greatness, one could have seen the ruin, the blood, the flames of Moscow, the ice of the Beresina and Leipsic, Fontainebleau, Elba, Saint Helena, and finally the death of this prince at the age of twenty, in exile, without one of the crowns he wore that day upon his head, and the many revolutions once more to raise his family after overthrowing it! What a blessing that the future is hidden from man! But what a stumbling-block for his prudence, charged to conjecture the morrow and to guard against it with all one's wisdom."

When the governess had again taken the Prince, she courtesied to the Emperor, and the King of Rome, with his retinue, left the church, to be taken to the Archbishop's, whence he returned to the Tuileries. Then the Grand Almoner intoned the *Te Deum*, which, was performed by the choir, and followed by the *Domine, fac salvum imperatorem*. The Emperor and the Empress were conducted with the same ceremonies as at their entrance, to the church door, where they got into their carriage amid the cheers of the crowd, and drove to the entertainment at the Hôtel de Ville.

"The people of Paris admitted to this festivity," says Thiers, "were able to see Napoleon at table, his crown on his head, surrounded by the kings of his family and a number of foreign princes, eating in public, like the old Germanic Emperors, the successors of the Emperors of the West. The Parisians applauded in their delight at this brilliant spectacle, imagining that durability was united with grandeur and with glory! They did well to rejoice, for these joys were the last of the reign. Henceforth our story is but one long lamentation."

Napoleon and Marie Louise reached the Hôtel de Ville at eight in the evening. The Prefect of the Seine, after welcoming them with an address, led them to the rooms prepared for them, and the Emperor received four sets of presentations. The Grand Marshal of the Palace announced that dinner was ready. The Imperial banquet was thus arranged: in the middle of the table, the Emperor; on his left, the Empress, the Queen of Holland, Princess Borghese, the Grand Duke of Würzburg, the Grand Duke of Frankfort; on his right, his mother, the King of Spain, the King of Westphalia, Prince Borghese, the Viceroy of Italy. The table was on a dais. A canopy overhung the chairs of the Emperor and Empress. The ladies of the Palace and the Imperial retinue sat below the platform, opposite the table, The officers of the Emperor's household waited on the table. The hall was decorated with the coats-of-arms of the forty-nine chosen cities, Paris, Rome, and Amsterdam being the first; the rest were in alphabetical order. After the dinner, the sovereigns went into the record-room, where a concert was given, in which was sung a cantata, called "Ossian's Song," with words by Arnault, and music by Méhul. Then, after talking to a number of people in the throne-room, Napoleon and Louise went into the garden which had been constructed about the courtyard of the Hôtel de Ville, where the Tiber was represented by abundant streams of cool water. They left at eleven, and thereupon was opened a ball which lasted till daybreak. In the morning poor young girls, with dowries given by the city, had been married to soldiers in every arrondissement. The whole city was alive with enthusiasm. Food had been given away on the Champs Élysées, there had been sports in the square of Marigny, tournaments, greased poles, public balls, balloon ascension, fireworks, a general illumination, and everything of the sort for the amusement of the populace.

On the 9th of June there were grand festivities in the large towns of the Empire, in honor of the baptism of the King of Rome. At Antwerp all the arts and trades contributed to making six chariots, which made an imposing procession. The first represented France crowned by Immortality; the second, the marriage of the Emperor and Empress; the third, the birth of the King of Rome; the fourth, his cradle; the fifth, Religion, Innocence, and Charity praying Heaven for a long life to the sovereigns and their son; the sixth, France representing the young Prince as King to the city of Rome. This procession of chariots was preceded by the giant, the whale, the frigate, the car of Neptune, that of Europe, and other figures called in their language *den grooten hommegang*.

At Rome, the city of the Prince, festivities began in the night of June 8, being announced by guns of the fleet of Civita Vecchia, which had sailed up the Tiber, all beautifully decorated. The Capitol, the Forum, the Coliseum, the arches of Septimius and Constantine, the temples of Concord, of Peace, of Antoninus, and Fausta, the Column of Jupiter Stator, were all brilliantly illuminated. In the morning of the 9th all the authorities went to Saint Peter's to hear the *Te Deum* sung before an immense multitude. In the course of the day there was a horse-race, and in the evening the dome of Saint Peter's and the Colonnade were illuminated, and there were fireworks at the Castle of Saint Angelo. The Rome of the Cæsars and the Popes, the Eternal City, celebrated the baptismal day of its young King with great splendor.

XXII
SAINT CLOUD AND TRIANON

The Emperor had determined that there could not be too much rejoicing at his son's baptism; consequently he gave an entertainment himself, June 23,1811, in the palace and park of Saint Cloud. The palace, with its magnificent halls, its drawing-rooms of Mars, Venus, Truth, Mercury, and Aurora, its Gallery of Apollo, and Room of Diana, adorned with Mignard's frescoes; the park, with its fine trees, its wonderful stretches, its greensward, and abundant flowers; the two grand views from the upper windows, one towards Paris, the other towards the garden; the waterfalls, set in a tasteful frame, and rushing down step by step, breaking into a white foam, sparkling in the sunlight or with the reflection of a thousand torches, formed a marvellous setting for a festival both by night and by day. More than three hundred thousand persons went to Saint Cloud; they began to arrive in the morning, and filled every avenue, covered every bit of rising ground. Food was publicly distributed; the fountains ran wine. Games and sports of all kinds were played, and the Imperial Guard gave an open-air banquet to the garrison of Paris.

At six in the evening Napoleon and Marie Louise drove in an open barouche through the park, without guard or escort, to the great delight of the applauding multitude. The orange house, which had been stripped of its contents for the decoration of the front of the palace, was adorned with stuffs of fine colors. Temples and kiosks had been set up in the shrubbery. At nightfall six illuminated launches, manned by sailors of the Imperial Guard, performed various evolutions and discharged fireworks, which made a brilliant show upon the river. Meanwhile the illuminations began throughout the park, along the terraces, and the amphitheatre, and in the palace. It was a most fairy-like sight; the large cascade with its half-lying statues of the Seine and the Loire; the lower cascade beneath; the fountain rising twenty-seven metres; the large square basin with the ten little shell-shaped basins and the nine fountains spurting from gilded masques; the green lawns, the flower-beds, the shrubbery,—all lit up by the blazing fireworks. At nine o'clock Madame Blanchard went up in a balloon, discharging fireworks from the car, which formed a starlike crown set at a great height; she seemed like a magician in a fiery chariot. Fireworks were then set off by the artillery of the Imperial Guard from the middle of the Plain of Boulogne; they were visible from Paris as from Saint Cloud, and from all the hills bordering the Seine from Calvaire to Meudon. Next to the row of columns opened the illuminated garden, with waterfalls, trees, and porticoes, forming a most brilliant spectacle. The Emperor and Empress walked through the park, and Marie Louise was continually reminded of her beloved Austria, of Schoenbrunn, of the Burg, of Laxenburg, by the wonderful panorama. There were many bands stationed among the trees, playing waltzes, and dancers from the opera, dressed as German shepherds and shepherdesses, were dancing. An interlude, "The Village Festival," words by Étienne, set to music by Nicolo, was given in the open air, on the grass. When the Empress came to a column supporting a basket of flowers, a dove alit at her feet and offered her an ingenious motto.

The weather had been tolerably pleasant all day; but it became stormy in the evening; the air grew heavy: there could be seen neither moon nor stars. There had just been illuminated, opposite the grand cascade, a model of the palace intended for the King of Rome,—this palace the Emperor meant to build on the high ground of Chaillot, with the Bois de Boulogne for its park,—when suddenly the storm that had been slowly gathering burst upon the heads of the vast crowd in the park. There were there deputations from all the large towns of the vast empire which reached from Cuxhaven to Rome; the men in costly velvet coats, the women in dresses of embroidered silk. The Emperor at the moment happened to be talking in the doorway between the drawing-room and the garden; near him was the Mayor of Lyons, to whom he said, "I am going to benefit your manufactures." Then he remained standing in the doorway. The courtiers received the shower with bare heads and smiling faces. Possibly some might have said that the rain of Saint Cloud, like the rain of Marly, did not wet.

Of course no one had an umbrella. Prince Aldobrandini, the Empress's First Equerry, managed to procure one, which he held over her. Count Rémusat found another, and for an hour he was coming and going, between the park and the palace, to bring as many ladies as possible under shelter. The entertainment could not go on; every one was wet through. The musicians could not play on their dripping instruments. The Emperor and the Empress withdrew at eleven, and both the court and the people had gloomy memories of this festivity which began so well and ended so badly. Superstitious and ill-disposed persons fancied that they saw an evil omen in this; they recalled the disastrous ball at the Austrian Embassy, and said that the storm broke just at the very moment when the palace of the King of Rome was illuminated. But what difference could a simple shower make to a people accustomed to streams of blood?

August 15, 1811, there was a brilliant celebration at Saint Cloud and Paris, as well as throughout the Empire, of the festival of the great and the small Napoleon. August 25 was the birthday of the Empress Marie Louise, and this was celebrated at the two Trianons, which were full of memories of Louis XIV. and of Marie Antoinette. The Grand Trianon, graceful and majestic, though but a single story high, and the Little Trianon, charming, though but a simple small square, of no regal aspect, were enchanted palaces on Marie Louise's birthday. The two buildings, the belvedere, the little lakes, the island and Temple of Love, the village, the octagonal pavilion, the theatre, were all aglow. It seemed as if Marie Antoinette were alive again, and to the Empress Delille's lines could have applied as well as to the Queen:—

> "Like its August and youthful deity,
> Trianon combines grace with majesty:
> For her it adorns itself, is by her adorned."

It was only twenty-two years since Marie Antoinette had been there, and many of the lords and ladies who adorned Napoleon's court as they had adorned that of Louis XVI. could not see without emotion this fairy-like recall of the brilliant days of the old régime. The French nobility had an opportunity to make many reflections on revisiting the Little Trianon which aroused many memories. It was less than eighteen years since there had perished on the scaffold the charming sovereign who had been the idol, the goddess, of this little temple; and now new festivities were beginning; another Austrian archduchess occupied the place of the martyred Queen. There was the Swiss village, of which Louis XVI. had been the miller, the Count of Provence the schoolmaster, the Count of Artois the gamekeeper, the village with its merry mill, the dairy where the cream filled porphyry vessels on marble tables, the laundry where the clothes were beaten with ebony sticks, the granary to which led mahogany ladders, the sheep-house where the sheep were shorn with golden shears. They saw once more the grass sprinkled with flowers, the clear water, the trees of all colors from dark green to cherry-red; larches and pink acacias, cedars of Lebanon, sophoras from China, poplars from Athens, and they said that Time, which shatters a sceptre, respects a shrub. Everything else had changed; the garden was still the same.

All day long the gloomy solitude of Versailles had been crowded anew as if by magic. A countless multitude thronged its long, wide avenues, which had been almost deserted since October, 1789. The festivities of the former monarchy appeared to have begun again. At three in the afternoon a rather heavy shower had fallen, and it seemed as if the day and evening would end gloomily; but on the contrary, the rain was but brief and only freshened the air, and made the festival pleasanter. The setting sun lit up the great king's town, and at night many-colored lamps decorated the Grand Trianon. Six hundred women in rich dresses, and ablaze with jewelry, gathered in the gallery of that palace. The Empress spoke to many of them, and it was noticed how well she had become acquainted with French society, although she had been in the country but fifteen months; and with what kindness and dignity she addressed them.

Then they went to the theatre of the Little Trianon, a perfect jewel, a gem, with its two Ionic columns, its pediment in which Love is holding a lyre and a laurel wreath; and its ceiling representing Olympus, the work of Lagrenée; and its curtain, on which are two nymphs supporting Marie Antoinette's coat-of-arms. It was there that, August 19, 1785, the Queen played Rosina, in "The Barber of Seville," and that the Count of Artois uttered those ominous words as Figaro, "I try to laugh at everything, lest I should have to weep at everything." Before Napoleon and Marie Louise there was given a piece composed for the occasion by Alissan de Chazet: it was called "The Gardener of Schoenbrunn." After it was a pretty ballet given by the dancers of the Opera.

When this was over, the Emperor and Empress walked through the gardens of the Little Trianon, which were illuminated. Napoleon, with his hat in his hand, gave his arm to Marie Louise. They visited the island and the marble Temple of Love, in which is Bouchardon's statue of Love carving his bow into the club of Hercules. There was soft music from concealed performers, which seemed to rise from the bottom of the lake, on which floated illuminated boats full of children disguised as cupids. Then they walked further in the garden, and watched a *tableau vivant*, representing Flemish peasants. This was succeeded by groups representing the people of the different provinces of the Empire in their national dress, from the Tiber to the North Sea. The celebration ended with a supper in the gallery of the Grand Trianon. All those who had known the place in the old régime agreed that the festival was a perfect success; and Marie Louise, who was becoming more and more at home in France, was sure that her birthday had never been celebrated with anything like such magnificence.

XXIII
THE TRIP TO HOLLAND

A short time after Wagram Napoleon had been heard, in a levee at which his generals were present, to lament the bloody campaigns in which he always lost some of his early companions. "I have been a soldier long enough," he went on; "it's time for me to be a king." During 1811 he seemed faithful to this new programme. The soldier had become a monarch, and the hero of so many battles seemed to be desirous of the glories of peace. He determined to make a trip in Belgium and Holland and along the banks of the Rhine, where he should see for himself what the happiness of the people required. The Empress made the journey with him, but Napoleon started from Compiègne without her, September 19; she was to join him on the 30th at Antwerp. At this time she was so attached to him that she could not endure a separation of only a few days, and she wrote to her father: "My husband has left to-night to go to the island of Walcheren, which has the worst climate in the world, so that I could not go with him, for which I am extremely sorry." While the Emperor was visiting Boulogne, Ostend, and Flushing, the Queen made her way, with a magnificent court, to Belgium. She left Compiègne, September 22, and took up her residence at the castle at Laeken, near Brussels. She often visited the Belgian capital, which then was only the chief town of a French department,—the department of the Dyle. Napoleon made a great point of her appearing in all splendor in the provinces which had previously been governed by the house of Austria. She went to the theatre, where she was warmly greeted, and purchased a hundred and fifty thousand francs' worth of lace to revive the manufactures of the city. September 30 she joined her husband at Antwerp. The *Moniteur* thus spoke of the way the Emperor had transformed this city: "Antwerp may be considered as a fortress of the rank of Metz and Strasbourg. The work which has been done there is enormous. On the left bank of the Scheldt, where two years ago there was only a redoubt, there has risen a city twelve thousand feet long, with eight bastions.... The view from the dockyard is unparalleled; twenty-one men-of-war, eight of them three-deckers, are building. The arsenal is fully provided with provisions of all sorts brought down the Rhine and the Meuse.

"Seven years ago," continues the *Moniteur*, "there was not a single quay in Antwerp, and the houses came down to the river's edge. To-day, in the place of these houses, are superb quays, of service to the commerce and to the defence of the place. Six years ago there was no basin, but only a few canals where boats drawing ten or twelve feet could scarcely enter. To-day there is a basin twenty-six feet deep at the bank, able to hold ships-of-the-line, with a lock for the admission of ships carrying a hundred and twenty guns."

The formal entrance into Amsterdam took place October 9, 1811. The former capital of Holland was merely the chief town of a French department,—the department of the Zuyder Zee. The Dutch were suffering a good deal from the Embargo, and sorely missed King Louis Bonaparte, who had in vain tried to alleviate their sufferings. When they came under the dominion of the Emperor, he had appointed Lebrun, Duke of Piacenza, their governor general. Of him, Count Beugnot says in his Memoirs, "He was doubtless a superior man, but he found it easier to translate Homer and Tasso, and to treat with wonderful ease the most difficult questions of political economy, than to console a Dutchman for the loss of ten florins."

The discontent of the Dutch only strengthened Napoleon's desire to please and win them. "It seemed at that time," M. Beugnot goes on, "as if Heaven had given him every means of securing happiness. A son had just been born to him, whose future the poets were justified in foretelling in their own way. The child who inspired the Mantuan poet with the idyl, or rather with the magnificent prophecy, *Sicelides Musae*, etc., was but an humble creature by the side of this infant, who to the most impressive pride of race added enormous, newly acquired glory, such as the world had never seen." The happy Emperor fancied that by showing himself with the mother of the King of Rome to the Dutch and Germans, he should silence their complaints, wipe out their memories of national independence, and arouse an enthusiasm that would make them forget their sufferings and losses. Their welcome was of a sort to confirm him in this belief. The peaceful populace of Amsterdam forgot their usual phlegm, and cheered the mighty monarch and his young wife. The Empress entered the city in a gilded carriage with glass sides, and she was met by a guard of honor composed of young men belonging to the first families of Holland. The Emperor followed on horseback, surrounded by a brilliant staff. Their stay at Amsterdam was marked by extraordinary pomp; the company of the Théâtre Français was brought thither from Paris, and Talma appeared as Bayard and as Orosmane. The court made a stay of a fortnight, the Emperor making short excursions to Helder, one of his creations, to Texel, and to the dykes of Medemblik, which protect the country against the Zuyder Zee.

General de Ségur, who went on the journey, thus describes it: "It might naturally be supposed, that in going through Holland, after the last two attempted assassinations, Napoleon would have taken precautions against such frequent attacks; but, far from it, he was full of confidence, and went about alone among these worst victims of the continental system, mingling every day with the dense crowd that gathered about him. His sole thought was to study their needs, their manners, and habits, anxious to see for himself and trusting thoroughly in them. These northern people hide warm hearts beneath a cold exterior; they are impressed by greatness, and give it their confidence. Their feelings are slow, but for that reason surer when once aroused. The Emperor's enormous fame had preceded him; and the appearance among them of this genius, all fire and flame, who had come, as he said, to adopt them, warmed their phlegmatic nature. They were at once filled with admiration; his presence, his trust in them, his consoling and encouraging words, the good works at once begun by his active and able administration, filled them with enthusiasm."

During the three days of the Emperor's absence Marie Louise visited the neighborhood of Amsterdam. She went to the village of Broek, which lies a league from the port, on the shores of a little basin surrounded with flowers and grass, and is in communication with the Zuyder Zee by means of a small canal. This village is famous as a perfect model of the attractive luxury and the over-zealous neatness of the Dutch. It is of a circular shape. The houses, of wood and one story high, are built around and upon a lake, and are decorated outside with frescoes. Through the window-glass, which is remarkably clear, it is easy to see the curtains of Chinese figured silk or of Indian stuff. Within the houses are large Gothic sideboards, full of costly Japanese porcelain. There are no signs of use or of wear upon the furniture; every house looks as if it were the house of the Sleeping Beauty. There are no barns, or stables, or granaries, or kitchens. Everything connected with animals is banished from this fairy-like enclosure. Posts at the ends of every street bar the way against carriages. The pavement is in mosaic, and is covered with a fine sand, on which are designs of flowers. The inhabitants carry their sense of neatness so far that they compel every visitor to take off his shoes and put on slippers on entering a house. One day, when the Emperor Joseph II. happened to appear in a pair of boots before one of these curious houses, he was told that he would have to take them off before he could go in. "I am the Emperor," he said. "Well, if you were the burgomaster of Amsterdam, you couldn't come in with boots on," was the reply. Another time Hortense, then Queen of Holland, was not allowed to enter one of the houses, and King Louis approved, because the Queen had not sent word that she was coming.

When Marie Louise visited this famous village, the burgomaster, in view of the importance of the occasion, consented to break the rigid rules and to permit the Imperial carriage to drive over the mosaic pavement to his house, where he presented his respects to the Empress. At this house, as in every one in the village, there are two doors,—one for daily use, the other opened only for baptisms, marriages, and funerals. This door, which is called the fatal door, opens into a room which is always kept shut except on these three occasions. "The Empress," says M. de Bausset, "asked to have the fatal door opened. We crossed the threshold with gratified vanity, in the presence of many inhabitants, who feared to follow us, but who were almost tempted to admire the ease and courage with which we went in and out. After visiting, admiring, and praising everything, we left these worthy people delighted with the touching graces and amiable kindness of their young sovereign."

The Emperor and Empress visited Saardam, where Peter the Great spent ten months as a workman, to study shipbuilding. Napoleon fell into meditation before the hut of the famous Czar, as he had done before the tomb of Frederick the Great. "That is the noblest monument in Holland!" he said; and in memory of Peter the Great he ordered Saardam to be made a city.

Napoleon and Marie Louise also spent a few hours at Harlem, a half-Gothic, half-Japanese town, celebrated by the passion of its inhabitants for flowers, especially for tulips. October 26, they arrived at Rotterdam, at Loo on the 27th, and spent the night of the 28th at The Hague, whence they went to visit the banks of the Rhine. The Emperor carried away with him a most favorable impression of the Dutch, whose seriousness, morality, love of order, and industry had continually struck him, so that he shared his brother Louis's partiality for a nation as interesting in the present as in the past.

November 2, Napoleon and his wife reached Düsseldorf. This pretty town, which is picturesquely placed at the junction of the Düssel with the Rhine, was at that time the capital of the Grand Duchy of Berg, and had been under the rule of Murat before he was appointed King of Naples; on this visit the Emperor assigned it to the oldest son of Louis Bonaparte. Count Beugnot was then ruling the principality, which contained less than a million inhabitants. He it was who said in his curious and witty Memoirs: "How easy it would have been to secure the allegiance of the Germans, who are unable to withstand the attraction of military glory, for whom an oath of allegiance is a mere nothing, and who felt for France an affection which we cruelly drove out of them!... Germany, which always admires the marvellous, long preserved its admiration for the Emperor. At that time this was so general, that a breath would have blown over the Prussian monarchy, which neither the armies nor the memories of the great Frederick, together with the invincible legion of the successor of Peter the Great, could defend."

At Düsseldorf, Napoleon, in accordance with his usual custom, received all the authorities, civil and military, as well as representatives of all sects. Among these last was an old white-bearded rabbi a hundred years old, who was so anxious to see the Emperor that he had himself carried to the reception. He entered, supported on one side by the parish priest, on the other, by the Protestant clergyman. This union of the three creeds in homage to their sovereign did not displease the Emperor, strange as it was. Count Beugnot's Memoirs must be consulted for a full account of the activity, the interest in details, the minuteness of the administrative investigations which, at Düsseldorf as everywhere else, characterized Napoleon in these laborious journeys, on which, under pretext of seeking distraction, he kept himself in almost as active movement as if he were at war. The Count who once played whist at Düsseldorf with Marie Louise for his partner, against the Duchess of Montebello and the Prince of Neufchâtel, says in speaking of the occasion: "As often happens, the game was carelessly played; all watched the cards only with their eyes, and gave their attention to what was going forward about the table, to which the Emperor came every few minutes to say a few pleasant words to the Empress or to joke with the Prince of Neufchâtel and me. I was too busy, both during the dinner and while we were playing, to make any study of the Empress's tastes or to form from them a judgment about her character. The journey had been long; she seemed tired and out of sorts. She answered the Emperor only in monosyllables, and the other by a somewhat monotonous nod of the head. I may be mistaken, but I am inclined to believe that Her Majesty is not free from the awe which her August husband inspires in all who approach him."

After resting for two days at Düsseldorf, Napoleon and Marie Louise went on to Cologne, when they visited the Chapel of the Eleven Thousand Virgins, and a grand *Te Deum* was sung in the famous Cathedral, They returned by Liège, Givet, Mézières, and Compiègne, reaching Saint Cloud after an absence of nearly three months, — the longest visit that the Emperor had made in the provinces of either the old or the new France. Everywhere he had met with the expression of two distinct but somewhat different sentiments: for the Empress, an affectionate respect; for himself, the sort of violent sensation that a man who is a living wonder always produces.

XXIV
NAPOLEON AT THE HEIGHT OF HIS POWER

At the beginning of 1812 Napoleon had reached the height of his power. Before we watch his decline, it may be well to consider him at the summit of his fortune, in the fulness of his force, might, and glory. In his career there were two distinctly marked periods,—the democratic and the aristocratic. In the early days of the Empire the first one had not yet come to an end. The coins of that time still bore the stamp, "French Republic. Napoleon Emperor." He himself resembled Caesar rather than Charlemagne: he granted no hereditary titles, and associated with but few of the émigrés; he was still, in many ways, a man of the Revolution. In 1812, on the other hand, he had given his authority a sort of feudal character, and revived many points of resemblance with the Carlovingian epoch. Charlemagne had become his model, his ideal. The saviour of the Convention, the friend of the young Robespierre, was busily introducing much of the imperial and military splendor of the Middle Ages. The continental sovereigns treated him with so much consideration that he regarded himself as their superior rather than as an equal. He called them his brothers; but he thought that he was more than a brother—something like the head of a family of kings. The Kings of Bavaria, of Würtemberg, of Saxony, of Spain, of Naples, of Westphalia, who all owed their crowns to him, were indeed his subordinates. As the Princes of the Confederation of the Rhine, the vassals of their protector, they despatched their contingents to him with as much zeal and punctuality as if they had been plain prefects of the Empire.

The émigrés crowded the drawing-rooms of the Tuileries. One might have thought one's self at Coblenz. Those men who belonged to the old régime were especially appreciated. The one of his aides-de-camp who most pleased the Emperor was perhaps the Count of Narbonne, knight of honor of one of the daughters of Louis XV., Minister of War under Louis XVI. The most rigid, the most precise etiquette prevailed in the Imperial residences. The high dignitaries and marshals concealed their plebeian names under pompous titles of princes and dukes. Madame de Mailly, the widow of a marshal of the royal period, had been admitted to the rank and privileges of the wives of the grand officers of the crown, and had figured as a marshal's widow, at the reception of January 1, 1811. The court of Versailles appeared to have revived.

Napoleon preferred to derive his power from divine right than from the will of the nation. "He was much struck," Metternich says in his Memoirs, "by the idea of ascribing the origin of supreme power to divine choice. One day at Compiègne, soon after his marriage, he said to me, 'I notice that when the Empress writes to her father, she addresses him as His Holy Imperial Highness. Is that your usual way?' I told him he was so addressed from the tradition of the old Germanic Empire, and because he also wore the apostolic crown of Hungary. Napoleon then said with some solemnity, 'It is a noble and excellent custom. Power derives from God, and that is the only way it can be secure from human assault. Some time or other I shall adopt the same title.'"

At about the same time, in conversation with M. Molé about the houses building in Paris, on being asked when he intended to give his attention to the Church of the Madeleine, the Emperor said, "Well, what is expected of me?" M. Molé told him that he had heard that it was intended for a Temple of Glory. "That's what people think, I know," said Napoleon; "but I mean it for a memorial in expiation of the murder of Louis XVI." He said to Metternich: "When I was young I favored the Revolution out of ignorance and ambition. When I came to the age of reason I followed its counsels and my own instinct, and crushed the Revolution." At another time he said: "The French throne was empty. Louis XVI. had not been able to hold it. If I had been in his place, in spite of the immense progress it had made in men's minds during the previous reigns, the Revolution would not have triumphed. When the King fell, the Republic took its place; and I set that aside. The former throne was buried under the ruins; I had to make a new one."

According to Prince Metternich, "One of Napoleon's keenest and most persistent regrets was that he could not appeal to the principle of legitimacy as the foundation of his power. Few men have felt like him the fragility and precariousness of authority without this basis, and its vulnerability to attacks." One day, in speaking to the Austrian statesman about the letter he wrote when First Consul to Louis XVIII., he said: "His answer was dignified and rich in impressive traditions. In Legitimists there is something which lies outside of their intelligence. If he had consulted his intellect alone, he would have come to terms with me, and I should have treated him most generously."

The Emperor had come to regard himself as the glorious personification of divine right, and as the defender of all the monarchies. In his eyes the

King of Prussia was only a revolutionary monarch. If we may believe Chateaubriand, "Frederick William's great crime, according to Bonaparte the Republican, was this, that he abandoned the cause of the kings. The negotiations of the Berlin court with the Directory indicated, Bonaparte used to say, a timid, selfish, undignified policy, which sacrificed his own position and the general monarchical interests to petty advantages. When he used to look at the new Prussia on the map he would say, 'Is it possible that I have left that man so much territory?'"

The philosophers aroused as much horror in Napoleon as the Jacobins. In his eyes strong minds were weak minds; and though he persecuted the Pope, he denounced with equal severity attacks on the throne and attacks on the Church. He especially detested the Voltairian irony, regarding it as both blasphemous and treasonable. To quote once more from Prince Metternich: "He had a profound contempt for the false philosophy as well as for the false philanthropy of the eighteenth century. Of all the founders of the doctrine it was Voltaire who was his pet aversion, and he carried his hate so far as to attack on every occasion his general literary reputation."

Napoleon thought, spoke, and acted as if he had always been Emperor and King. In the whole world there was no court so magnificent and brilliant as his. Many kings were admitted to it only as French princes, high dignitaries of the Empire: Joseph, King of Spain, was a Great Elector; Murat, King of the Two Sicilies, Lord High Admiral; Louis Bonaparte, deprived of the throne of Holland, figures in the Imperial Almanac of 1812 in his capacity of Constable. The other high dignitaries at this epoch were Cambacérès, Duke of Parma, Lord High Chancellor of the Empire; Lebrun, Duke of Piacenza, Lord High Treasurer, Governor General of the Departments of Holland; Prince Eugene de Beauharnais, Viceroy of Italy, Lord High Chancellor of State; Prince Borghese, Governor General of the Departments beyond the Alps; Marshal Berthier, Prince of Neufchâtel and of Wagram, Vice Constable; Talleyrand, Prince of Benevento, Vice Great Elector. At the head of his military household, the Emperor had four colonel-generals of the Imperial Guard, all four marshals of France, Davoust, Duke of Auerstadt and Prince of Eckmühl; Soult, Duke of Dalmatia; Bessières, Duke of Istria; Mortier, Duke of Treviso. Moreover, there were ten aides-de-camp, nine of whom were generals of divisions, and thirteen orderly officers. For Grand Almoner he had Cardinal Fesch, Archbishop of Lyons, aided by four ordinary almoners, two archbishops, and two bishops; for Grand Marshal of the Palace, Duroc, Duke of Frioul; for High Chamberlain, the Count of Montesquiou Fezensac; for First Equerry, General de Caulaincourt, Duke of Vicenza; for Chief Huntsman, Marshal Berthier, Prince of Neufchâtel and of Wagram; for Grand Master of Ceremonies, the Count of Ségur, formerly the

Ambassador of Louis XVI. to the great Catherine of Russia. The Emperor had no fewer than ninety chamberlains, among whom figured these among other great names of the old régime: an Aubusson de la Teuillade, a Galard de Béarn, a Marmier, a d'Alsace, a Turenne, a Noailles, a Brancas, a Gontaut, a Gramont, a Beauvau, a Sapicha, a Radziwill, a Potocki, a Choiseul-Praslin, a Nicolay, a Chabot, a La Vieuville. This aristocratic court knew no lack of amusements. The winter of 1811-12 was one long succession of pleasures. "It was in the whirl of these entertainments and festivities of all sorts," says Madame Durand, first lady-in-waiting to the Empress, "that Napoleon formed his plan for the conquest of Russia. The spoiled child of fortune, intoxicated with flattery, never dreaming of the possibility of defeat, seemed to be calculating his victories in advance, and to regard pleasures as the preparations for war. Not a day passed without a play, a concert, or a masked ball at court." The theatrical representations on the Tuileries' stage were most impressive. The Emperor and Empress occupied a box opposite the stage. The princes and princesses sat on each side of them or behind; on the right was the box of the foreign ambassadors; on the left, that of the French Ministers. A large gallery was reserved for the ladies of the court, who all dressed magnificently and wore sparkling jewels. A number of distinguished men filled the pit, all in court dress, with small-sword, and ribbons and orders. During the entr'actes the Emperor's liveried footmen carried about ices and refreshments of various kinds. The hall was most brilliantly lit. The balls in the great rooms of the first floor, and the dinners in the Diana Gallery, were equally sumptuous. The Emperor, however, especially delighted in the masked balls, when, changing his Imperial robes for a simple domino, he whose police system was so perfect, who knew and saw everything, used to baffle the women, and tease or surprise their husbands and lovers.

Everywhere Napoleon used to make himself feared, at a ball as well as in a meeting of his Ministers. At an entertainment he won as much glory as on the battle-field. Even those who hated him had to admire him, for he had a most wonderful power of astounding and fascinating every one. His aide, General de Narbonne, had an old mother, who maintained her allegiance to the old royalty. "See here, my dear Narbonne," the Emperor said one day, "it's a bad thing for me that you see your mother so often. I understand that she doesn't like me." "True," replied the crafty courtier, "she hasn't got beyond admiration." This same Count de Narbonne had been off to preside at an electoral meeting in a department some distance from Paris. "What do they say about me in the different departments you have been through?" asked the Emperor. "Sire," replied M. de Narbonne, "some say you are a god, and others say you are a devil; but all agree that you are something more than a human being."

A witty observer, who was inclined to witticism rather than to enthusiasm, said of the Napoleon of 1811: "His genius controlled every one's thoughts. I believed that he was born to rule Fortune, and it seemed to be natural enough that people should prostrate themselves before his feet; that became, in my eyes, the normal way of the world." Count Beugnot, who was at that time ruling the Grand Duchy of Berg, adds: "I worked all night with extraordinary zeal, and thereby surprised the inhabitants, who did not know that the Emperor performed for all his officers, at whatever distance they might be, the miracle of real presence. I imagined that I saw him before me, when I was working alone in my room, and this impression, which sometimes inspired me with ideas far beyond my powers, more often preserved me from lapses due to negligence or carelessness. An ancient writer has said that it was of great service for a man's conduct of life, if he could feel himself in the presence of a superior being; and I am inclined to believe, that the Emperor was generally so well served, because, whether through the precautions he took, or through the influence of his name, which was uttered everywhere and all the time, every one of his servants saw him continually at his side."

If Napoleon produced such an effect even at a distance, what an impression he must have made on those who were near him! Count Miot de Mélito thus describes an Imperial reception in 1811: "Never had the Tuileries displayed more pomp and magnificence. Never had a greater number of princes, ambassadors, distinguished foreigners, generals, splendid in gold, and purple, and jewels, ablaze with orders and ribbons of every color, offered more obsequious homage or sought with more eagerness at Versailles for the favor of a word or of a glance. The Emperor alone seemed free and unconstrained. With an assured step he passed through the throng of courtiers, who respectfully made way before him. With a look he transported with rapture or crushed those who approached him; and if he deigned to speak to any one, the happy mortal thus honored stood with bowed head and attentive ear, scarcely daring to breathe or to reply."

Napoleon had then given France so much glory that the loss of liberty was hardly perceived.

December 19, 1832, Victor Hugo, in a speech before the Court of Commons, where he was trying to compel the government to let "Le Roi s'amuse" be given, spoke thus of the Imperial government: "Then, sirs, it is great! The Empire, in its administration and government, was, to be sure, an intolerable tyranny, but let us remember that our liberty was largely paid for with glory. At that time France, like Rome under Caesar, maintained an attitude at once submissive and proud. It was not the France we desire, free, ruling itself, but rather a France, the slave of one man, and mistress of the world. It used to be said, 'On such a day, at such an hour, I shall enter that capital,' and they entered that day and at that hour. All sorts of kings used to elbow one another in his ante-chambers. A dynasty would be dethroned by a decree in the *Moniteur*. If a column was wanted, the Emperor of Austria used to furnish the bronze. The control of the French comedians was, I confess, a little arbitrary, but their orders were dated from Moscow. We were shorn of all our liberties, I say; there was a rigid censorship, our books were pilloried, our posters were torn down; but to all our complaints a single word sufficed for a magnificent reply; they could answer us with Marengo! Jena! Austerlitz!"

And the poet thus ended his speech: "I have but a few more words to say, and I hope that you will remember them when you proceed to your deliberations. They are these: 'In this century there has been only one great man—Napoleon; and only one great thing—Liberty. We no longer have the great man; let us try to have the great thing.'"

Certainly he exceeded the common measure, that man of whom Chateaubriand, his implacable foe, said: "The world belongs to Bonaparte. What that destroyer could not finish, his fame has seized. Living, he missed the world; dead, he possesses it. You may protest, but generations pass by without hearing you." When some one asked the illustrious author why, after so violently attacking Napoleon, he admired him so much, the answer was, "The giant had to fall before I could measure his height."

Those who were nearest to Napoleon regarded him as an almost supernatural being. The Baron of Méneval, who, before he was the private secretary of Marie Louise, when regent, had been secretary of the First Consul and Emperor, thus writes: "By the influence which Napoleon exercised on his age he was more than a man. Never perhaps will a human being accomplish greater things than did this privileged creature in so few years, in the face of so many obstacles; yet these were inferior to those of which the plans lay in his mighty head. The memory of that time, of the hours I spent with this wonderful man, seems to me a dream. In the deep feeling which he arouses in me, I have to bow before the impenetrable decrees of Providence, which, after inspiring this wonderful instrument of its plans, tore him from his uncompleted work. Possibly God did not wish him to anticipate the time He had established by an invariable order. Possibly He did not wish a mortal to exceed human proportions!"

If Napoleon was thus admired, even after the terrible catastrophes which wrought his ruin, even after the retreat from Russia, after the two invasions, after Waterloo, what an impression he must have made on his enthusiastic partisans when he was the incarnation of success and glory, when there was no spot on the sun of his omnipotence, and, protected by some happy fate, he had disarmed envy, discouraged hate, and so far bound Fortune that she seemed to tremble before him like an obedient slave!

In spite of the glory which surrounded him in 1812, Napoleon, who is often represented as infatuated with himself and his glory, yet even at this moment of colossal power and unheard-of prosperity, had moments when he judged himself with perfect impartiality. He knew human nature thoroughly, and he indulged in no illusions about his family, which he distrusted, or about his marshals, whose desertion he seemed to anticipate, or about his courtiers, whose flatteries did not deceive him. Being convinced that interest is generally the sole motive of human actions, he expected neither devotion nor gratitude. "One day, in speaking to my father," says General de Ségur, "he asked him what he thought people would say about him after his death, and my father began to enlarge on the way we should mourn for him. 'Nothing of the sort!' interrupted the Emperor; 'you would all say, "Ah!"' and he accompanied this word with a consolatory gesture which expressed 'at last we can take a long breath and be at peace.'" It was not after his defeats that the Emperor said this, but in 1811, when still mighty and successful.

"The Emperor," says General de Ségur again, "was not so blind as some have thought, as to the fate that awaited his gigantic work. He was often heard to say that his heir would be crushed by the vast bulk of his empire. 'Poor child!' he said, as he gazed on the King of Rome, 'what a snarl I leave to you.' ... Every one knows the gloomy impression it makes, when to the vigor and activity of youth there succeeds, with advancing years, the benumbing influence of stoutness. This transition, a melancholy warning, came over Napoleon at the end of 1810. Doubtless this warning of physical decline and weakness rendered him anxious about the future of a work founded on force. This was apparent when he told my father: 'The shortest ride now tires me;' and to M. Mollier: 'I am mortal, and more so than many men;' and again, 'My heir will find my sceptre very heavy.' As he regarded the future, the only power that seemed to threaten this sceptre and this heir was Russia, and it may be that as he began to feel himself grow old, he repented that he had enlarged its territory both on the north and the south, to the Gulf of Bothnia and to the Danube. Hence, possibly, this eager desire to deal the country a blow arose from a spirit of preservation rather than from one of conquest, and the charge of an overweening and uncontrollable ambition is thus somewhat refuted." This observation is not wholly inaccurate. It may be that if the Emperor had had no son, he would not have made the Russian campaign, and possibly it was more by a mistaken calculation than by pride, that he was drawn into this colossal war which, he hoped, would bring the whole continent, and consequently England, under his control.

A great deal has been said about Napoleon's pride; but in discussing the matter it is necessary to distinguish between two very different personages,—the man as he appeared in public, and the man as he was in private. In public, he was obliged to display more majesty than any other sovereign. The novelty of his grandeur made additional formality necessary. When the general became Emperor, he was compelled to keep at a distance his old fellow-soldiers who had formerly been his equals and intimates, for familiarity would have lowered his glory and have lessened his authority. He had to appear before his court like a living statue that never descended from its pedestal. It was hard to detect a human heart beating under the sovereign's Imperial robes. Yet in private life he was by no means what he seemed in public; when he returned to his own rooms, he laid aside his official seriousness as if he were taking off a fatiguing uniform, and became affable and familiar. He used to joke, and sometimes even noisily. He was no longer a haughty potentate, a terrible conqueror, but rather a good husband who was kind to his wife, and a good father who played with his child. He used to tease the companions of Marie Louise wittily, and without malice; he would take an interest in their dresses, and often give them bits of good advice in the gentlest manner. He took as much interest in the minutest details as in the greatest questions. He was indulgent and generous to his officials, and knew how to make himself loved by them. He and Marie Louise lived most happily together, as his valet de chambre, Constant, tells us, "As father and husband he might have been a model for all his subjects." He simply adored his son, and knew how to play with him better than did the Empress. As Madame Durand says: "Being without experience with children, Marie Louise never dared to hold or pet the King of Rome; she was afraid of hurting him: consequently, he became more attached to his governess than to his mother—a preference which at last made Marie Louise a little jealous. The Emperor, on the other hand, used to take him in his arms every time he saw him, play with him, hold him before a looking-glass, and make all sorts of faces at him. At breakfast, he used to hold him on hi knees, and would dip one of his fingers in a sauce, and let the child suck it, and rub it all over its face. If the governess complained, the Emperor would laugh, and the child, who was almost always merry, seemed to like his father's noisy caresses. It is a noteworthy fact that those who had any favor to ask of the Emperor when he was thus employed were almost sure of a favorable reception. Before he was two years old the young Prince was always present at Napoleon's breakfast."

At this period of his life Napoleon was really happy. The two years that he spent in the society of the young Empress formed a blessed rest in his stormy career; he loved his wife and thought that she loved him. He was grateful to her for being an archduchess, for her beauty, youth, and health; for having given him an heir to the Empire. He continually rejoiced in a marriage which, to be sure, inspired him with many illusions, but yet gave him at least some moments of moral repose and domestic calm, which are of importance in the life of such a man. Why was he not wise enough to stop and give thanks to Providence, instead of continuing his perilous course and forever tempting fortune? How many evils he would have spared France, Europe, and himself! A few concessions would have disarmed his adversaries, have satisfied Germany, have consolidated the Austrian alliance, strengthened the thrones, and brought about a lasting and general peace. We may say that Napoleon was his own worst enemy, and that when he held his happiness in his hand he willingly let it drop on the ground. It was not his second marriage that ruined him, but rather the over-bold combination which led him to extend the line of his military operations from Cadiz to Moscow.

XXV
MARIE LOUISE IN 1812

Empress Marie Louise was twenty, December 12, 1811. Early in 1812 she, like Napoleon, was at the summit of her fortune. During the two years of her reign she had received nothing but homage in France, and no woman in the whole world held so lofty a position. We will try to draw a portrait of her at this time when she had reached the top of the wave of human prosperity.

Rather handsome than pretty, Marie Louise was more impressive than charming. Her most striking quality was her freshness; her whole person bespoke physical and moral health. Her face was more gentle than striking; her eyes were very blue and full of animation; she had a rich complexion; her hair was light yellow, but not colorless; her nose, slightly aquiline; her red lips were a trifle thick, like those of all the Hapsburgs; her hands and feet were models of beauty; she had an impressive carriage, and was a little above the medium height. When she arrived in France, she was a little too stout, and her face was a little too red; but after the birth of her child these two slight imperfections disappeared. With a more delicate figure she became more graceful, and no woman ever had a finer complexion. Being endowed with a most sturdy constitution, she owed all her beauty to nature and nothing to artifice; her face needed no paint, her wit no coquetry; with no fondness for luxury or dress, possessing simple and quiet tastes, never striving for effect, always preferring half-tints to a blaze of light, her expression and demeanor always had a quality of simplicity and directness which fascinated Napoleon, who was very glad to turn from experienced coquettes to a really natural person.

Those who had supervised Marie Louise's education rightly thought that the greatest charm in a young girl was innocence. She had been brought up with the most scrupulous care. The books to be placed in the hands of the archduchesses were first carefully read, and any improper passages or even words were excised; no male animals were admitted into their apartments, but only females, these being endowed with more modest instincts. Napoleon, who was accustomed to the women of the end of the eighteenth century and to the heroines of the court of Barras, was delighted to find a girl so pure and so carefully trained.

On grand occasions Marie Louise bore no resemblance to the Marie Louise in private life; she assumed a coldness which was mistaken for disdain. She became imposing; she weighed every word; and careless observers attributed to haughtiness what was really due to reserve and timidity. The young Empress had every reason to distrust the French court. She knew what it had cost her great-aunt, Marie Antoinette, to try to live on the throne like a private person, and to carry kindliness even to familiarity. The best way for the Empress to escape malevolence and criticism was by saying very little. She knew French very well, but it was not her mother-tongue, and however well acquainted with its grammar, she could not know perfectly the fine shades of the language. Her fear of employing possibly correct but unusual expressions made her timid about speaking. Besides, her husband would not have liked to see her taking part in long conversations. Political subjects were forbidden to her, and her great charm in Napoleon's eyes was that she did not interfere in such matters. She never tried to pass for a witty woman. Although she was well-read, she lacked the delicate observation, the ingenious comparisons, the jingling of brilliant phrases or words which compose what in France is called wit. She had no confidence in the character of the prominent Frenchwomen, of the romantic but unsentimental beauties who always expressed more than they felt, who knew how to faint when fainting would be of use to them, and who in their drawing-rooms, and especially in their boudoirs, bore too close a resemblance to actresses upon the stage. Marie Louise never assumed any feelings or ideas which were not genuine. She was always natural. Comparing his two wives, Napoleon at Saint Helena said: "One was art and grace; the other, innocence and simple nature. My first wife never, at any moment of her life, had any ways or manners that were not agreeable and attractive. It would have been impossible to find any fault with her in this respect; she tried to make only a favorable impression, and seemed to attain her end without study. She employed every possible art to adorn herself, but so carefully that one could only suspect their use. The other had no idea that there was anything to be gained by these innocent artifices. One was always a little inexact; her first idea was to deny everything: the other never dissimulated, and hated everything roundabout. My first wife never asked for anything, but she ran up debts right and left; my second always asked for more when she needed it, which was seldom. She never bought anything without feeling bound to pay for it on the spot. But both were kind, gentle, and devoted to their husband."

Marie Louise did not shine in a drawing-room like Josephine; that would have required a French tact which she did not in the least possess. The first Empress was thoroughly familiar with French society, which the second did not know at all. Josephine had seen the last brilliancy of the old regime and the golden days of the Revolution; she had been a conspicuous figure in that brilliant but, above all, amusing period, of which Talleyrand said, "No one who did not live before 1789 knows how charming life can be." As Viscountess of Beauharnais, she was intimate with the most intelligent persons in Paris. Though far less educated than Marie Louise, her conversation was more animated and had a wider range. No subject was too deep for her; and although she never said anything very important, she always could give what she had to say an agreeable turn. Her most ardent desire was to make people forget, by her fascinations, that she was not born to the throne, and she seemed always endeavoring to be pardoned for her elevation into the society of the Faubourg Saint Germain. The names of the great French families always made much more impression on her, who had risen from the people, than on Marie Louise, who by birth as well as position could look down on all the French ladies without exception. It was not those who had belonged to the old régime whom she preferred; Madame Lannes was far more congenial to her than the Princess of Beauvau or the Countess of Montesquieu. She never sought to flatter the Faubourg Saint Germain, but rather kept it at a distance, making none of the advances to which it was accustomed at the hands of the first Empress. She felt that the Royalists secretly blamed her for attaching her old coat-of-arms to the new fortune of Bonaparte. She belonged to a race which had never felt a warm love for the Bourbons; while Josephine, who was born in a family of Royalists, had remained faithful, even when on the Imperial throne, to her devotion to the old Royalty. Marie Louise indulged in no illusions. She knew that the courtiers, under the appearance of adoration which amounted to servility, were really concealing a depth of malice and ill-will, which was the more dangerous the more it was hidden, and that the very ones who were burning incense before her would be the most delighted to catch her tripping. Hence she was always on her guard, and in public steadily maintained an attitude of cold benevolence and discreet reserve. Napoleon loved her, for the very reason that her qualities were the exact opposite of those of Josephine; and if she had striven to copy the former Empress, she would only have sunk in her husband's estimation. He had bidden her never to forget that she was a sovereign, as he was always Emperor: she obeyed him, and she did right to obey him. Strong in her husband's approval,—for he never had occasion for the slightest reproach,—she persisted in the very prudent and dignified line of conduct that she had adopted on entering France. She had every reason to be proud of her success; for so long as she lived with Napoleon, no whisper of calumny attacked her, no faintest insinuation was breathed against her morality. At Saint Helena, the Emperor said, "Marie Louise was virtue itself."

The untiring precision of her demeanor and of her words protected the Empress from criticism, but aroused no enthusiastic praise. She was more esteemed than loved; and, in spite of her precocious wisdom, she aroused no fervent sympathy, none of the enthusiastic admiration which less reserved, more amiable queens have inspired. Still, no one found fault with her. Count Miot de Mélito, in describing a reception at the Tuileries in 1811, says: "The Empress entered…. Her face wore a dignified but somewhat disdainful expression. She walked round the room, accompanied by the Duchess of Montebello, and spoke agreeably and pleasantly with a number of people whom she had introduced to her, and all were gratified by their kindly reception."

The Duke of Rovigo, the Minister of Police, speaks thus in his Memoirs: "Marie Louise aroused enthusiasm whenever she opened her mouth. Her success in France was entirely her own work; for I declare, on my honor, the authorities never adopted any particular methods to secure for her a warm welcome from the public. When she was to appear in a procession or at the theatre, all the authorities did was to provide against the slightest breach of order or propriety; beyond that, nothing was done. For example, when I was told that she was going to the theatre, I used to take all the boxes opposite the one she was to occupy, and all others from which people might stare at her. Then I took the precaution of sending the tickets for these boxes to respectable families, who were very glad to use them. In this way I filled the balcony on the days when the Empress meant to be present. As to any steps towards insuring a warm welcome from the pit, I simply did not take any. The Empress Marie Louise was accustomed, when she came before the public, to make three courtesies, and so gracefully that the applause always broke out with great warmth before the third. It was she herself who bade me take no active steps on such occasions." After thus greeting the audience, the Empress used to sit modestly in the back of the box. To be gazed at through all the opera-glasses always annoyed her. Her lofty rank, the pride of her position, which would have filled other women with rapture, left her almost indifferent.

Marie Louise was certainly attached to Napoleon, but we may doubt whether she was really in love with him. He was twenty-two years her senior; and if she was a wife who suited him in every particular, probably he was not the husband of whom she had dreamed. He possessed too much power, too much genius, too much majesty; a quiet home would have pleased her better than the Imperial Olympus, of which he was the Jupiter, and she the Juno. Doubtless his glory was unrivalled, but he had won the best part of it through Austrian defeats. Arcola and Marengo, Austerlitz and Wagram, were names that wounded Austrian ears. Had she been free to choose, she would perhaps have preferred to this all-powerful Emperor any petty German prince, who possessed neither great wealth nor vast territories, but who shared her memories, ideas, and hopes. Yet she had resolved to love her husband, and she easily succeeded in so doing. She was grateful for his kindness, his consideration, his respect; and in her affectionate but not passionate devotion there was no trace of reluctance. She sincerely thought that she would always be faithful to him. She was not only attached to him, she was also jealous of him; the proximity of Josephine annoyed and disturbed her. In fact, there was something singular in the simultaneous presence in France of two empresses sharing almost equally the official honors. Marie Louise knew how popular Josephine was; and this offended her, although she pitied a woman of whom the rigid laws of public policy had required so cruel a sacrifice. Possibly, too, she feared that she could not count too absolutely on the feelings of a man who, for reasons of state, had abandoned a wife whom a short time before he had really loved. Who knows, indeed, but what she dreaded the same fate for herself, in case she should bear no children? She felt really sure only when she had borne a son. Before that she was so jealous that one day when she heard that Napoleon had made a visit to Josephine, she was seen to shed tears, for the first time since her arrival in France. Another time, when the Emperor had suggested to her to take advantage of the absence of the first Empress, who had gone to Aix, in Savoy, and to visit Malmaison, her face suddenly became so sad that Napoleon at once abandoned the plan. But after the birth of King of Rome, Marie Louise was no longer jealous. Under the conviction that she had finally reconciled Austria and France, and that her son was the pledge of the peace and happiness of all Europe, she thought that she had so well accomplished her destiny that she could always count on her husband's affection and gratitude.

Judging by the words of Cardinal Maury, who had been so famous in the Constituent Assembly, and had been made Archbishop of Paris by the Emperor, Napoleon was very much in love with his young wife. "It would be impossible," he wrote to the Duchesa of Abrantes, "to make you understand how much the Emperor loves our charming Empress. It is love, but a good love this time. He is in love with her, I tell you, and as he never was with Josephine; for, after all, he never knew her when she was young. She was over thirty when they married, while this wife is young and as fresh as the spring. You will see her, and you will be delighted with her.... And then if you knew how gay she is, how pleasant, and, above all, how thoroughly at her ease with all those whom the Emperor honors with his intimacy! You will see how lovable she is. People used to talk about the *soirées* of the Queen of Holland. I assure you the Empress is very charming for those whom the Emperor admits informally into the Tuileries. They go there of an evening to pay their court, they play with Their Majesties reversis or billiards; and the Empress is so charming, so fascinating, that it is easy to see from the Emperor's eyes that he is dying to kiss her."

Probably there is some exaggeration in Cardinal Maury's enthusiasm. Doubtless Marie Louise pleased Napoleon very much, but had she been a young woman of humble rank, he probably would not have noticed her. What he especially admired in her was the Archduchess, the daughter of the German Caesars, and in the feeling she aroused in him there was perhaps more gratified vanity than real love. He certainly was not attracted to her by one of those tempests of passion which had drawn him towards Josephine; he would not have written to his second wife burning letters like those he wrote to Josephine during the first campaign in Italy. In his affection for Marie Louise there was something calm and reasonable, almost paternal; it was the reflection of maturity succeeding to the impetuous ardor of youth. Yet he had more deference and regard for the second Empress than for the first. Shortly after her marriage Marie Louise said to Metternich: "I am sure that in Vienna people think a great deal about me, and imagine that I live in continual anguish. The truth often seems improbable. I am not afraid of Napoleon, but I am beginning to think that he is afraid of me."

It has been said that the Emperor was not perfectly constant to Marie Louise; but even if he was ever unfaithful, he kept the fact from her knowledge, and never made his second wife as unhappy as he had made his first. He used to boast that he cared only for honest men and virtuous women, and he was anxious that no one should be able to charge him with setting a bad example. His court had become very strict, at least in appearance. Decorum prevailed there as rigidly as etiquette.

Marie Antoinette had in fact known less happiness than Marie Louise. From the moment she entered France she encountered a sullen enmity which Marie Louise never experienced. The Empress was never denounced for her Austrian birth as the Queen had been by the opposition. Marie Antoinette was surrounded by snares and pitfalls which were never prepared for Marie Louise. Who would have dared to treat Napoleon's wife as the Cardinal de Rohan treated the wife of Louis XVI.? What could there have been under the Empire to compare with the affair of the necklace? The Queen was attacked by pamphlets of all sorts. The Empress was not once insulted or slandered. The bitterest foes of her husband respected her. Moreover, Napoleon was far more attractive than Louis XVI., and Marie Louise was soon a mother, while Marie Antoinette long endured a barrenness for which she was not to blame.

The happiness of Marie Louise lasted but little more than two years, but it was all without a cloud. The mistake that historians always make in discussing celebrities is that they try to make a single portrait instead of a series of portraits, according to the different ages and circumstances. What was true in 1812 was no longer true in 1813, still less so in 1814. Human life has its seasons like the year. Is anything less like a brilliant spring day than a gloomy winter's day? In his history of the Restoration, Lamartine has drawn a picture of the Empress Marie Louise which seems tolerably exact for the period after the calamities that befell the Empire, but inapplicable to the happy days of the mother of the King of Rome. "Marie Louise," he writes, "sought refuge in ceremony, in retreat and silence from the ill-will that pursued her at every step.... Napoleon loved her from a feeling of superiority and pride. She was a sign of his alliance with great races; the mother of his son; and thus she perpetuated his ambition. ... The public did wrong to demand of Marie Louise passionate returns and devotion when her nature could inspire her only with a feeling of duty and respect for a soldier who had regarded her only as a German hostage and a pledge of posterity. Her constraint lessened her natural charms, darkened her expression, dimmed her wit, and burdened her heart. She was looked upon as a foreign decoration attached to the columns of the throne. Even history, written in ignorance of the truth, and inspired by the resentment of Napoleon's courtiers, has slandered this sovereign. Those who knew her will restore, not the stoical, theatric glory which was demanded of her, but her real nature.... The alleged emptiness of her silence hid feminine thoughts and mysteries of feeling which transported her far from this court. Magnificent though cruel exile!... She could not pretend anything, either during the days of her grandeur, nor after her husband's overthrow; that was her crime. The theatrical world of the court wanted to see a pretence of conjugal affection in a victor's captive. She was too natural to simulate love where she felt only obedience, terror, and resignation. History will blame her; nature will pity her.... She was expected to play a part; she failed as an actress, but as a woman she has survived."

The Marie Louise who is thus described by Lamartine is not the Marie Louise of the beginning of 1812; then the young Empress did not regard herself as "a victor's captive," nor as "a foreign decoration attached to the columns of the throne." Napoleon did not inspire her with terror, and she knew none of the constraint which "lessened her natural charms, darkened her expression, dimmed her wit, and burdened her heart." She did not look upon her court as a "magnificent but rude exile." These thoughts may have occurred to her in misfortune, but hardly, we think, before the Russian campaign. If Lamartine had read the letters which she wrote to her father in 1810, 1811, and the beginning of 1812, he would doubtless have acknowledged that for some time Napoleon's second wife was happy on the French throne.

To this portrait drawn by the great poet we prefer the one we find in Méneval's Memoirs: "The better Napoleon learned to know the Empress, the more he applauded his choice. Her character seemed made for him; she brought him happiness and consolation amid the cares of his stormy career. In ordinary life she was simple and kindly, yet with no loss of dignity. No word of complaint or blame ever crossed her lips. Gentle, but reserved and discreet, she never expressed her feelings with any vivacity. She was kind and generous, simple and astute at the same time; her gayety was gentle, her wit without malice. Though well-informed, she made no parade of her acquirements, fearing to be accused of pedantry. Her wifely devotion had won the Emperor's affection, and her unfailing gentleness had attracted all his friends. In this estimate I am confirmed by my recollections, and I am not inspired by any partiality, by what has happened, or by any present interest. It would be a mistake to suppose that her duty and her inclinations were at variance; she was perfectly natural and could not conceal her real impressions; but events have shown that while she inclined to virtue when it was easy, she yet lacked the strength to practise it when it was hard."

Marie Louise did not have the character of her great-grandmother Marie Thérèse, or that of her great-aunt Marie Antoinette. She rather resembled the wife of Louis XIV. or that of Louis XV. She would have led a calm, modest, harmless life, like those two queens, if her fate had not placed her amid unforeseen and terrible events, the shock of which she could not endure. In 1812 we see her a loving mother, a faithful wife, a worthy sovereign. If Napoleon had adopted a less imprudent policy, all that would have lasted. Doubtless that is what he said to himself when, at Saint Helena, he impartially examined his career, and he had no angry thought, no bitter word, for the woman who has been so severely judged by others.

XXVI
THE EMPRESS'S HOUSEHOLD

We have just tried to draw a picture of the appearance and character of Marie Louise in 1812, when at the summit of her fortune; let us turn our attention to the organization of her household at this epoch, and to the details of her daily life. Her first almoner was Count Ferdinand de Rohan, formerly Archbishop of Cambrai; her knight-of-honor was the Count of Beauharnais, who had held the same position to the Empress Josephine, a relative of his. Napoleon had at first meant to appoint the Count of Narbonne to this place, but Marie Louise had dissuaded him. M. Villemain says in his *Life* of M. de Narbonne: "The Empress Marie Louise, generally so yielding to her husband, on this occasion manifested great opposition. Whether through womanly kindness or through her pride as a sovereign, possibly through some superstitious scruple as a second wife, she insisted on the retention in this post of the Count of Beauharnais; she was unwilling on any terms to seem to exclude, in the person of this relative of Josephine, the first name of the Princess whom she succeeded on the French throne. On the other hand, it is fair to suppose that in the dashing and attractive Count of Narbonne she was willing to keep away certain things which were unfamiliar and so alarming to her, such as the lighter graces, the jesting spirit of the old court, and doubtless too the melancholy presentiments attached, in her mind, to everything that recalled Versailles and the daughters of Louis XV., who had become the aunts of Marie Antoinette. In a word, Marie Louise, cold and calm, was inflexible in her opposition to the choice which the Emperor announced to her. He at once yielded the point, and smoothed matters over by appointing M. de Narbonne one of his aides, an odd favor for a man fifty-five years old, a relic of the former court, suddenly made a member of the most warlike and most active staff in Europe." For first equerry Marie Louise had Prince Aldobrandini, and for master of ceremonies, the Count de Seyssel d'Aix.

The maid-of-honor was Madame Lannes, Duchess of Montebello, the widow of the famous marshal who was killed in Austria in the first war. Méneval tells us that Napoleon in making this appointment hesitated between this lady and the Princess of Beauvau. "The fear of introducing into his court influences hostile to the national ideas, such as a German princess might have favored, with the prejudices of her birth and position, made him give up this idea. He decided for the Duchess, thinking this an honor due to the memory of one of his oldest and bravest comrades." It was a most happy choice. Madame de Montebello was ten years older than the Empress; very handsome, stately, above reproach, of whom the Emperor said when he appointed her, "I give the Empress a real lady-of-honor."

In the purity of her features, the Duchess of Montebello recalled Raphael's Virgins. There was in her appearance, and in her life, a quality of calmness, of regularity, which greatly pleased Marie Louise, who was also much touched by her untiring devotion at the time of her child's birth, when for nine whole days Madame de Montebello remained in the Empress's room, sleeping at night on a sofa, and the Empress was grateful to her for having rigorously performed what could be demanded only of affection or devotion.

Madame Durand says that Marie Louise felt the need of a friend, and that the Duchess won her confidence and good graces to such an extent that the Empress could not do without her; she got to love her like a sister, and tried to prove her affection by great confidence to her and to her children. She was always delighted to choose presents that the Duchess would like, and offered them to her with charming amiability. Naturally a preference of this sort aroused a great deal of jealousy, especially among the ladies of the palace, most of whom belonged to older families than did the Duchess, and were somewhat annoyed that she was preferred to them. Whenever the Emperor was away, Madame de Montebello used to stay with the Empress, and every morning Marie Louise used to go to her room to chat with her, and in order to avoid passing through the drawing-room, where the other ladies had assembled, she used to go through a dark passage, which greatly offended these ladies. According to Madame Durand, Madame de Montebello scorned to hide her real opinions about any one of whom she was talking, and gave her opinion clearly and frankly. This openness—a virtue rare in courts—inspired the Empress's confidence, but earned her many enemies; but they, in spite of their ill-will, could not injure her reputation. The lady of the bedchamber to the Empress was the Countess of Luçay, who had been a lady-in-waiting since the beginning of the Consulate. She was a gentle, modest, distinctly virtuous person, who enjoyed general esteem and sympathy. The Emperor set great store by her. "In private life," says General de Ségur, "Napoleon was gentle and confiding, and especially fond of honorable people, whose delicacy and uprightness were above suspicion, and of women of the best reputation; he was a good judge, and he demanded a great deal. This was undeniably true, and the exceptions were very few: the way he chose his council and the officers attached to his person, shows it. In corroboration I will quote first the Grand Marshal Duroc with all the household of the palace, whose affairs were managed more honestly and better than those of any private house that can be named. As to the ladies of the court, it will be enough to name Madame de Luçay, my mother-in-law, the Lady of the Bedchamber, and Madame de Montesquiou, governess of the King of Rome, whom the Emperor chose when my mother declined the position from ill-health. His confidence, when once given, was unlimited."

The Countess of Montesquiou, the governess of the King of Rome, was the wife of the Emperor's Grand Chamberlain. The Baron de Méneval thus speaks of her: "Madame de Montesquiou, who was of high birth, received the highest consideration and thoroughly deserved it. She was forty-six years old when she was appointed governess of the Imperial children; her reputation was above reproach. She was a woman of great piety, yet indifferent to petty formalities; her manners had a noble simplicity, her whole nature was dignified but benevolent, her character was firm, and her principles were excellent. She combined all the qualities that were required for the important position which the Emperor, of his own choice, had given her." Madame Durand speaks as warmly about the Countess of Montesquiou: "It would have been hard to make a better choice. This lady, who belonged to an illustrious family, had received an excellent education; to the manners of the best society she added a piety too firmly fixed and too wise to run into bigotry. Her life had been so well ordered that she escaped any breath of calumny. Some were inclined to call her haughty, but this haughtiness was tempered by politeness and the most gracious consideration for others. She took the most tender and constant care of the young Prince, and there could be nothing nobler and more generous than the devotion which led her later to leave the country and her friends, to follow the lot of this young Prince whose hopes had been destroyed. Her sole reward was bitter sorrow and unjust persecution.

"The Duchess of Montebello and the Countess of Montesquieu had little sympathy for each other, but they never betrayed any coolness. Even had they desired it, they would have been held in awe by fear of Napoleon, who insisted on harmony in his court. Still, there could be distinguished at the Tuileries two parties in occult opposition, belonging respectively to the old and to the new nobility. At the head of the first stood the Count and the Countess of Montesquieu; of the second, the Duchess of Montebello, to whom the Empress's preference gave great authority. Madame Durand says that all the influence which the Grand Chamberlain and his wife, the governess of the King of Rome, enjoyed was exercised in obtaining pardon, favors, pensions, and places for the nobles, whether they had left France or not; they assured the Emperor that this was the best way of attaching them to his person, of making them love his government. They said this because they really thought it; and since they believed that the destiny of France was firmly fixed, they were anxious to secure for the ruler of this Empire those men whom they regarded as its strongest support. Since he had seen Madame de Montesquiou's unwearying devotion to his son, it was seldom that he refused her whatever she asked."

The new nobility, which was jealous of the old, had a representative in the Duchess of Montebello, who was very proud, and did not admit the superiority of the old aristocracy to the illustrious plebeians, who, like her husband, had no ancestors, but were destined to become ancestors themselves. She thought that the title of Duke was not enough for her valiant husband, and that the Emperor, in not making him a prince like Davout, Masséna, and Berthier, had been unjust, and that Marshal Lannes was of more account than all the dukes and marquises of the Versailles court.

There was at court, between these two groups of the old and the new nobility, a third party, the military party, headed by the Grand Marshal of the Palace, Duroc, Duke of Frioul, who, seeing honor and glory only in the career of a soldier, looked down on all other occupations. The Emperor secretly favored him, but he nevertheless remained true to his usual system of neutralizing all opinions, by trying to balance their forces. Each one of the three rival parties kept an eye on the other two, and thus everything of interest came to the Emperor's ears.

In 1812, the ladies-in-waiting were the Duchess of Bassano, the Countess Victor de Mortemart, the Duchess of Rovigo, the Countesses of Montmorency, Talhouet, Law de Lauriston, Duchâtel, of Bouillé, Montalivet, Perron, Lascaris Vintimiglia, Brignole, Gentile, Canisy, the Princess Aldobrandini, the Duchesses of Dalberg, Elchingen, Bellune, Countesses Edmond de Périgord and of Beauvau, Mesdames de Trasignies, Vilain XIV., Antinori, Rinuccini, Pandolfini Capone, and the Countesses Chigi and Bonacorsi. They accompanied the Empress in her walks and drives and at the theatre. They were real women-chamberlains, always at her side when she appeared in public, but they had no part in her domestic life and did not reside in the Imperial palaces. This privilege belonged to only six other women, who occupied a humbler position in the court hierarchy, but yet saw much more of the Empress.

In her time Josephine had four other ladies who held a position of something like female ushers, and whose duty it was to announce the persons who came to her apartments. These four ladies had numerous squabbles with the ladies-in-waiting over points in etiquette; and Napoleon, to put a stop to these heart-burnings, decided to substitute for them four new ladies, who should be chosen from those who had charge of Madame Campan's school at Ecouen for the daughters of members of the Legion of Honor.

Among those thus appointed was the widow of a general, Madame Durand, whose curious Memoirs we have often consulted. Some months later the Emperor raised their number to six, and appointed two of the pupils of this school, a daughter and a sister of distinguished officers, Mesdemoiselles Malerot and Rabusson.

These six ladies had an important position. Not only did they announce all the Empress's visitors; they also had actual charge of the domestic service, with six chambermaids under their orders, who only entered the Empress's rooms when she rang for them, while they, four, being in attendance every day, spent all their time with Marie Louise. They went to the Empress as soon as she was up, and did not leave her till she had gone to bed. Then all the doors of the Empress's room were locked, except one, leading into the next room, where slept the one of the ladies in charge, and Napoleon himself could not go into Marie Louise's room at night without passing through this room. No man, with the exception of the Empress's private secretary, her keeper of the purse, and her medical attendants, could enter her apartment without an order from the Emperor. Even ladies, other than the Lady of Honor and the Lady of the Bedchamber, were not received there except by appointment. The six ladies we have mentioned had charge of the enforcement of these rules, and were responsible for their observance. One of them was present at the Empress's drawing, music, and embroidery lessons. They wrote at her dictation, or under her orders. The same etiquette prevailed when the court was on its travels. Always one of these six ladies slept in the next room to the Empress, and that was the only approach to her chamber.

Madame Durand tells vis the goldsmith Biennais had made for the Empress a letter-case with a good many secret drawers which she alone could know, and he asked to be allowed to explain it to her. Marie Louise spoke about it to the Emperor, who gave her permission to receive him. Biennais was consequently summoned to Saint Cloud and admitted into the music-room, where he stood at one end with the Empress, while Madame Durand was in the same room, but so far off that she could not overhear his explanation. Just when this was finished the Emperor came in, and seeing Biennais, he asked who that man was; the Empress hastened to tell him, to explain the reason of his coming, mentioning that he had himself given him permission. This the Emperor absolutely denied, and pretended that the lady-in-waiting was to blame; he scolded her so severely that the Empress could scarcely stop him, although she said, "But, my dear, it is I who ordered Biennais to come." The Emperor laughed, and told her that she had nothing to do about it; that the lady was responsible for every one she admitted, and was alone to blame; and that he hoped that nothing of the sort would ever happen again.

Another time, when M. Paër was giving Marie Louise a music-lesson, the lady, who was present as usual at the lesson, had an order to give. She opened the door and was leaning half out to give the order, when Napoleon came in. At first he did not see her, and thought she was not present. The music-master went out. "Where were you when I came in?" the Emperor asked. She called his attention to the fact that she had not left the room. He refused to believe her, and gave her a long sermon in the course of which he said that he was unwilling that any man, no matter what his rank, should be able to flatter himself that he had been two seconds alone with the Empress. He added with some warmth: "Madame, I honor and respect the Empress; but the sovereign of a great empire must be placed above any breath of suspicion."

The gynæceum of Marie Louise was thus guarded with the greatest care and submitted to a very severe discipline. Napoleon entered freely into his wife's room whenever he pleased, and she never complained; for having absolutely nothing to conceal from him, she had no desire to be unfaithful to him even in her thoughts.

Madame Durand tells us that the Emperor, who desired to rule in important matters, endured, and even liked to be contradicted on minor matters. "When he was with Marie Louise, he used to be forever teasing her ladies about a thousand things; it often happened that they stood up against him, and he would carry on the discussion and laugh heartily when he had succeeded in vexing the young girls, who, in their frankness and ignorance of the ways of the world and the court, made very lively and unaffected answers which were amusing for those to whom they were addressed."

The nearness of these six ladies to the Empress aroused much jealousy. The name by which they were to be called was often changed. For some time they were allowed to call themselves First Ladies of the Empress; but this title offended the ladies of the palace, who wanted to call them First Chambermaids, which made them very angry. The Emperor at last gave them the name of *Lectrices*. They had under them six ordinary chambermaids who had no position in the court; these dressed the Empress, put on her shoes and stockings, and did her hair every morning; they were, in fact, chambermaids.

This is the way in which Marie Louise passed the day: At eight in the morning her window shutters were thrown open, and the curtains of her bed pushed back. The newspapers were brought to her, and she took her first breakfast in bed. At nine she dressed, and received intimate friends. At twelve she ate her second breakfast. Then she would practise a little, or draw, or sew, or play billiards. At two, if the weather was pleasant, she would drive out with the Duchess of Montebello, the Knight of Honor, and two ladies-in-waiting. Sometimes she rode on horseback; it was Napoleon who had given her lessons at Saint Cloud. "He used to walk by her side, holding her hand, while an equerry led the horse by the bridle; he allayed her fear and encouraged her. She profited by her lessons, became bolder, and at last rode very well. When she did credit to her teacher, the lessons went on, sometimes in the avenues of the private park just outside of the family drawing-room, so called because it was adorned with portraits of the Imperial family. When the Emperor had a moment's leisure after breakfast, he used to have the horses brought around, would get on one himself in his silk stockings and silver-buckled shoes, and ride by the Empress's side. He would urge her horse on, get it to gallop, laughing heartily at her terrified cries, although all danger was guarded against by the presence of a line of huntsmen ready to stop the horse and prevent a fall."

On returning, Marie Louise often took a lesson in music or painting. She was a real musician, and had a real talent for the piano. Prudhon and Isabey, who taught her drawing and painting, praised her talents. As Lamartine says: "When she entered her own rooms or the solitude of the gardens, she was once more a German woman. She cultivated poetry, drawing, singing. Education had perfected these talents in her, as if to console her, far from her country, for the absence and the sorrows to which the young girl would be one day condemned. She excelled in these things, but for herself alone. She used to read and recite from memory the poets of her own language and country." Marie Louise busied herself with charities, but without ostentation, almost secretly; hence she never won the credit for it that she deserved. Her generosity did not limit itself to the ten thousand francs which she set aside out of her allowance of fifty thousand francs a month; she never heard of a case of suffering without at once trying to relieve it.

In private life Marie Louise was kind and amiable. She was very polite and gentle; unlike many princesses, she was not given to fickle preferences and to infatuations as intense as they were brief; she was not unjust, violent, or capricious. She was never angry; she did not give empty promises, or affect any excessive interest, but she could always be depended on; she never distressed or humiliated any one. Having been trained from her infancy to court life, she was a kind mistress, for she had learned to combine two qualities that are often irreconcilable—dignity and gentleness. All who were thrown into her society agree in this. Sometimes, according to Madame

Durand, when she was in company her face had a melancholy expression inspired by the demands of etiquette that were made upon her; but "when she had returned to her own quarters, she was gentle, merry, affable, and adored by all who were with her every day.... Nothing was more gracious, more amiable, than her face when she was at her ease, quietly at home in the evening, or among those to whom she was particularly attached."

Marie Louise gave a great deal of care to her son, whom she tenderly loved. She had him brought to her every morning, and she kept him with her until she had to dress. In the course of the day, in the intervals of her lessons, she used to visit the little King in his apartment, and sit by his side and sew. Often she took him and his nurse to the Emperor; the nurse would stop at the door of the room in which Napoleon was, and Marie Louise would enter, with the child in her arms, always afraid that she was going to drop him. Then the Emperor would run up, take the child, and cover him with kisses.

The Baron de Méneval writes thus: "Sometimes he was seated on his favorite sofa, near the mantel-piece, on which stood two magnificent bronze busts, of Scipio and Hannibal, and was busily reading an important report; sometimes he went to his writing-desk, hollowed in the middle, with two projecting shelves, covered with papers, to sign a despatch, every word of which had to be carefully weighed; but his son, sitting on his knees, or held close to his chest, never left him. He had such a marvellous power of concentration that he could at the same time give his attention to important business and humor his son. Again, laying aside the great thoughts which haunted his mind, he would lie down on the floor by the boy's side, and play with him like another child, eager to amuse him and to spare him every annoyance."

M. de Méneval also tells us that the Emperor had had made little blocks of mahogany, of different lengths and various colors, with one end notched, to represent battalions, regiments, and divisions, and that when he wanted to try some new combination of troops, he used to set out these blocks on the floor. "Sometimes," adds M. de Méneval, "we used to find him seriously occupied in arranging these blocks, rehearsing one of the able manuvres with which he triumphed on the battle-field. The boy, seated at his side, delighted by the shape and color of the blocks, which reminded him of his toys, would stretch out his hand every minute and disturb the order of battle, often at the decisive moment, just when the enemy was about to be beaten; but the Emperor was so cool and so considerate of his son, that he was not disturbed by the confusion introduced into his manoeuvres, but he would begin again, without annoyance, to arrange the blocks. His patience and his kindness to the boy were inexhaustible."

Napoleon was also very kind to Marie Louise. He did everything that he could to make his wife happy and respected. He arranged matters in such a way that etiquette should not interfere with her favorite occupations. She dined alone with him every evening, and when he was absent, she dined with the Duchess of Montebello. After dinner there was generally a small reception or a little concert. At eleven Marie Louise withdrew to her own apartment, and her life was monotonous, but agreeable. She generally spent the summer at Saint Cloud and the winter at the Tuileries. At Saint Cloud, where the park was a great attraction to her, she slept in a room on the first floor, which had been occupied by Marie Antoinette and Josephine. (In the time of Napoleon III. it was the Council Hall of the Ministers.) At the Tuileries, her rooms were on the ground floor, between the Pavilion of the Clock, and that of Flora, and had also been occupied by the Queen and the first Empress. They looked out on the garden, and consisted of a gala apartment and a private one. The first consisted of an ante-chamber, a first and second drawing-room, a drawing-room of the Empress, a dining-room, and a concert-room; the second, of a bedchamber, the library, the dressing-room, the boudoir, and the bathroom. A rigid etiquette controlled the entrance to the Empress's as well as the Emperor's apartment. Napoleon lived on the first floor, where he had the bedroom which had been previously occupied by Louis XV. and by Louis XVI.; but there was a little private staircase, which he used constantly, leading to his wife's apartment.

Marie Louise was on good terms with the princes and princesses of the Imperial family, who were less offended by the superiority of an archduchess than they had been by that of a woman of humble origin, like Josephine. In accordance with her husband's directions, the second Empress was always polite and affable in her relations with his family, but she was never too familiar. No one of her sisters-in-law was as intimate with her as was the Duchess of Montebello. One incident, for which Marie Louise was in no way responsible, threw a little coolness on her relations with the princesses, although it was of but brief duration. Soon after the birth of the King of Rome the Emperor noticed that near the bed on which the Empress was to lie there had been placed three armchairs,—one for his mother, the other two for the Queens of Spain and of Holland. He found fault with this arrangement, saying that since his mother was not a queen, she ought not to have an armchair, and that none of them should have one. Accordingly, for the armchairs he had three handsome footstools substituted. When the three ladies came in, they noticed, with some annoyance, the change that had been made, and soon left. They would have done wrong to blame the Empress; for it was the Emperor who was responsible, and when Napoleon gave an order, no one, not even his wife, could have thought of saying a word. In matters of etiquette he controlled the minutest details and regarded them as very important. Nothing came of this little incident, and in general the members of the Emperor's family got on better with the second Empress than with the first.

In short, what did Marie Louise lack in the beginning of 1812? She had a husband, at the height of his fame and glory, who gave her more affection, regard, and consideration than any one else in the world. She was the mother of a superb child, whom every one admired. Around her she saw respect on every face. For maid-of-honor she had a real friend, a woman whom she would herself have chosen, so highly did she value her character and manners. Her household consisted of the flower of the French aristocracy. She followed her own tastes, studied with the best masters, distributed alms as she pleased, lived in the handsomest palaces in Europe. There were no discomforts, no difficulties, in her position. She had no conflicting duties, no occasion to decide between her father and her husband, between the country of her birth and that of her adoption, none of those struggles and heartrending perplexities which so cruelly beset her afterwards. At that time the Emperor Francis was well contented with his son-in-law, and corresponded with him in a most friendly way. At that happy moment the Frenchwoman could be an Austrian without injury to her mission and her duty. The path she was to follow was clearly traced. Alas! it was not for long that she was to enjoy this calm and equable happiness, so well suited to her timid nature, which was made to obey, not to rule. She had then no cause to blame her fate or herself. As a young girl, as a wife, as a mother, she had nothing to ask for. Her satisfaction was furthered by the thought that she was soon to see again her father, her family, her country; and apart from the matter of feeling, she must have been gratified by the thought that she was to appear again in Austria with a brilliancy and splendor such as no other woman in the world could show. Her stay in Dresden was the crowning point of her brief grandeur, the end of the swift but dazzling period of prosperity and good fortune which may be described as the happy days of the Empress Marie Louise.

XXVII
DRESDEN

The *Moniteur* of May 10, 1812, contained the following announcement: "Paris, May 9. The Emperor left to-day to inspect the Grand Army assembled on the Vistula. Her Majesty the Empress will accompany His Majesty as far as Dresden, where she hopes to have the pleasure of seeing her August family. She will return in July at the latest. His Majesty the King of Rome will spend the summer at Meudon, where he has been for a month. He has finished his teething, and enjoys perfect health. He will be weaned at the end of the month."

It will be acknowledged that it was a somewhat singular thing to announce thus in the same article the speedy weaning of a baby and the beginning of the most colossal campaign of modern times. Not a word had been said about war. Never had the departure for an army seemed more like a pleasure trip. Followed by a great part of his court, Napoleon, like a Darius or a Louis XIV., had left Saint Cloud, May 9, in the same carriage as the Empress. The Republican general had disappeared before a magnificent monarch surrounded by Asiatic pomp. The possibility of defeat occurred to no one. One would have supposed that he was starting on a long ovation, a triumphal progress.

At every step the all-powerful Emperor and his young wife seemed to be tasting the onsets of grandeur and glory. May 9 he slept at Châlons; the 10th he entered Metz, where he at once got on horseback, reviewed the troops, and visited the fortifications. The 11th he was at Mayence, where he received the Grand Duke and the Grand Duchess of Hesse Darmstadt, as well as the Prince of Anhalt-Köthen. The 13th he crossed the Rhine, stopped a moment to see the Prince Primate at Aschaffenburg, met in the course of the day the King of Würtemberg and the Grand Duke of Baden, and spent the night at Würzburg, the sovereign of which was the former Grand Duke of Tuscany, the brother of the Emperor of Austria. Marie Louise was delighted to see her uncle again, who was to join her at Dresden. The 14th they slept at Bayreuth, the 15th at Plauen, and on the 16th they reached Dresden.

As Thiers says, Napoleon had passed through Germany amid an unprecedented throng of the populace, whose curiosity equalled their hatred. "Never, indeed, had the potentate whom they abhorred appeared more surrounded with glory. People talked with mingled surprise and terror of the six hundred thousand men who had gathered at his command from all parts of Europe. They ascribed to him plans far more extraordinary than those he had formed. They said he was going by Russia to India. They spread abroad a thousand fables far wilder than his real designs, and almost believed them accomplished, so much had his continual success discouraged hatred from hoping for what it desired. Vast heaps of wood were prepared along his path, and at nightfall these were set on fire to light his road; so that what was really curiosity produced almost the same effect as love and joy."

The Emperor's intention in going to Dresden was to spend two or three weeks there before taking command of his armies, and to dazzle all Europe by the sumptuous court which he should hold in the Saxon capital. For some weeks Marie Louise had been hoping to meet her father at Dresden, and the thought filled her with joy. She had written to him, March 15: "The Emperor sends all sorts of kind messages to you. He bids me tell you also that if we have war, he will take me to Dresden, where I shall spend two months, and where I hope soon to see you too. You cannot imagine, dear father, the pleasure I take in this hope. I am sure that you will not refuse me the great pleasure of bringing my dear mamma and my brothers and sisters. But I beg of you, dear papa, don't say anything about it, for nothing is decided." Marie Louise was at the height of happiness when she reached Saxony. At that moment she was very proud of being Napoleon's wife. She entered Dresden with him, May 16, 1812, at eleven in the evening, escorted by the King and Queen of Saxony, who had gone to Freiberg to meet them.

The next morning at eight, Napoleon, who was staying in the grand apartment of the royal castle, received the sovereign princes of Saxe-Coburg, Saxe-Weimar, and Dessau, as well as the high officials of the Saxon court. The King of Westphalia and the Grand Duke of Würzburg arrived in the course of the day, and at once presented their respects.

At one o'clock in the afternoon of the 18th the Emperor and Empress of Austria arrived in Dresden. "What a moment for Marie Louise!" writes Madame Durand. "She found herself once more in her father's arms, and appeared before the dazzled eyes of her family, the happiest of wives, the first of sovereigns! Her August father could not hide his emotion. He tenderly kissed his son-in-law, and recognizing the claims he had upon his heart, told him more than once that he could count on him and on Austria for the triumph of the common cause." Possibly these assurances were not perfectly sincere, but Napoleon believed in them, or pretended to believe in them. As for Marie Louise, she never interfered in politics, and gave herself up to family joys.

The period of Napoleon's stay at Dresden was the culmination of his power. Possibly no mortal had ever attained so high a position as this new Agamemnon. "It is at Dresden," says Chateaubriand, "that he united the separate parts of the Confederation of the Rhine, and for the first and last time set in motion this machine of his own creation. Among the exiled masterpieces of painting which sadly missed the Italian sun, there took place the meeting of Napoleon and Marie Louise with a crowd of sovereigns, great and small. These sovereigns tried to make out of their different courts subordinate circles of the first court, and rivalled with one another in vassalage. One wanted to be the cup-bearer of the ensign of Brienne; another, his butler. Charlemagne's history was put under contribution by the erudition of the German chancellor's officers. The higher they were, the more eager their demands. As Bonaparte said in Las Cases, a lady of the Montmorencys would have hastened to undo the Empress's shoes." The monarchs were more like Napoleon's courtiers than his equals. Princes and private citizens, rich and poor, nobles and plebeians, friends and enemies, crowded to get a look at him. Night and day there was an immense throng gazing at the doors and windows of the palace in which lodged the predestined being, in hope of being able to say, "I have seen him." The French waited on him with idolatry. The Germans had a complex feeling about him, in which admiration was stronger than hate.

General de Ségur, who was at Dresden with Napoleon, represents him as moderate and even eager to please, but with visible effort and manifestations of the fatigue which he experienced. As to the German princes, their attitude, their words, even the tone of their voice, showed the ascendancy he exercised over them. They were all there solely on his account. They scarcely ventured to discuss anything, being always ready to recognize his superiority of which he was himself only too conscious. "His reception," adds the General, "presented a remarkable sight. Sovereign princes flocked thither to await an audience of the Conqueror of Europe; they so crowded his officers, that these last often had to remind one another to take care not to offend these new courtiers who were crowding among them. Napoleon's presence thus removed the differences, for he was as much their chief as he was ours. This common dependence seemed to level everything about him. Then possibly the ill-concealed military pride of many French generals offended these princes, when the former seemed to think that they were elevated to royal rank; for whatever the dignity and position of the conquered, the conqueror is his equal."

May 18, the day of the arrival of the Emperor and the Empress of Austria, it was the King of Saxony who gave a dinner to his guests; but on the other days it was Napoleon who assumed the duties of hospitality, as if he had been at home in Dresden. He wanted to receive, not to be received. The sovereigns ate at his table, and it was he who fixed the hours and all the details of etiquette. Since he was unwilling that his stay should inconvenience the King of Saxony, who was not rich, he was preceded and followed by his household, which was supplied with everything necessary for a magnificent representation. Part of the handsome vermilion table service presented to him by the city of Paris, on the occasion of his marriage, had been carried to Dresden, and there was all the luxury of the Tuileries.

At Saint Helena the beaten conqueror recalled the memory of his past splendors with a certain satisfaction. "The interview at Dresden," he said in his Memorial, "was the moment of Napoleon's highest power. Then he appeared as the king of kings. He was compelled to point out that some attention should be paid to his father-in-law, the Emperor of Austria. Neither this monarch nor the King of Prussia had his household with him; nor did Alexander at Tilsit or Erfurt. There, as at Dresden, they ate at Napoleon's table. These courts, the Emperor used to say, were mean and middle-class; it was he who arranged the etiquette and set the tone. He invited Francis to visit him and dazzled him with his splendor. Napoleon's luxury and magnificence must have made him seem like an Asiatic satrap. There, as at Tilsit, he covered with diamonds every one who came near him." He had brought after him the best actors of the Théâtre Français, and, as at Erfurt, Talma played before a pit full of kings.

What were the real feelings of these princes, who were so obsequious to Napoleon? The King of Saxony, the patriarch of these monarchs, was a frank, loyal man, of a keen sense of honor, and he was thoroughly sincere in the devotion he professed to the Emperor, to whom he thought he owed a great debt. Napoleon, who was very fond of this king, would have no other guards at Dresden than the Saxon soldiers. Even after Leipsic he retained a pleasant memory of them, and at Saint Helena he said to those who charged him with excessive confidence in them, "I was then in so kind a family, with such good people, that there was no risk; every one loved me, and even now I am sure that the King of Saxony says every day a *Pater* and an *Ave* for me."

Unlike the Saxon king, the Emperor of Austria, in spite of the family ties, had but very moderate affection for Napoleon. Metternich, who was at Dresden, says in his Memoirs, "The attitude of the two sovereigns was such as their respective positions demanded, but was yet very cool." Thiers describes the Emperor Francis as opening his arms almost sincerely to his son-in-law, displaying a sort of inconsistency, which is more frequent than is generally imagined, torn between delight at seeing his daughter so exalted and pain at Austria's losses; promising Napoleon his assistance after having promised Alexander that this assistance would be nothing, saying to himself that after all he had adopted a wise course, by making himself sure whichever party should be victorious, yet with more confidence in Napoleon's success, from which he sought to get profit in advance.

As to the Empress of Austria, the step-mother of Marie Louise, she concealed beneath formality and perfect politeness a profound antipathy to the conqueror. It required almost a formal order from her husband to bring her to Dresden. She was then a pretty woman, twenty-four years old, witty, and proud of her birth and her crown. Napoleon she looked on as an upstart, a vainglorious adventurer, the cause of all the humiliations inflicted on the Austrian monarchy; and the splendor which surrounded the hero of Marengo, of Austerlitz, of Wagram, aroused in her a resentment all the keener because she was compelled to hide it. Napoleon in his pique determined to win over the step-mother of Marie Louise.

The health of the Empress of Austria was so delicate that she was unable to walk through the long row of rooms. Consequently Napoleon used to walk in front of her, one hand holding his hat, while the other rested on the door of her sedan-chair, talking in the liveliest way with his witty enemy. General de Ségur, like every one else, noticed the hostility which the Empress in vain tried to conceal. "The Empress of Austria," he says, "whose parents had been dispossessed by Napoleon in Italy, was noticeable for her aversion which she vainly essayed to hide; it made itself at once manifest to Napoleon, and he met it with a smiling face; but she made use of her intelligence and charm to win over hearts and to sow the seeds of hate of him."

In fact, the Empress of Austria was jealous of the Empress of the French. She distinctly recalled the time when she used to have her under her control, and she was annoyed to see her former pupil taking precedence of every queen and empress. She would have liked to be able to give her advice, as she had done in the past, and to exercise her authority as step-mother in criticising her; but she did not dare to do this, and the restraint was not agreeable. The careful observer finds life in a palace what it is in the house of a humble citizen. As La Bruyère has said: "At court, as in the town, there are the same passions, the same pettinesses, the same caprices, the same quarrels in families and between friends, the same jealousies, the same antipathies: everywhere there are daughters-in-law and mothers-in-law, husbands and wives, divorces, ruptures, and ineffectual reconciliations; everywhere eccentricity, anger, preferences, tattling, and tale-bearing. With good eyes it is easy to see town life, the Rue Saint Denis transported to Versailles or Fontainebleau."

Count de Las Cases has said in the Memorial: "One of us ventured to ask if the Empress of Austria was not the sworn enemy of Marie Louise. It was nothing else, said the Emperor, than a pretty little court hatred, a heartfelt detestation, concealed under daily letters, four pages long, full of affection and endearment. The Empress of Austria was very attentive to Napoleon and was very coquettish with him, so long as he was in her presence, but as soon as his back was turned she was busy with trying to detach Marie Louise from him by the vilest and most malicious insinuations; she was much annoyed that she could get no power over him. 'Besides,' said the Emperor, 'she is witty and intelligent enough to embarrass her husband, who was sure that she cared very little for him. Her face was agreeable and bright with a charm of its own. She was like a pretty nun.'"

Napoleon kept busy at Dresden. Men were continually coming and going, and the Emperor was actively working over the details, political and military, of the vast expedition he was getting ready. Marie Louise, who wished to avail herself of his few moments of leisure, scarcely left the palace, and it was to no purpose that her step-mother, the Empress of Austria, tried to represent this devotion as something ridiculous.

There was a sort of hidden rivalry between the two Empresses. Napoleon had had all the crown diamonds brought to Dresden, and Marie Louise was literally covered by them. General de Ségur says: "She completely effaced her step-mother by the splendor of her jewels. If Napoleon demanded less display, she resisted him, even with tears, and the Emperor yielded the point from affection, fatigue, or distraction. It has been said that, in spite of her birth, this princess mortified the pride of the Germans by some thoughtless comparisons between her new and her former country. Napoleon blamed her for this, but very gently. The patriotism with which he had inspired her gratified him; he tried to set matters right by numerous presents." The Empress of Austria was compelled to conceal her ill-will. She was present almost every morning when Marie Louise was dressing, ransacked her step-daughter's laces, ribbons, stuffs, shawls, and jewels, and carried something off almost every day.

The Emperor Francis pretended not to notice the jealousies of his wife and his daughter. He spent a good part of every day in walking about the town, and was somewhat surprised at the enormous amount of work which his son-in-law did. He sought to gratify the mighty Emperor by telling him that in the Middle Ages the Bonaparte family had ruled over Treviso; that he was sure of this, for he had seen the authentic documents that proved it. Napoleon replied that he took no interest in it, that he preferred being the Rudolph of Hapsburg of his family. The little genealogical flattery produced its effect, nevertheless, and Marie Louise was much pleased by it.

Napoleon was on the point of leaving Dresden, when Frederic William, King of Prussia, arrived there. A treaty, signed February 24, 1812, bound this prince to furnish for the next campaign twenty thousand men, under a Prussian general, but bound to obey the commander of the French army corps to which they should be assigned. Austria, by a treaty concluded March 14, had promised to furnish a corps of thirty thousand men, commanded by an Austrian general, under Napoleon's orders. Prussia especially suffered under such a condition of things, and the memory of Jena had never been keener or more distressing. The occupation of Spandau and Pillau by the French, and the ravages inflicted on the kingdom by the troops marching towards Russia, had much disturbed and grieved Frederic William, who imagined that Napoleon meant to dethrone him. Being very anxious to have early information about the lot that awaited him, he sent to Dresden M. von Hatzfeld, the great Prussian nobleman whom Napoleon had wanted to have shot in 1806, and to whom he had later become much attached, which shows, as Thiers has said, that it is well to think twice before having any one shot. Through M. von Hatzfeld the King of Prussia requested an interview with the Emperor in Berlin. The Emperor made answer that Berlin was not on his road, that he could not go there, but that he would be glad to see the King in Dresden.

Frederic William regarded the invitation as a command, and set out forthwith. He reached the capital May 26, accompanied by Baron von Hardenberg and Count von Goltz, Ministers of State, Prince von Witgenstein, High Chamberlain, M. von Jagou, First Equerry, Baron von Krumsmarck, Prussian Minister to Paris, and was joined the next day, the 27th, by the Crown Prince. Father and son were very well received. Napoleon consented to credit Prussia with the supplies taken by the troops on their march, and promised to enlarge the boundaries of the kingdom if the war with Russia should be successful. For his part, the King proposed to the Emperor to take the Crown Prince with him as aide-de-camp, and introduced him to the other aides, asking them to treat their new comrade kindly. According to the Memoirs of the Baron de Bausset, who was present at the Dresden interview, "Everything which has been written about the coldness of the King of Prussia's reception is false. He was welcomed, as he had the right to expect, as a powerful ally, who, by a recent treaty, had just united his troops with those of France." The young Crown Prince, who was making his first appearance in the world, attracted general attention by his elegance and distinction. As to the King, he affected a content of which the curious despatch given below was the official expression.

Nothing more clearly shows the ascendancy which Napoleon exercised at this time than this circular addresssed, June 2, 1812, by Count von Goltz to the diplomatic agent of Prussia: "Sir, it will be interesting for you to learn with certainty the main incidents of the recent journey of the King, our Sovereign, to Dresden. Since I had the honor to accompany His Majesty, I give myself the pleasure of seizing the moment of my return to inform you about them. On receipt of a letter from His Majesty, the Emperor Napoleon, brought to the King May 24, by the Count of Saint Marsan, which contained the most obliging and friendly invitation to visit that monarch at Dresden, His Majesty resolved to depart at once; and having set forth very early in the morning of the 25th, he arrived that evening at Grossenhain, whither His Majesty the King of Saxony had sent Lieutenant von Zeschaud and Colonel von Reisky to meet him. His entrance into Dresden took place on the 28th, at ten in the morning. It was desired to make this a formal occasion, but His Majesty deemed it better to decline the profound honors. Nevertheless, a squadron of the mounted body-guard had awaited His Majesty at a good quarter of a league from the city, and accompanied him to the palace of Prince Antony, a part of the castle in which His Majesty is lodged, amid a countless throng of spectators, who with one accord gave the King the most marked tokens of their respectful devotion.

"His Majesty was received at the foot of the staircase, and in the most flattering way, by His Majesty the King of Saxony, accompanied by all his court, his ministers, and the most distinguished citizens. After a brief interview in the King's apartment, His Majesty having announced his visit to the two Emperors, they paid him the friendly attention of announcing their own. The Emperor Napoleon was the first to arrive, and the two monarchs, having embraced, had at once an interview which lasted more than half an hour. The Emperor of Austria then arrived, and greeted His Majesty in the most considerate and friendly manner."

The Prussian Minister, expressing the most unbounded satisfaction, abounded with praise of the courtesy and kindness of Napoleon. He concluded his circular despatch thus: "I am obliged to abstain from going into further details with regard to our Sovereign's reception, and the subsequent interviews, as well as the court ceremonies and festivals of this day and the two following; but what I can and must add as an eye-witness, is, that in general there could have been nothing more considerate and more friendly than this reception, as well on the part of His Majesty the Emperor Napoleon, as on that of Their Majesties the Emperor of Austria and the

King of Saxony and their August families, and that the King has been much gratified by it. The friendship and the personal confidence of these monarchs and the reciprocal conviction of the sincerity of their feelings have affirmed themselves in the most solid way; and especially, the close bonds uniting our Sovereign with that of France have acquired a new character of cordiality and strength. I have to add that His Royal Highness the Crown Prince, who reached Dresden on the 27th, has equally received the suffrages of the Sovereigns there assembled, and that the Emperor Napoleon greeted him with affectionate cordiality." Count von Goltz was evidently anxious that all this should be bruited abroad. The last sentence of the despatch ran thus, "Although these details are primarily intended for you, Sir, you are obviously free to make such use of them as you may see fit." Possibly this sentence meant that when these details might not be agreeable, that is to say, to the friends of Russia or England, it might not be well to communicate them.

In fact, not a single Prussian had forgotten Jena; there was not one who did not yearn for revenge. King Frederic William, who had at first resolved to withdraw to Silesia, in order not to be in Potsdam under the cannon of Spandau, or in Berlin under the authority of a French governor, consented to return to his usual quarters. Although his minister, Count von Goltz, had represented him as "perfectly satisfied with the precious days he had spent at Dresden, and deeply touched by the repeated proofs of friendship, esteem, and attachment that he had received," this sovereign, though he bowed to the exigencies of the hour, waited only for a favorable moment to reappear in the front ranks of his conqueror's foes. In 1816 Napoleon thus judged him: "The King of Prussia, as a man, is loyal, kind, and honest, but in his political capacity he is naturally ruled by necessity; so long as you have the strength, you are his master."

People of intelligence who were with Napoleon in Dresden were not deceived about the real feelings of Germany and nearly all its rulers. "The wisest of us," says General de Ségur, "were alarmed; they said, though not aloud, that one must think one's self something supernatural to destroy and displace everything in this way without fear of being caught in the general overthrow. They saw monarchs leaving Napoleon's palace, with their eyes and hearts full of the bitterest resentment. They imagined that they heard them at night pouring forth to their trusty ministers the agony which filled their souls. Everything intensified their grief. The crowd through which they had to make their way, in order to reach the door of their proud conqueror, was a source of distress; for all, even their own people, seemed to be false to them. When his happiness was proclaimed, their misfortunes were insulted. They had collected at Dresden to make Napoleon's triumph more brilliant, for it was he who triumphed. Every cry of admiration for him was one of reproach to them, his exaltation was their abasement, his victories were their defeats! They thus fed their bitterness, and every day hatred sank deeper into their hearts."

The Duke of Bassano, at that time Minister of Foreign Affairs, was unwilling to perceive this latent hostility, which was carefully concealed under protestations of devotion. He wrote, May 27, 1812, to Count Otto, French Ambassador at Vienna: "Their Royal and Imperial Majesties will probably leave Dresden day after to-morrow. Their stay in this city has been marked by reciprocal proofs of the most perfect intelligence and the greatest intimacy. Now the two Emperors know and appreciate each other. The embarrassment and timidity of the Emperor of Austria have left him in face of Napoleon's frankness and simple character. Long conversations have taken place between the two monarchs. All the interests of Austria have been discussed, and I believe the Emperor Francis will have received from his journey a fuller confidence in the feelings of the Emperor Napoleon towards him, as well as a large crop of good counsels." With all his optimism, the Minister of Foreign Affairs was compelled to notice the secret feelings of the Empress of Austria. After saying in his despatch to Count Otto that the Emperor Francis had been able to see with his own eyes how happy Marie Louise was, he went on: "This sight, so agreeable to a father, has produced on another August person more surprise than emotion. However, if the real feelings are not changed, there will be at least a perceptible amelioration, since the illusions inspired and fed by a coterie will have disappeared." The Duke ended his despatch by these words of praise for the Crown Prince of Prussia: "The King of Prussia arrived here day before yesterday. He was followed yesterday by the Crown Prince, who is making his entrance into the world. He comports himself with prudence and grace."

The Dresden festivities were drawing to a close. Not only the Germans, even the French, were growing weary of them. "I pass over the ceremonies of etiquette," says the Baron de Bausset, who took part in these so-called rejoicings; "they are the same at every court. Great dinners, great balls, great illuminations, always standing, even at the eternal concerts, a few drives, long waitings in long drawing-rooms; always serious, always attentive, always busy in defending one's powers or one's pretensions, … that is to what these envied, longed-for pleasures amount." All this machinery of alleged distractions concealed serious anxieties and the keenest uneasiness.

Napoleon had desired that the Dresden interview should preserve a pacific appearance. Possibly he had for a moment hoped that the Czar, on seeing the force assembled about the Emperor of the French, King of Italy, and Protector of the Confederation of the Rhine, the ally of Prussia and Austria, would accept whatever conditions so great a potentate might offer, and abandon the struggle before it was begun. The military element was kept in the background. Court dresses were more numerous in Dresden than uniforms. Napoleon assumed the appearance of a sovereign rather than of a general. Murat and King Jerome were despatched to their courts. But every one knew perfectly well that the storm was gathering. One would have said that the first cannon fired in that tremendous campaign—the Russian campaign—were going to disturb and then to extinguish the sound of trumpets and bands. The entertainments were on the surface; the war was in the depths.

It was a terrible, lamentable war towards which the hero of so many battles was plunging with a lowered head, as if drawn into the abyss by a deadly fascination. Sometimes, amid the fumes of power and pride, some mysterious voice warned him of his peril; but he would reassure himself by recalling his former victories and thinking of his star. As General de Ségur has said: "It seemed as if in his doubts of the future, he buried himself in the past, and that he felt it necessary to arm himself against a great peril with all his most glorious recollections. Then, as he has since done, he felt the need of forming illusions about the alleged weakness of his rival. As he made ready for this great invasion, he hesitated to regard the result as certain; for he no longer was conscious of his infallibility, nor had that military assurance which the force and fire of youth give, nor had he that conviction of success which makes it sure." There had been no lack of warnings. Those of his advisers who knew Russia well, such as the Count of Ségur and the Duke of Vicenza, ambassadors at Saint Petersburg, one under the King, the other under the Empire, had said to him: "Everything will be against you in this war. The Russians will have their patriotism and love of independence, all public and private interests, including the secret wishes of our allies. We shall have for us, against so many obstacles, nothing but glory alone, even without the cupidity which the terrible poverty of those regions cannot tempt." General Rapp, who was in command at Dantzic, had thought it his duty to inform Marshal Davoust of the alarming symptoms which he had discovered among the German populace: "If the French army suffers a single defeat, there will be one vast insurrection from the Rhine to the Niemen." Davoust forwarded this information to Napoleon with this single indorsement: "I remember, Sire, in fact, that in 1809, had it not been for Your Majesty's miracles at Regensburg, our situation in Germany would have been very difficult," The Emperor listened to no one. He did not suspect that the King of Prussia, seemingly his ally, had sent word secretly to the Czar:

"Strike no blow at Napoleon. Draw the French into the heart of Russia; let fatigue and famine do the work." Meanwhile the sun was drying the roads; the grass was beginning to grow. Nature was preparing the earth for the common extermination of its people. And, oddly enough, at the moment when the slaughter was about to begin, Napoleon had no feeling of hate or wrath towards his adversary, the Russian monarch. He was of the opinion that a war between sovereigns, that is to say, between brothers by divine right, could in no way affect their friendship. He had written, April 25, 1812, to the Emperor Alexander: "Your Majesty will permit me to assure you, that if fate shall render this war between us inevitable, it cannot alter the feelings with which Your Majesty has inspired me; they are secure from all vicissitude and all change."

Napoleon rightly spoke of fate; for was it not that which lured him, by its irresistible power, towards the icy steppes where his power and glory sank beneath the snow? If at times a swift and sombre anticipation of evil crowned his mind, what was that presentiment by the side of the terrible reality? What would the conqueror have said if, in the misty future, he had seen anything of his own fate? Among the courtiers of every nationality who were gathering around the great Emperor at Dresden, there was an Austrian general, half a military man, half a diplomatist, but not a striking figure in any way. One evening the Empress Marie Louise, on her way to the theatrical performance, spoke a few empty words to him, merely because she happened to meet him. He was the Count of Neipperg. How astonished Napoleon would have been if any one had told him that one day this unknown officer would succeed him as the husband of Marie Louise. The young Empress would have been equally amazed if any one had prophesied so strange a thing. Of these two personages, then so brilliant, the all-powerful Emperor and the radiant Empress, one was in a few years to be a prisoner at Saint Helena; the other was to be the morganatic wife of an Austrian general.

XXVIII
PRAGUE

May 29, 1812, at three o'clock in the morning, Napoleon left Dresden to put himself at the head of his armies. He kissed Marie Louise most warmly, and she seemed sorely distressed at parting from him. The 30th, at two in the morning, he reached Glogan, in Silesia, whence he started at five to enter Poland. The Emperor of Austria passed the whole of the 29th with his daughter, trying to console her for Napoleon's departure, and he left Dresden that evening. He was going to Prague, where she was to rejoin him in a few days, and he was meaning to put the last touches to the preparations of the reception he designed for her. Marie Louise looked forward with pleasure to passing a few weeks at Prague with her family; and the Austrian ruler, for his part, acted both as a kind father and an astute statesman in offering to his daughter attentions and tokens of deference by which his son-in-law could not fail to be flattered.

· After the departure of her husband and her father, Marie Louise remained still five days in the capital of Saxony, profiting by them to visit the wonderful museum, the castle of Pilnitz, and the fortress of Königstein, on the banks of the Elbe, upon a steep rock. June 4, in the early morning, she left Dresden accompanied by her uncle, the Grand Duke of Würzburg. The royal family and the Saxon court escorted the young Empress to her carriage, and she set forth amid the roar of cannon and the pealing of all the bells. Her journey was one long ovation. The Saxon cuirassiers escorted her to the Austrian frontier; there she found waiting to receive her Count Kolowrat, Grand Burgrave of Bohemia, and Prince Clary, the Emperor Francis's Chamberlain. A detachment of light horse of the Klenau regiment took the place of the Saxon cuirassiers. At midday Marie Louise arrived at Töplitz; there she rested two hours; then they drove in the magnificent palace gardens of Prince Clary, into which the populace had been admitted. Then she visited the suburbs, the park of Turn, Schlossberg. Everywhere there were triumphal arches, bands of music, girls presenting flowers. In the evening the whole town of Töplitz was illuminated. The miners assembled before the palace in which the Empress was staying, to sing one of their songs, each verse of which ended with a cheer and a swinging of their lanterns.

While the Emperor Francis was at Prague, waiting for his daughter, he was joined by Count Otto, the French Ambassador at Vienna. This diplomatist sent to the Duke of Bassano this curious despatch: "Prague, June 5, 1812. My Lord,—I arrived here the night of the 3d. The Emperor of Austria had given orders that I and my suite should be conducted to a house prepared for me by the side of the palace. I was at once informed on arriving that I was at liberty to dispose of all the service of the court, including the carriages,—a very agreeable attention, because on the mountain on which the castle of Prague is built there are no provisions for strangers. The next day the Grand Chamberlain wrote to me to say that Their Majesties would be very glad to receive me at a private audience, after which I should have the honor of dining with them. I found the Emperor extremely satisfied with all he had seen and heard at Dresden. He congratulated himself on having made more thorough acquaintance with his August son-in-law, and spoke with real emotion of the happiness of his dear Louise. He was impatiently awaiting her arrival at Prague, and anticipating her surprise at the picturesque and magnificent view from the castle overhanging the broad river, full of islands, above the brilliantly illuminated city. The Empress of the French would enjoy a spectacle which could scarcely be equalled anywhere, and the more striking because she had never seen Prague. Knowing that the Emperor preferred to speak German, I addressed him in that language, and I was glad that I did. The monarch expressed himself at length in a way that touched me deeply. He told me that he wanted to keep his August daughter with him as long as she should care to stay at Prague, and that he would escort her to the frontier. 'To-morrow,' he added, 'I shall go to meet her with the Empress; I shall make the most of every moment she can give me, and I shall part with her with the sincerest regret.'

"Then talking about the state of affairs, the Emperor said that he could not understand the conduct of Russia; that they must be beside themselves at Saint Petersburg to wish to measure their strength with a power like France. 'Your army,' he went on, 'is stronger by at least a hundred thousand men; you have far abler officers; your Emperor alone is worth eighty thousand men.'"

After the audience of the Emperor Francis, came the Empress's. The ambassador described that too, but not without noticing the systematic reserve she showed in speaking directly or indirectly about the state of affairs. "When I was introduced to Her Majesty the Empress, she received me with the same flattering consideration. She made me sit down by her, and spoke at some length of the excellent health of our Empress, and of her delight that she was still going to stay for some time with her. The rest of the conversation was about matters of art and literature, which interest Her

Majesty very much. She talked easily and pleasantly, but confined herself to literature and philosophy, making no reference to the events of the day or to those which are preparing." In spite of this shadow which the ambassador was acute enough to notice, the despatch on the whole bore witness to his complete content. "On rising from the table," he added, "the Emperor spoke to me in the kindest way, and asked some of the noblemen who were present to show me the curiosities of the city and the neighborhood. He afterwards sent me word by the High Chamberlain that he had set aside for me one of the principal boxes of the theatre during my stay. This court, which is generally so informal, is to be very magnificent during the visit of Her Majesty the Empress. The Emperor is going to meet her with the principal members of the court; the guards of the castle and of the city have been largely reinforced; the Hungarian Guard has been ordered from Vienna. The young Imperial family will arrive some time to-morrow; preparations are making for grand illuminations, balls, and other festivities to celebrate this interesting reunion. I have been invited again to dine with Their Majesties, and everything is in readiness to receive our Sovereign. The hearts of this good people of Bohemia are flying to meet her. Speaking of the loyalty of this nation, the Emperor told me that it is ready to do whatever is asked of it. General Klenau added that if he were allowed to make use of the influence of Saint Nepomuc, whose bronze statue is saluted every day by those who cross the Prague bridge, he could raise two hundred thousand Bohemians in a very short time. I have mentioned General Klenau, and I must say that he is full of gratitude for the kindness with which His Majesty has been treated at Dresden. He speaks of him most enthusiastically and regrets that he is not able to serve under the greatest general the world has ever seen. The Prince and Princess Anthony of Saxony arrived this morning, and are now setting forth to meet Her Majesty the Empress."

June 5, Marie Louise made an early start from Töplitz for Prague. At five in the afternoon a salute of fifty cannon announced that she had arrived at the White Mountain. The Emperor and Empress of Austria, followed by their household in gala attire, had met her at the Abbey of Saint Margaret. She got into their carriage, and with them made a triumphal entry into Prague amid blazing torches. The capital of Bohemia was brilliantly illuminated. The garrison and the guilds, bearing their banners, formed a double line. The Empress of Austria had given up to her step-daughter her place to the right on the back seat, and the Emperor sat on the front seat with his brother, the Grand Duke of Würzburg. A countless multitude cheered them most enthusiastically.

When they had reached the castle, Marie Louise was conducted to her apartments by the Emperor and the Empress, and there she found awaiting her, to present their respects, the authorities of the city, the canonesses of the two noble chapters of the province, those of the court who had not gone to meet her, and a large household chosen by the Emperor from his most distinguished chamberlains. She dined at her father's table with the Grand Duke of Würzburg, Prince Anthony of Saxony, the Duchess of Montebello, the Duchess of Bassano, the Count of Montesquiou, etc. The Emperor and the Empress of Austria gave up to her the first place at the table, as they had done in the carriage, and during her whole stay at Prague she received the honors reserved for the Austrian sovereigns on grand occasions. Prince Clary was put at the head of the household chosen for her, which included besides, Counts Neipperg, von Nestitz, von Clam, Prince von Auersperg, Prince von Kinsky, Counts von Lutzow, von Paar, von Wallis, von Trautmannsdorf, von Clam-Martinitz.

In the postscript of his despatch of June 5, 1812, which we have quoted, Count Otto gave the following details about Marie Louise's entrance into Prague: "Her Majesty the Empress arrived here at about seven in the evening. Ever since eleven in the morning, the troops, the corporation, the civic guards, the University, and nearly all the inhabitants of the town, had turned out to meet her, forming a line which it was most interesting to see, on account of the kindliness and affection which animated the multitude. The procession was very imposing and worthy of the two sovereigns. It had been arranged that Her Majesty should arrive in an open carriage, which was driven very slowly so that the vast crowd should be able to get a good look at her. Incessant cheers mingled with the pealing bells, the cannon, and the military music. The whole court had gathered to welcome the Empress, at the foot of the grand staircase of the castle. Her Majesty seemed very little tired by the journey, though she had a slight cold, which did not mar her pleasure or keep her from expressing to her parents her delight at being with them."

June 7, the Archduke Charles reached Prague. That evening there was a state dinner in the apartment of the Emperor of Austria. Marie Louise sat at the middle of the table with the Emperor on her right, and the Empress on her left. This was the place always assigned to her, both at home and at her father's. At this dinner she was waited on by Prince Clary, who was entrusted with the functions of her High Chamberlain.

The same day (June 7), the Duke of Bassano, who had accompanied Napoleon, wrote to Count Otto: "Sir,—I have the honor of informing you that His Majesty, who left Dresden May 29, reached Thorn the 2d inst. He stopped forty-eight hours at Posen, leaving at four o'clock for Dantzic in order to review on his way several of the army corps. His health is perfect, and everywhere he has received the expression of the enthusiasm and admiration he inspires. The army is magnificent. The soldiers are in good trim, and all the corps are conspicuous for their fine bearing and their discipline. The weather is faultless, the roads are in good condition, and the country amply supplies all that the army needs, without its calling on its abundant reserves. I propose, Sir, to write to you twice a week, to give you the news about His Majesty, and details about the operations of the army. These communications will enable you to contradict the idle rumors which malicious persons may spread."

At Prague the festivities continued without interruption: June 10, the Empress of France gave a dinner, and at the Court Theatre there was a performance of a German play, Kotzebue's "American"; on the 11th, the Emperor of Austria gave a dinner; on the 12th, they visited the Imperial Library, the Drawing-School, the Museum of Machinery, and in the evening there was a concert; the 10th, the Archdukes Anthony and Reinhardt arrived; in the afternoon Marie Louise gave a ball in honor of her sisters, the three young Archduchesses; the 14th, they visited the Park of Bubenet; the 15th, the gardens of Count Wratislau, and the estate of Count von Clam; the 16th, a picnic at Count von Chotek's castle, seven leagues from Prague, a sail in the boats, return to Prague, and the arrival of Archduke Albert. The 18th, the Empress Marie Louise rode in the riding-school of the Wallenstein Place; the Prince of Ligne arrived, of whom the Baron de Bausset says: "This amiable Prince had all the qualities needed for social success; he was witty, dignified without haughtiness, affectionate, and most gracious and polite; his fancy was quick and fertile; his conversation was animated though kindly and always in good taste; he was continually saying clever things which amused but gave no pain, and was full of good stories and interesting reminiscences. His face was handsome, his expression noble, and he was very tall. Every one began with loving him, and ended with loving him still more."

June 18th, in the evening, a grand ball was given by Count von Kolowrat, Grand Burgrave of Bohemia. The 19th, arrived Archduke Joseph, Palatine of Hungary; the 20th, visit to the wild and picturesque grotto of Saint Procopius, which lies amid woods and rocks; the 21st, reception of the Princes of Mecklenburg and Hesse-Homburg, state dinner and grand ball at the castle. The 22d, the Empress Marie Louise rode with her father, who, when he saw that she liked her horse, made her a present of it. Marie Louise gave it the name of Hradschin, which is the name of the mountain on which the castle of Prague is built. The 23d, visit to the Hermitage of Saint Ivan and to the old castle of Carlstein; the 24th, a grand performance at the theatre; the 25th, arrival of Archduke Rudolph; the 26th, arrival of the young Archdukes, Ferdinand and Maximilian, ball given by the Empress of

France; the 27th, dinner given by the Emperor of Austria; the 30th, festival on the island of the Arquebusiers, setting out at half-past six in the evening from the right bank of the Moldau, landing at the end of the island, where a triumphal arch had been built, and young girls threw flowers before Their Majesties' path.

July 1, Marie Louise, accompanied by her father the Emperor, left Prague at six in the morning. The garrison and the civic guard were under arms. The nobles who were at court escorted the Empress of the French to her carriage, and amid pealing bells and roaring cannon, the cheers and blessings of the crowd, the young sovereign departed. That evening she slept at Schöffin; the next day, July 2, at Carlsbad; the 4th, she visited the tin mines of Frankenthal, descending more than six hundred feet in a chair, placed at the mouth and controlled by balance-weights; the chair was then sent up, the Emperor Francis went down as well as all the ladies, one after another; the 5th they left Carlsbad, and reached Franzbrunn, where they were entertained by national songs and dances. The 6th, Marie Louise parted from her father, whom she was not to see again till after the fall of the Empire; she spent the night at Bamberg, in the palace of the Duke William of Bavaria. The next day, the 7th, she reached Würzburg, where her uncle, the Grand Duke, gave her a magnificent reception. After a few excursions to the castle of Werneck, many boating-parties, illuminations, and concerts led by the Duke himself, she continued her journey. She reached Saint Cloud July 18, 1812: and at six in the evening the cannon of the Invalides announced to the Parisians the return of their Empress.

Marie Louise, who was not yet twenty years and six months old, had been for two years and four months Empress of the French and Queen of Italy. In her thoughts she recalled everything that had happened since her pathetic departure from Vienna,—the moving ceremony at Braunau, where she was given over to the French; her first meeting with Napoleon before the church of Courcelles; her triumphal entry into Paris by the Avenue of the Champs Élysées; her magnificent marriage in the *salon carré* of the Louvre; the brilliant festivities, the journeys, continual ovations; the ball at the Austrian Embassy, a gloomy warning amid so much prosperity; her sufferings ending with a great joy, with the birth of a son; the enthusiasm which this event aroused throughout the world; then more recently, the wonderful splendor of the Dresden interview. For two years nothing but flattery, homage, applause, music, triumphal arches, magnificence, splendid festivities; and, after all, how poor and empty it all was!

So far from her husband, her guide and protector, Marie Louise felt alone and strange in the grand palace of Saint Cloud. It was then that she began to suffer from those attacks of homesickness which made her long for the neighborhood of Vienna. Up to that day there had been nothing but fairy-like splendor; the young sovereign had seen only the brilliant side of the Empire. A vague presentiment made her fear that she was to see the other side. Napoleon had not been able to make his wife share his boundless confidence in himself. She would have been tempted to apply to all she saw these words from the "Imitation": "The glory which comes from men passes quickly away…. The glory of this world is never void of sorrow." Napoleon had just said in his last proclamation: "Russia is led by fatality. She must fulfil her destiny." Alas! it was not Russia, it was France; it was the Emperor who was led by fatality. The army had crossed the Niemen June 24. As the national historian has said, "We shall find glory at every step; but we must not look for good fortune beyond the Niemen." Up to this point every one looked upon Napoleon as invincible, and his young wife had imagined that he was the incarnation of success. This false idea soon vanished. Marie Louise's happy days were over.

In our book about the Empress Josephine we regretted that Napoleon had not oftener sought her advice. We may say the same thing regarding the second Empress. Marie Louise was very young and inexperienced, especially in matters of statesmanship and diplomacy. Yet her husband, genius as he was, would have done well to take counsel of her. She loved peace, did not care for adventure, and she would have dissuaded him from the Russian campaign. She who had known from infancy the prejudices, passions, and rancors of the Viennese court, would have warned him against blind confidence in Austrian promises. But would she have dared to give even one word of advice to her powerful husband? Had a woman of twenty ventured to advise the great Napoleon, the modern Caesar, the second Charlemagne, he would have received the presumptuous child with a smile. Yet it was she who would have been right, and she would have prevented the lamentable wreck of the gigantic Empire. How small a thing is genius, that word we utter with such respect and emphasis! How petty before God is the greatest of men!